THE NEW-ENGLAND PRIMER
Introduction by Paul Leicester Ford

BENJAMIN FRANKLIN ON EDUCATION
Edited by John Hardin Best

THE COLLEGES AND THE PUBLIC
1787–1862
Edited by Theodore Rawson Crane

TRADITIONS OF AFRICAN EDUCATION
Edited by David G. Scanlon

NOAH WEBSTER'S AMERICAN SPELLING BOOK
Introductory Essay by Henry Steele Commager

VITTORINO DA FELTRE
AND OTHER HUMANIST EDUCATORS
By William Harrison Woodward
Foreword by Eugene F. Rice, Jr.

DESIDERIUS ERASMUS
CONCERNING THE AIM AND METHOD
OF EDUCATION
By William Harrison Woodward
Foreword by Craig R. Thompson

JOHN LOCKE ON EDUCATION
Edited by Peter Gay

CATHOLIC EDUCATION IN AMERICA
A Documentary History
Edited by Neil G. McCluskey, S.J.

THE AGE OF THE ACADEMIES
Edited by Theodore R. Sizer

HEALTH, GROWTH, AND HEREDITY
G. Stanley Hall on Natural Education
Edited by Charles E. Strickland and Charles Burgess

TEACHER EDUCATION IN AMERICA
A Documentary History
Edited by Merle L. Borrowman

THE EDUCATED WOMAN IN AMERICA
Selected Writings of Catharine Beecher,
Margaret Fuller, and M. Carey Thomas
Edited by Barbara M. Cross

EMERSON ON EDUCATION
Selections
Edited by Howard Mumford Jones

ECONOMIC INFLUENCES UPON EDUCATIONAL
PROGRESS IN THE UNITED STATES, 1820–1850
By Frank Tracy Carlton
Foreword by Lawrence A. Cremin

QUINTILIAN ON EDUCATION
Selected and Translated by William M. Smail

ROMAN EDUCATION FROM CICERO
TO QUINTILIAN
By Aubrey Gwynn, S.J.

HERBERT SPENCER ON EDUCATION
Edited by Andreas M. Kazamias

JOHN LOCKE'S *OF THE CONDUCT
OF THE UNDERSTANDING*
Edited by Francis W. Garforth

STUDIES IN EDUCATION DURING THE
AGE OF THE RENAISSANCE, 1400–1600
By William Harrison Woodward
Foreword by Lawrence Stone

JOHN AMOS COMENIUS ON EDUCATION
Introduction by Jean Piaget

HUMANISM AND THE SOCIAL ORDER
IN TUDOR ENGLAND
By Fritz Caspari

VIVES' *INTRODUCTION TO WISDOM*
Edited by Marian Leona Tobriner, S.N.J.M.

THE THEORY OF EDUCATION IN
THE *REPUBLIC* OF PLATO
By Richard Lewis Nettleship
Foreword by Robert McClintock

UTOPIANISM AND EDUCATION
Robert Owen and the Owenites
Edited by John F. C. Harrison

The Supreme Court and Education

THIRD EDITION

Edited, with an Introduction and Notes, by
DAVID FELLMAN

☆

CLASSICS IN

No. 4

EDUCATION

☆

TEACHERS COLLEGE PRESS
TEACHERS COLLEGE, COLUMBIA UNIVERSITY
NEW YORK AND LONDON

Foreword

"It is, of course, quite true that the responsibility for public education is primarily the concern of the States, but it is equally true that such responsibilities, like all other state activity, must be exercised consistently with federal constitutional requirements as they apply to state action." Thus has the United States Supreme Court defined one of the central political problems of our time: the task of reconciling the traditional localism of American education with the rights and liberties guaranteed by the Fourteenth Amendment to the Federal Constitution. In a score of recent opinions, most of them handed down since 1945, the Court has worked resolutely at this task, with prodigious results for schools at all levels. Professor Fellman has gathered together excerpts from the more important of these opinions—minority as well as majority—with a view to illuminating both the constitutional and the educational issues at stake. Readers will find here much more than formal legalistic argument; for the Court's opinions have embodied some of the most cogent and compelling discussions of educational policy set before the American public in recent years.

LAWRENCE A. CREMIN

Contents

Introduction

By DAVID FELLMAN

In the American federal system, education has always been primarily a function of the states and their local subdivisions. The national government, under the United States Constitution, is limited to the delegated powers enumerated therein, and no authority over education is given to it. Congress does have the power to "lay and collect taxes" in order "to pay the debts and provide for the common defence and general welfare of the United States," and the promotion of education is clearly for the country's general welfare. Accordingly, various types of federal aid to education take the form of expenditures authorized by Congress to promote the general welfare. In addition, Congress may give financial aid for education to carry out any other delegated power. Thus a recent great statute, which extends a variety of forms of financial assistance for education—the National Defense Education Act of 1958—was adopted to implement, from the legal point of view, the extensive national defense powers vested in Congress by the Constitution.

The oldest federal grant for educational purposes was the Land Ordinance of 1785, which set aside the sixteenth section of every township in the western territory "for the maintenance of public schools within the said township." Probably one of the most influential federal grants for educational purposes to date was the Morrill

Act of 1862 which created the land-grant colleges. Congress gave to the states many millions of acres of public land for the support of colleges offering programs in agriculture, engineering, and home economics. Since 1890 Congress has made regular annual appropriations of money for the promotion of education in the agricultural colleges. This educational program has been supplemented, since 1914, when the Smith-Lever Act was adopted, with federal support for the Agricultural Extension Service.

While Congress may spend money for the promotion of education, and attach conditions to its expenditures, it has no direct power to fix the standards of education except in those areas where it has direct legislative power —the District of Columbia, the territories and other possessions, and federal enclaves, such as forts and other military installations. The Office of Education, established by Congress in 1867, and since 1953 located in the Department of Health, Education, and Welfare, collects educational statistics, conducts research, advises and consults with state and local school officials, and administers various grants-in-aid to education and special programs. The Office also administers the national vocational education acts, the National Defense Education Act of 1958 and its later extensions and amendments, and the far-reaching education acts of 1965.

Actually, the commitments of the national government in the field of education are now considerable. On the international level it participates in the United Nations Educational, Scientific and Cultural Organization (UNESCO), maintains an international educational exchange service, gives technical assistance to foreign countries in various areas of educational activity, administers student visa problems, and supervises the admission to

American institutions of foreign students. On the national level the federal government has a wide variety of educational programs dealing with agriculture, the teaching of citizenship, education for the blind and the deaf, civil defense, health and nutrition, Indians, fisheries, botanical studies, various basic sciences, veterans, vocational training, and wildlife conservation. In addition it maintains a number of service academies for the military establishments.

But however considerable federal activity may be, it is still true that the national government has relatively little to do with most of the country's educational system. The overwhelming majority of American students attend schools maintained by local school boards which function under the authority of state law. A considerable minority of students attend private schools which have only minimal connections with any government. The impact of the national government through legislation and appropriation upon the American educational system is at most tangential and indirect. The states and their local subdivisions, mainly school districts, support most of our schools through local taxation, and fix their own standards of operation. These are not, for the most part, matters of federal concern at all.

The United States Constitution, however, is the supreme law of the land, and as such is ultimately enforceable by the Supreme Court. Insofar as the Constitution imposes limitations on the states, the states are bound by them, and by the interpretations which the Supreme Court attaches to them.

Before the Civil War there was nothing in the federal Constitution which set limits to what the states could do in the field of education. If anyone had a grievance so far as a local educational activity was concerned, he had to be content with whatever appeals he could take within his state's judicial system. While the federal Bill of Rights has a number of provisions which might have a bearing on educational policy—such as the guaranty of religious freedom in the First Amendment, and of due process of law in the Fifth—it was established by the Supreme Court at a very early date, in *Barron* v. *Baltimore,* 7 Pet. 243 (1833), that the Bill of Rights was not intended to apply as limitations upon the states, but only upon the national government. If, for example, a state did something before the Civil War violative of one's religious freedom, he had no appeal beyond his highest state court. For state courts speak with finality regarding the meaning of state law, and the national Supreme Court may review state courts only where federal questions of law are involved.

A very drastic change was made in this traditional division of national and state power in 1868, when the states ratified the Fourteenth Amendment as one of the major legal consequences of the Civil War. This Amendment imposed on the states very broadly phrased limitations for the purpose of protecting the rights of individuals. "No State," Section 1 of the Fourteenth Amendment decrees, "shall make or enforce any law which shall abridge the privileges or immunities of citizens of the United States; nor shall any State deprive any person of life, liberty, or property, without due process of law; nor deny to any person within its jurisdiction the equal protection of the laws." What these sweeping clauses mean is a matter of interpretation, and ultimately for the Supreme Court to decide authoritatively and with finality.

The first of the three clauses of Section 1—which forbids the abridgment by the states of the privileges or immunities of United States citizens—got off to a bad start in the *Slaughterhouse Cases,* 16 Wall. 36 (1873), and has never amounted to very much, since the Court insisted on drawing a basic distinction between federal and state privileges and immunities, holding that the latter did not fall within the scope of the limitation. But the due process and equal protection clauses, which got off to a slow start, have become through a gradual process of interpretation the most important of all constitutional provisions from the point of view of federally enforceable limitations on the states.

It was not until 1925 that the Supreme Court ruled squarely, in *Gitlow* v. *New York,* 268 U.S. 652, that one of the liberties which states may not invade unreasonably and arbitrarily, in violation of the Due Process Clause, is the liberty of speech. In 1940, in *Cantwell* v. *Connecticut,* 310 U.S. 296, the Court held, for the first time, that freedom of religion is one of the liberties which falls within the ambit of the due process guaranty. In fact, today all the great guaranties of the First Amendment—freedom of religion, separation of church and state, freedom of speech and of the press, and the right of association—are treated by the Court as falling within the scope of the Due Process Clause of the Fourteenth Amendment. The Court has consistently refused to hold that the Fourteenth Amendment was intended to nationalize all the guaranties of the federal Bill of Rights as limitations upon the states and thus some of the purely procedural clauses, such as that dealing with the grand jury (*Hurtado* v. *California,* 110 U.S. 516 [1884]), do not apply to the states. But those clauses which have implications for education do apply to the states. If, for example, a state adopts a regulation for school children which violates their religious freedom, a federal remedy is available through appeal to the Supreme Court.

Although the limitations of the Fourteenth Amendment apply only to state action—"no State shall"—it is important to note that the Supreme Court takes a broad view of what constitutes state action. There is state action, of course, if the legislature passes a law, but there is also state action if the act is that of the governor or some other executive officer, a state board or commission, a state court, or any county, city, village, school board, or other local governmental body. In fact, any policeman who holds office by virtue of state law, or purports to act pursuant to state law, falls within the scope of the concept of state action. Whoever acts under color of state law is acting for the state and is therefore subject to the restraints of the Fourteenth Amendment.

The cases concerning education that have been decided by the United States Supreme Court are classified here under five headings. One group of cases deals with the impact of state educational policy on claims to religious liberty or appeals to the principle of the separation of church and state. A second series focuses on the ever-thorny question of racial segregation in the public schools. The third group of cases analyzes issues of academic freedom. A recent development—the Court's involvement in cases of students' rights—is featured in the fourth group. Finally, the courts in this country, state as well as national, are increasingly concerned with legal questions dealing with the financing of the public schools. On this general subject the Supreme Court has so far spoken out only once; this case appears as the fifth part of this book. The cases that appear in the appendixes are addenda to two of the original three groups of the earlier editions of this book: Appendix A to the first category, Appendix B to the second.

Educational policy often impinges on claims of religious conscience. In the first great Supreme Court decision on this subject, *Pierce* v. *Society of Sisters* (page 3), the Court had to face the question whether there was a federal constitutional right to operate a religious-oriented parochial school in the face of a state policy which was designed to compel all children to attend public schools through the eighth grade. Whether a taxpayer's property is taken without due process of law by supplying bus rides, *Everson* v. *Board of Education* (page 6), or textbooks, *Board of Education of Central School District* v. *Allen* (page 101), at public expense to students attending private schools has been adjudicated by the nation's highest court. More recently, in *Meek* v. *Pittenger* (Appendix A, page 301, the Court has had to pass judgment on the constitutionality of providing church-related schools with various auxiliary services at public expense. It has also ruled on the right of a local school board to compel school children to salute the flag and recite a pledge where such a ceremony is contrary to religious belief, *West Virginia State Board of Education* v. *Barnette* (page 32). Perhaps the most widely debated subject today is that of the use of public school facilities or school time for religious education. Here a position taken by the Court, in *Illinois* ex rel. *McCollum* v. *Board of Education* (page 48), aroused such a tremendous amount of controversy that the Court quickly withdrew to a less vulnerable position, in *Zorach* v. *Clauson* (page 62). Whether Bible-reading in the public schools can be squared with the no-establishment clause of the First Amendment was finally adjudicated by the Supreme Court in *Abington School District* v. *Schempp,* in 1963 (page 85). In 1962, the Court ruled against the recitation of prayers in the public school, in *Engel* v. *Vitale* (page 74). In November 1968, in *Epperson* v.

Arkansas (page 112), the Court finally had an opportunity to rule on the validity of a state statute forbidding the teaching of evolution in the schools and concluded that such laws are unconstitutional. Although the Justices did not all agree on the reasoning, they all concurred in the result. This decision will become an important milestone in the history of academic freedom in the United States, as well as in the history of religious freedom.

Whether racial segregation in the public schools is constitutional depends on how the Equal Protection Clause of the Fourteenth Amendment is interpreted. It is impossible to determine what the authors and ratifiers of the Fourteenth Amendment had in mind on this subject, since the public school system we now have scarcely existed at that time. The Supreme Court committed itself, in 1896, in the well-known case of *Plessy* v. *Ferguson,* 163 U.S. 537, to the proposition that the maintenance of racially separated transportation facilities did not violate the Equal Protection Clause so long as the facilities were equal. This marked the beginning of the stormy career of the "separate but equal" doctrine, but it is worth emphasizing that the *Plessy* decision was concerned with transportation and not with education.

Those who wished to break down the racial barriers which many state legislatures erected in the public schools had their first victories in the field of higher education. Thus in 1938 the Supreme Court held that Missouri could not legally close the state university's law school to Negroes by paying the tuition of resident Negroes to attend the law schools of other states (*Missouri* ex rel. *Gaines* v. *Canada,* 305 U.S. 337). Speaking for the Court, Chief Justice Hughes asserted that "manifestly, the obligations of the state to give the protection of equal laws can be performed only where its laws operate, that is, within its own jurisdiction. It is there that the equality of legal rights must be maintained." Ten years later the Supreme Court ordered open for a Negro student the doors of the School of Law of the University of Oklahoma (*Sipuel* v. *Board of Education,* 332 U.S. 631 [1948]), and in 1950 the Court rejected an attempt of the state of Texas actually to create a separate law school for Negro students, in *Sweatt* v. *Painter* (page 127). The great climax came when principles already established for higher education were applied to the grade schools in the spring of 1954, *Brown* v. *Board of Education* (page 133). The riotous events in Little Rock only served to stiffen the attitude of the Justices, *Cooper* v. *Aaron* (page 144).

While there was a considerable amount of compliance with the Supreme Court's rulings forbidding racial segregation in the schools, in various parts of the country, there has also been a great deal of resistance, and endless litigation in the federal courts. Accordingly, the Supreme Court has been deeply involved in the effort to protect the integrity of its commitments in the *Brown* Case. Thus in *Griffin* v. *County School Board of Prince Edward County* (page 156), the Court struck down an aspect of the "massive resistance" movement in Virginia by holding that it was constitutionally improper for a county to close its public schools and give tax money for the support of racially segregated private schools. While many school boards proceeded to experiment with various expedients, such as "freedom-of-choice," pupil placement, "free-transfer," and zoning, the Court served notice, in *Green* v. *School Board of New Kent County* (page 164), that the command of the Constitution was not satisfied unless the plan actually resulted in substantial racial integration, the decisive test being the concrete results and not the words used to describe it. The road to racial integration in our public schools, however, is a rocky one, as is suggested by the recent decision in *Milliken* v. *Bradley* (Appendix B, page 311), where a sharply divided Court refused to sanction compulsory busing of school children across school district lines in order to achieve a greater measure of racial balance.

Questions of academic freedom are increasingly litigated in our courts. For the most part, academic freedom does not even fall within the scope of the legal protection which is available to parties who go to court. It depends on administrative practices and understandings, and professional pressures, and falls outside the formal system of legal rights. Where issues involving academic freedom can be litigated at all, the outcome normally depends on the interpretation of state law by state courts. But in recent years, as a consequence of a rather excited search for security in an unsettled world, a few appeals have reached the Supreme Court in which the issue was basically one of academic freedom. A teacher whose job has been taken from him arbitrarily or whose freedom to teach has been invaded unreasonably does have a due process issue which he can seek to take to the United States Supreme Court. Although a few parties have succeeded in getting their appeals considered, the Court has been most reluctant to limit the state's power to inquire into the fitness of teachers for their positions, *Beilan* v. *Board of Education of Philadelphia* (page 181). Furthermore, the power of congressional committees to carry on investigations in the field of education was affirmed in 1959 in very sweeping terms, in *Barenblatt* v. *United States* (page 220). In *Board of Regents of State Colleges* v. *Roth* (page 230), however, the Court came to grips with some aspects of the problem of academic tenure, which is closely related to the concept of academic freedom.

The principal decisions of the Supreme Court which have vindicated claims to academic freedom have been concerned with various loyalty oaths imposed by states upon teachers. In *Wieman* v. *Updegraff* (page 175), the Court served notice that a loyalty oath was unconstitutional if it failed to distinguish between knowing and innocent membership in a subversive organization, while in *Shelton* v. *Tucker* (page 189) it held that a state may not interfere with associational freedom beyond what may be justified in the exercise of the state's right to look into the competency of its teachers. The decision in *Cramp* v. *Board of Public Instruction of Orange County, Florida* (page 195) made the important point that the language of a statute providing for a loyalty oath must not be too vague or ambiguous, and in *Keyishian* v. *Board of Regents of the University of the State of New York* (page 199) the Court declared unconstitutional a complicated scheme of statutes and administrative rulings which included the much-talked-about Feinberg Law. Finally, in *Pickering* v. *Board of Education of Township High School* (page 210) the Court made it clear that teachers enjoyed freedom of speech, and that if a school board dismissed a teacher merely because he criticized the board's policies in public, it was doing an arbitrary thing contrary to the due process guaranty.

Cases involving the legal rights of students under the Constitution have come to the United States Supreme Court only in very recent years. The first truly significant case was *Tinker* v. *Des Moines Independent Community School District* (page 241), decided in 1969, in which an aspect of the right of students to freedom of speech was explored by a divided Court. The exercise of the right of association by college students was analyzed in a very discriminating opinion in *Healy* v. *James* (page 251). A closely divided Court came to grips in 1975 with the vexing problem of the requirements of due process where students are suspended for allegedly improper conduct, in *Goss* v. *Lopez* (page 260). Finally, in another case decided in 1975, *Wood* v. *Strickland* (page 272), the Court was called upon to examine the nature of the immunity from damage suits which school boards enjoy under federal statute when sued by students, for an allegedly unlawful expulsion.

After the Supreme Court of California startled the educational world by holding that to the extent that school districts which are supported by property taxes have unequal tax resources to devote to public education, the pupils in the poorer districts are denied the equal protection of the laws, an appeal to the Supreme Court on the basis of the Equal Protection Clause of the Fourteenth Amendment was inevitable. A closely and sharply divided Court backed away from the problem in the important case of *San Antonio School District* v. *Rodriguez* (page 283).

Madison, Wisconsin
November 1975

Part I

EDUCATION AND RELIGION

1. Pierce v. Society of Sisters

268 U.S. 510 (1925)

Appeals from the District Court of the U.S. for the District of Oregon.

Mr. Justice McReynolds delivered the opinion of a unanimous Court.

These appeals are from decrees, based upon undenied allegations, which granted preliminary orders restraining appellants from threatening or attempting to enforce the Compulsory Education Act adopted November 7, 1922, under the initiative provision of her Constitution by the voters of Oregon. . . .

The challenged Act, effective September 1, 1926, requires every parent, guardian or other person having control or charge or custody of a child between eight and sixteen years to send him to "a public school for the period of time a public school shall be held during the current year" in the district where the child resides; and failure so to do is declared a misdemeanor. There are exemptions—not specially important here—for children who are not normal, or who have completed the eighth grade, or who reside at considerable distances from any public school, or whose parents or guardians hold special permits from the County Superintendent. The manifest purpose is to compel general attendance at public schools by normal children, between eight and sixteen, who have not completed the eighth grade. And without doubt enforcement of the statute would seriously impair, perhaps destroy, the profitable features of appellees' business and greatly diminish the value of their property.

Appellee, the Society of Sisters, is an Oregon corporation, organized in 1880, with power to care for orphans, educate and instruct the youth, establish and maintain academies or schools, and acquire necessary real and personal property. It has long devoted its property and effort to the secular and religious education and care of children, and has acquired the valuable good will of many parents and guardians. It conducts interdependent primary and high schools and junior colleges, and maintains orphanages for the custody and control of children between eight and sixteen. In its primary schools many children between those ages are taught the subjects usually pursued in Oregon public schools during the first eight years. Systematic religious instruction and moral training according to the tenets of the Roman Catholic Church are also regularly provided. . . .

No question is raised concerning the power of the State reasonably to regulate all schools, to inspect, supervise and examine them, their teachers and pupils; to require that all children of proper age attend some school, that teachers shall be of good moral character and patriotic disposition, that certain studies plainly essential to good citizenship must be taught, and that nothing be taught which is manifestly inimical to the public welfare.

The inevitable practical result of enforcing the Act under consideration would be destruction of appellees' primary schools, and perhaps all other private primary schools for normal children within the State of Oregon. These parties are engaged in a kind of undertaking not inherently harmful, but long regarded as useful and meritorious. Certainly there is nothing in the present records to indicate that they have failed to discharge their obligations to patrons, students or the State. And there are no peculiar circumstances or present emergencies which demand extraordinary measures relative to primary education.

Under the doctrine of *Meyer* v. *Nebraska,* 262 U.S. 390, we think it entirely plain that the Act of 1922 unreasonably interferes with the liberty of parents and guardians to direct the upbringing and education of children under their control. As often heretofore pointed out, rights guaranteed by the Constitution may not be abridged by legislation which has no reasonable relation to some purpose within the competency of the State. The fundamental theory of liberty upon which all governments in this Union repose excludes any general power of the State to standardize its children by forcing them to accept instruction from public teachers only. The child is not the mere creature of the State; those who nurture him and direct his destiny have the right, coupled with the high duty, to recognize and prepare him for additional obligations. . . .

The decrees below are *affirmed.*

2.   Everson v. Board of Education

330 U.S. 1 (1947)

Appeal from the Court of Errors and Appeals of New Jersey

MR. JUSTICE BLACK delivered the opinion of the Court.

A New Jersey statute authorizes its local school districts to make rules and contracts for the transportation of children to and from schools. The appellee, a township board of education, acting pursuant to this statute, authorized reimbursement to parents of money expended by them for the bus transportation of their children on regular busses operated by the public transportation system. Part of this money was for the payment of transportation of some children in the community to Catholic parochial schools. These church schools give their students, in addition to secular education, regular religious instruction conforming to the religious tenets and modes of worship of the Catholic Faith. The superintendent of these schools is a Catholic priest.

The appellant, in his capacity as a district taxpayer, filed suit in a state court challenging the right of the Board to reimburse parents of parochial school students. He contended that the statute and the resolution passed pursuant to it violated both the State and the Federal Constitutions. That court held that the legislature was without power to authorize such payment under the state constitution. . . . The New Jersey Court of Errors and Appeals reversed, holding that neither the statute nor the resolution passed pursuant to it was in conflict with the State constitution or the provisions of the Federal Constitution in issue. . . .

Since there has been no attack on the statute on the ground that a part of its language excludes children attending private schools operated for profit from enjoying State payment for their transportation, we need not consider this exclusionary language; it has no relevancy to any constitutional question here presented. Furthermore, if the exclusion clause had been properly challenged, we do not know whether New Jersey's highest court would construe its statutes as precluding payment of the school transportation of any group of pupils, even those of a private school run for profit. Consequently, we put to one side the question as to the validity of the statute against the claim that it does not authorize payment for the transportation generally of school children in New Jersey.

The only contention here is that the state statute and the resolution, insofar as they authorized reimbursement to parents of children attending parochial schools, violate the Federal Constitution in these two respects, which to some extent overlap. *First.* They authorize the State to take by taxation the private property of some and bestow it upon others, to be used for their own private purposes. This, it is alleged, violates the due process clause of the Fourteenth Amendment. *Second.* The statute and the resolution forced inhabitants to pay taxes to help support and maintain schools which are dedicated to, and which regularly teach, the Catholic Faith. This is alleged to be a use of state power to support church schools contrary to the prohibition of the

First Amendment which the Fourteenth Amendment made applicable to the states.

First. The due process argument that the state law taxes some people to help others carry out their private purposes is framed in two phases. The first phase is that a state cannot tax A to reimburse B for the cost of transporting his children to church schools. This is said to violate the due process clause because the children are sent to these church schools to satisfy the personal desires of their parents, rather than the public's interest in the general education of all children. This argument, if valid, would apply equally to prohibit state payment for the transportation of children to any nonpublic school, whether operated by a church or any other nongovernment individual or group. But, the New Jersey legislature has decided that a public purpose will be served by using tax-raised funds to pay the bus fares of all school children, including those who attend parochial schools. The New Jersey Court of Errors and Appeals has reached the same conclusion. The fact that a state law, passed to satisfy a public need, coincides with the personal desires of the individuals most directly affected is certainly an inadequate reason for us to say that a legislature has erroneously appraised the public need.

It is true that this Court has, in rare instances, struck down state statutes on the ground that the purpose for which tax-raised funds were to be expended was not a public one. . . . But the Court has also pointed out that this far-reaching authority must be exercised with the most extreme caution. *Green* v. *Frazier,* 253 U.S. 233, 240. Otherwise, a state's power to legislate for the public welfare might be seriously curtailed, a power which is a primary reason for the existence of states. Changing local conditions create new local problems which may lead a state's people and its local authorities to believe that laws authorizing new types of public services are necessary to promote the general well-being of the people. The Fourteenth Amendment did not strip the states of their power to meet problems previously left for individual solution. . . .

It is much too late to argue that legislation intended to facilitate the opportunity of children to get a secular education serves no public purpose. . . . The same thing is no less true of legislation to reimburse needy parents, or all parents, for payment of the fares of their children so that they can ride in public busses to and from schools rather than run the risk of traffic and other hazards incident to walking or "hitchhiking." . . . Nor does it follow that a law has a private rather than a public purpose because it provides that tax-raised funds will be paid to reimburse individuals on account of money spent by them in a way which furthers a public program. . . . Subsidies and loans to individuals such as farmers and home-owners, and to privately owned transportation systems, as well as many other kinds of businesses, have been commonplace practices in our state and national history.

Insofar as the second phase of the due process argument may differ from the first, it is by suggesting that taxation for transportation of children to church schools constitutes support of a religion by the State. But if the law is invalid for this reason, it is because it violates the First Amendment's prohibition against the establishment of religion by law. This is the exact question raised by appellant's second contention, to consideration of which we now turn.

Second. The New Jersey statute is challenged as a "law respecting an establishment of religion." The First

Amendment, as made applicable to the states by the Fourteenth, *Murdock* v. *Pennsylvania,* 319 U.S. 105, commands that a state "shall make no law respecting an establishment of religion, or prohibiting the free exercise thereof." These words of the First Amendment reflected in the minds of early Americans a vivid mental picture of conditions and practices which they fervently wished to stamp out in order to preserve liberty for themselves and for their posterity. Doubtless their goal has not been entirely reached; but so far has the Nation moved toward it that the expression "law respecting an establishment of religion," probably does not so vividly remind present-day Americans of the evils, fears, and political problems that caused that expression to be written into our Bill of Rights. Whether this New Jersey law is one respecting an "establishment of religion" requires an understanding of the meaning of that language, particularly with respect to the imposition of taxes. Once again, therefore, it is not inappropriate briefly to review the background and environment of the period in which that constitutional language was fashioned and adopted.

A large proportion of the early settlers of this country came here from Europe to escape the bondage of laws which compelled them to support and attend government-favored churches. The centuries immediately before and contemporaneous with the colonization of America had been filled with turmoil, civil strife, and persecutions, generated in large part by established sects determined to maintain their absolute political and religious supremacy. With the power of government supporting them, at various times and places, Catholics had persecuted Protestants, Protestants had persecuted Catholics, Protestant sects had persecuted other Protestant ects, Catholics of one shade of belief had persecuted Catholics of another shade of belief, and all of these had from time to time persecuted Jews. In efforts to force loyalty to whatever religious group happened to be on top and in league with the government of a particular time and place, men and women had been fined, cast in jail, cruelly tortured, and killed. Among the offenses for which these punishments had been inflicted were such things as speaking disrespectfully of the views of ministers of government-established churches, nonattendance at those churches, expressions of nonbelief in their doctrines, and failure to pay taxes and tithes to support them.

These practices of the old world were transplanted to and began to thrive in the soil of the new America. The very charters granted by the English Crown to the individuals and companies designated to make the laws which would control the destinies of the colonials authorized these individuals and companies to erect religious establishments which all, whether believers or nonbelievers, would be required to support and attend. An exercise of this authority was accompanied by a repetition of many of the old-world practices and persecutions. Catholics found themselves hounded and proscribed because of their faith; Quakers who followed their conscience went to jail; Baptists were peculiarly obnoxious to certain dominant Protestant sects; men and women of varied faiths who happened to be in a minority in a particular locality were persecuted because they steadfastly persisted in worshiping God only as their own consciences dictated. And all of these dissenters were compelled to pay tithes and taxes to support government-sponsored churches whose ministers preached inflammatory sermons designed to strengthen and consolidate the established faith by generating a burning hatred against dissenters.

These practices became so commonplace as to shock the freedom-loving colonials into a feeling of abhorrence. The imposition of taxes to pay ministers' salaries and to build and maintain churches and church property aroused their indignation. It was these feelings which found expression in the First Amendment. No one locality and no one group throughout the Colonies can rightly be given entire credit for having aroused the sentiment that culminated in adoption of the Bill of Rights' provisions embracing religious liberty. But Virginia, where the established church had achieved a dominant influence in political affairs and where many excesses attracted wide public attention, provided a great stimulus and able leadership for the movement. The people there, as elsewhere, reached the conviction that individual religious liberty could be achieved best under a government which was stripped of all power to tax, to support, or otherwise to assist any or all religions, or to interfere with the beliefs of any religious individual or group.

The movement toward this end reached its dramatic climax in Virginia in 1785-86 when the Virginia legislative body was about to renew Virginia's tax levy for the support of the established church. Thomas Jefferson and James Madison led the fight against this tax. Madison wrote his great Memorial and Remonstrance against the law. In it, he eloquently argued that a true religion did not need the support of law; that no person, either believer or nonbeliever, should be taxed to support a religious institution of any kind; that the best interest of a society required that the minds of men always be wholly free; and that cruel persecutions were the inevitable result of government-established religions. Madison's Remonstrance received strong support throughout Virginia, and the Assembly postponed consideration of the proposed tax measure until its next session. When the proposal came up for consideration at that session, it not only died in committee, but the Assembly enacted the famous "Virginia Bill for Religious Liberty" originally written by Thomas Jefferson. . . .

The "establishment of religion" clause of the First Amendment means at least this: Neither a state nor the Federal Government can set up a church. Neither can pass laws which aid one religion, aid all religions, or prefer one religion over another. Neither can force nor influence a person to go to or to remain away from church against his will or force him to profess a belief or disbelief in any religion. No person can be punished for entertaining or professing religious beliefs or disbeliefs, for church attendance or non-attendance. No tax in any amount, large or small, can be levied to support any religious activities or institutions, whatever they may be called, or whatever form they may adopt to teach or practice religion. Neither a state nor the Federal Government can, openly or secretly, participate in the affairs of any religious organizations or groups and *vice versa*. In the words of Jefferson, the clause against establishment of religion by law was intended to erect "a wall of separation between church and State." . . .

We must consider the New Jersey statute in accordance with the foregoing limitations imposed by the First Amendment. But we must not strike that state statute down if it is within the State's constitutional power even though it approaches the verge of that power. . . . New Jersey cannot consistently with the "establishment of religion" clause of the First Amendment contribute tax-raised funds to the support of an institution which teaches the tenets and faith of any church. On the other hand, other language of the amendment commands that New Jersey cannot hamper its citizens in the free exercise of their own religion. Consequently, it cannot exclude individual Catholics, Lutherans, Mohammedans, Baptists, Jews, Methodists, Non-believers, Presbyterians, or the members of any other faith, *because of their faith, or lack of it,* from receiving the benefits of public welfare legislation. While we do not mean to intimate that a state could not provide transportation only to children attending public schools, we must be careful, in protecting the citizens of New Jersey against state-established churches, to be sure that we do not inadvertently prohibit New Jersey from extending its general state law benefits to all its citizens without regard to their religious belief.

Measured by these standards, we cannot say that the First Amendment prohibits New Jersey from spending tax-raised funds to pay the bus fares of parochial school pupils as a part of a general program under which it pays the fares of pupils attending public and other schools. It is undoubtedly true that children are helped to get to church schools. There is even a possibility that some of the children might not be sent to the church schools if the parents were compelled to pay their children's bus fares out of their own pockets when transportation to a public school would have been paid for by the State. The same possibility exists where the state requires a local transit company to provide reduced fares to school children including those attending parochial schools, or where a municipally owned transportation system undertakes to carry all school children free of charge. Moreover, state-paid policemen, detailed to protect children going to and from church schools from the very real hazards of traffic, would serve much the same purpose and accomplish much the same result as state provisions intended to guarantee free transportation of a kind which the state deems to be best for the school children's welfare. And parents might refuse to risk their children to the serious danger of traffic accidents going to and from parochial schools, the approaches to which were not protected by policemen. Similarly, parents might be reluctant to permit their children to attend schools which the state had cut off from such general government services as ordinary police and fire protection, connections for sewage disposal, public highways and sidewalks. Of course, cutting off church schools from these services, so separate and so indisputably marked off from the religious function, would make it far more difficult for the schools to operate. But such is obviously not the purpose of the First Amendment. That Amendment requires the state to be a neutral in its relations with groups of religious believers and nonbelievers; it does not require the state to be their adversary. State power is no more to be used so as to handicap religions than it is to favor them. . . .

The First Amendment has erected a wall between church and state. That wall must be kept high and impregnable. We could not approve the slightest breach. New Jersey has not breached it here.

Affirmed.

Mr. Justice Jackson, dissenting.

I find myself, contrary to first impressions, unable to join in this decision. I have a sympathy, though it is not ideological, with Catholic citizens who are compelled by

law to pay taxes for public schools, and also feel con
strained by conscience and discipline to support other
schools for their own children. Such relief to them a
this case involves is not in itself a serious burden to tax
payers and I had assumed it to be as little serious in
principle. Study of this case convinces me otherwise
The Court's opinion marshals every argument in favor
of state aid and puts the case in its most favorable light,
but much of its reasoning confirms my conclusions that
there are no good grounds upon which to support the
present legislation. In fact, the undertones of the opinion, advocating complete and uncompromising separa
tion of Church from State, seem utterly discordant with
its conclusion yielding support to their commingling in
educational matters. The case which irresistibly comes to
mind as the most fitting precedent is that of Julia who,
according to Byron's reports, "whispering 'I will ne'er
consent,'—consented." . . .

The Township of Ewing is not furnishing transportation to the children in any form; it is not operating
school busses itself or contracting for their operation;
and it is not performing any public service of any kind
with this taxpayer's money. All school children are left
to ride as ordinary paying passengers on the regular
busses operated by the public transportation system.
What the Township does, and what the taxpayer complains of, is at stated intervals to reimburse parents for
the fares paid, provided the children attend either public schools or Catholic Church schools. This expenditure
of tax funds has no possible effect on the child's safety
or expedition in transit. As passengers on the public
busses they travel as fast and no faster, and are as safe
and no safer, since their parents are reimbursed as before.

In addition to thus assuming a type of service that

does not exist, the Court also insists that we must close our eyes to a discrimination which does exist. The resolution which authorizes disbursement of this taxpayer's money limits reimbursement to those who attend public schools and Catholic schools. That is the way the Act is applied to this taxpayer.

The New Jersey Act in question makes the character of the school, not the needs of the children, determine the eligibility of parents to reimbursement. The Act permits payment for transportation to parochial schools or public schools but prohibits it to private schools operated in whole or in part for profit. Children often are sent to private schools because their parents feel that they require more individual instruction than public schools can provide, or because they are backward or defective and need special attention. If all children of the state were objects of impartial solicitude, no reason is obvious for denying transportation reimbursement to students of this class, for these often are as needy and as worthy as those who go to public or parochial schools. Refusal to reimburse those who attend such schools is understandable only in the light of a purpose to aid the schools, because the state might well abstain from aiding a profit-making private enterprise. Thus, under the Act and resolution brought to us by this case, children are classified according to the schools they attend and are to be aided if they attend the public schools or private Catholic schools, and they are not allowed to be aided if they attend private secular schools or private religious schools of other faiths. . . .

It is no exaggeration to say that the whole historic conflict in temporal policy between the Catholic Church and non-Catholics comes to a focus in their respective school policies. The Roman Catholic Church, counseled by experience in many ages and many lands and with all sorts and conditions of men, takes what, from the viewpoint of its own progress and the success of its mission, is a wise estimate of the importance of education to religion. It does not leave the individual to pick up religion by chance. It relies on early and indelible indoctrination in the faith and order of the Church by the word and example of persons consecrated to the task.

Our public school, if not a product of Protestantism, at least is more consistent with it than with the Catholic culture and scheme of values. It is a relatively recent development dating from about 1840. It is organized on the premise that secular education can be isolated from all religious teaching so that the school can inculcate all needed temporal knowledge and also maintain a strict and lofty neutrality as to religion. The assumption is that after the individual has been instructed in worldly wisdom he will be better fitted to choose his religion. Whether such a disjunction is possible, and if possible whether it is wise, are questions I need not try to answer.

I should be surprised if any Catholic would deny that the parochial school is a vital, if not the most vital, part of the Roman Catholic Church. If put to the choice, that venerable institution, I should expect, would forego its whole service for mature persons before it would give up education of the young, and it would be a wise choice. Its growth and cohesion, discipline and loyalty, spring from its schools. Catholic education is the rock on which the whole structure rests, and to render tax aid to its Church school is indistinguishable to me from rendering the same aid to the Church itself.

It is of no importance in this situation whether the beneficiary of this expenditure of tax-raised funds is primarily the parochial school and incidentally the pupil, or whether the aid is directly bestowed on the pupil with indirect benefits to the school. The state cannot maintain a Church and it can no more tax its citizens to furnish free carriage to those who attend a Church. The prohibition against establishment of religion cannot be circumvented by a subsidy, bonus or reimbursement of expense to individuals for receiving religious instruction and indoctrination. . . .

It seems to me that the basic fallacy in the Court's reasoning, which accounts for its failure to apply the principles it avows, is in ignoring the essentially religious test by which beneficiaries of this expenditure are selected. A policeman protects a Catholic, of course—but not because he is a Catholic; it is because he is a man and a member of our society. The fireman protects the Church school—but not because it is a Church school; it is because it is property, part of the assets of our society. Neither the fireman nor the policeman has to ask before he renders aid "Is this man or building identified with the Catholic Church?" But before these school authorities draw a check to reimburse for a student's fare they must ask just that question, and if the school is a Catholic one they may render aid because it is such, while if it is of any other faith or is run for profit, the help must be withheld. To consider the converse of the Court's reasoning will best disclose its fallacy. That there is no parallel between police and fire protection and this plan of reimbursement is apparent from the incongruity of the limitation of this Act if applied to police and fire service. Could we sustain an Act that said the police shall protect pupils on the way to or from public schools and Catholic schools but not while going to and coming from other schools, and firemen shall extinguish a blaze in public or Catholic school buildings but shall not put out a blaze in Protestant Church schools or private schools operated for profit? That is the true analogy to the case we have before us and I should think it pretty plain that such a scheme would not be valid. . . .

This freedom was first in the Bill of Rights because it was first in the forefathers' minds; it was set forth in absolute terms, and its strength is its rigidity. It was intended not only to keep the states' hands out of religion, but to keep religion's hands off the state, and, above all, to keep bitter religious controversy out of public life by denying to every denomination any advantage from getting control of public policy or the public purse. Those great ends I cannot but think are immeasurably compromised by today's decision. . . .

But we cannot have it both ways. Religious teaching cannot be a private affair when the state seeks to impose regulations which infringe on it indirectly, and a public affair when it comes to taxing citizens of one faith to aid another, or those of no faith to aid all. If these principles seem harsh in prohibiting aid to Catholic education, it must not be forgotten that it is the same Constitution that alone assures Catholics the right to maintain these schools at all when predominant local sentiment would forbid them. *Pierce* v. *Society of Sisters,* 268 U.S. 510. Nor should I think that those who have done so well without this aid would want to see this separation between Church and State broken down. If the state may aid these religious schools, it may therefore regulate them. Many groups have sought aid from tax funds only to find that it carried political controls with it. . . .

MR. JUSTICE FRANKFURTER joins in this opinion.

MR. JUSTICE RUTLEDGE, with whom MR. JUSTICE FRANK-
FURTER, MR. JUSTICE JACKSON, and MR. JUSTICE BUR-
TON agree, dissenting.

Not simply an established church, but any law respecting an establishment of religion is forbidden. The
Amendment was broadly but not loosely phrased. It is
the compact and exact summation of its author's views
formed during his long struggle for religious freedom.
In Madison's own words characterizing Jefferson's Bill
for Establishing Religious Freedom, the guaranty he put
in our national charter, like the bill he piloted through
the Virginia Assembly, was "a Model of technical precision, and perspicuous brevity." Madison could not have
confused "church" and "religion," or "an established
church" and "an establishment of religion."

The Amendment's purpose was not to strike merely
at the official establishment of a single sect, creed or
religion, outlawing only a formal relation such as had
prevailed in England and some of the colonies. Necessarily it was to uproot all such relationships. But the
object was broader than separating church and state in
this narrow sense. It was to create a complete and permanent separation of the spheres of religious activity
and civil authority by comprehensively forbidding every
form of public aid or support for religion. In proof the
Amendment's wording and history unite with this Court's
consistent utterances whenever attention has been fixed
directly upon the question. . . .

No provision of the Constitution is more closely tied
to or given content by its generating history than the
religious clause of the First Amendment. It is at once
the refined product and the terse summation of that
history. The history includes not only Madison's author-

ship and the proceedings before the First Congress, but also the long and intensive struggle for religious freedom in America, more especially in Virginia, of which the Amendment was the direct culmination. In the documents of the times, particularly of Madison, who was leader in the Virginia struggle before he became the Amendment's sponsor, but also in the writings of Jefferson and others and in the issues which engendered them is to be found irrefutable confirmation of the Amendment's sweeping content.

For Madison, as also for Jefferson, religious freedom was the crux of the struggle for freedom in general. . . . Madison was co-author with George Mason of the religious clause in Virginia's great Declaration of Rights of 1776. He is credited with changing it from a mere statement of the principle of tolerance to the first official legislative pronouncement that freedom of conscience and religion are inherent rights of the individual. He sought also to have the Declaration expressly condemn the existing Virginia establishment. But the forces supporting it were then too strong.

Accordingly Madison yielded on this phase but not for long. At once he resumed the fight, continuing it before succeeding legislative sessions. As a member of the General Assembly in 1779 he threw his full weight behind Jefferson's historic Bill for Establishing Religious Freedom. That bill was a prime phase of Jefferson's broad program of democratic reform undertaken on his return from the Continental Congress in 1776 and submitted for the General Assembly's consideration in 1779 as his proposed revised Virginia code. With Jefferson's departure for Europe in 1784, Madison became the Bill's prime sponsor. Enactment failed in successive legislatures from its introduction in June, 1779, until its adoption in January, 1786. But during all this time the fight for religious freedom moved forward in Virginia on various fronts with growing intensity. Madison led throughout, against Patrick Henry's powerful opposing leadership until Henry was elected governor in November, 1784.

The climax came in the legislative struggle of 1784–1785 over the Assessment Bill. . . . This was nothing more nor less than a taxing measure for the support of religion, designed to revive the payment of tithes suspended since 1777. So long as it singled out a particular sect for preference it incurred the active and general hostility of dissentient groups. It was broadened to include them, with the result that some subsided temporarily in their opposition. As altered, the bill gave to each taxpayer the privilege of designating which church should receive his share of the tax. In default of designation the legislature applied it to pious uses. But what is of the utmost significance here, "in its final form the bill left the taxpayer the option of giving his tax to education."

Madison was unyielding at all times, opposing with all his vigor the general and nondiscriminatory as he had the earlier particular and discriminatory assessments proposed. The modified Assessment Bill passed second reading in December, 1784, and was all but enacted. Madison and his followers, however, maneuvered deferment of final consideration until November, 1785. And before the Assembly reconvened in the fall he issued his historic Memorial and Remonstrance.

This is Madison's complete, though not his only, interpretation of religious liberty. It is a broadside attack upon all forms of "establishment" of religion, both general and particular, nondiscriminatory or selective. Reflecting not only the many legislative conflicts over the

Assessment Bill and the Bill for Establishing Religious Freedom but also, for example, the struggles for religious incorporations and the continued maintenance of the glebes, the Remonstrance is at once the most concise and the most accurate statement of the views of the First Amendment's author concerning what is "an establishment of religion." Because it behooves us in the dimming distance of time not to lose sight of what he and his coworkers had in mind when, by a single sweeping stroke of the pen, they forbade an establishment of religion and secured its free exercise, the text of the Remonstrance is appended at the end of this opinion for its wider current reference, together with a copy of the bill against which it was directed. [The Remonstrance and the bill are not included in this volume.]

The Remonstrance, stirring up a storm of popular protest, killed the Assessment Bill. It collapsed in committee shortly before Christmas, 1785. With this, the way was cleared at last for enactment of Jefferson's Bill for Establishing Religious Freedom. Madison promptly drove it through in January of 1786, seven years from the time it was first introduced. This dual victory substantially ended the fight over establishments, settling the issue against them. . . .

The next year Madison became a member of the Constitutional Convention. Its work done, he fought valiantly to secure the ratification of its great product in Virginia as elsewhere, and nowhere else more effectively. Madison was certain in his own mind that under the Constitution "there is not a shadow of right in the general government to intermeddle with religion" and that "this subject is, for the honor of America, perfectly free and unshackled. The government has no jurisdiction over it." Nevertheless he pledged that he would work for a Bill of Rights, including a specific guaranty of religious freedom, and Virginia, with other states, ratified the Constitution on this assurance.

Ratification thus accomplished, Madison was sent to the first Congress. There he went at once about performing his pledge to establish freedom for the nation as he had done in Virginia. Within a little more than three years from his legislative victory at home he had proposed and secured the submission and ratification of the First Amendment as the first article of our Bill of Rights.

All the great instruments of the Virginia struggle for religious liberty thus became warp and woof of our constitutional tradition, not simply by the course of history, but by the common unifying force of Madison's life, thought and sponsorship. He epitomized the whole of that tradition in the Amendment's compact, but nonetheless comprehensive, phrasing.

As the Remonstrance discloses throughout, Madison opposed every form and degree of official relation between religion and civil authority. For him religion was a wholly private matter beyond the scope of civil power either to restrain or to support. Denial or abridgment of religious freedom was a violation of rights both of conscience and of natural equality. State aid was no less obnoxious or destructive to freedom and to religion itself than other forms of state interference. "Establishment" and "free exercise" were correlative and coextensive ideas, representing only different facets of the single great and fundamental freedom. The Remonstrance, following the Virginia statute's example, referred to the history of religious conflicts and the effects of all sorts of establishments, current and historical, to suppress religion's free exercise. With Jefferson, Madison believed that to tolerate any fragment of establishment would be by so much to perpetuate restraint upon that freedom. Hence he sought to tear out the institution not partially but root and branch, and to bar its return forever.

In no phase was he more unrelentingly absolute than in opposing state support or aid by taxation. Not even "three pence" contribution was thus to be exacted from any citizen for such a purpose. . . .

In view of this history no further proof is needed that the Amendment forbids any appropriation, large or small, from public funds to aid or support any and all religious exercises. But if more were called for, the debates in the First Congress and this Court's consistent expressions, whenever it has touched on the matter directly, supply it. . . .

Does New Jersey's action furnish support for religion by use of the taxing power? Certainly it does, if the test remains undiluted as Jefferson and Madison made it, that money taken by taxation from one is not to be used or given to support another's religious training or belief, or indeed one's own. Today as then the furnishing of "contributions of money for the propagation of opinions which he disbelieves" is the forbidden exaction; and the prohibition is absolute for whatever amount may be sought or given to that end.

The funds used here were raised by taxation. The Court does not dispute, nor could it, that their use does in fact give aid and encouragement to religious instruction. It only concludes that this aid is not "support" in law. But Madison and Jefferson were concerned with aid and support in fact, not as a legal conclusion "entangled in precedents." Remonstrance, Par. 3. Here parents pay money to send their children to parochial schools and funds raised by taxation are used to reimburse them. This not only helps the children to get to school and the parents to send them. It aids them in a substantial way to get the very thing which they are sent to the particular school to secure, namely, religious training and teaching. . . .

Finally, transportation, where it is needed, is as essential to education as any other element. Its cost is as much a part of the total expense, except at times in amount, as the cost of textbooks, of school lunches, of athletic equipment, of writing and other materials; indeed of all other items composing the total burden. Now as always the core of the educational process is the teacher-pupil relationship. Without this the richest equipment and facilities would go for naught. . . . But the proverbial Mark Hopkins conception no longer suffices for the country's requirements. Without buildings, without equipment, without library, textbooks and other materials, and without transportation to bring teacher and pupil together in such an effective teaching environment, there can be not even the skeleton of what our times require. Hardly can it be maintained that transportation is the least essential of these items, or that it does not in fact aid, encourage, sustain and support, just as they do, the very process which is its purpose to accomplish. No less essential is it, or the payment of its cost, than the very teaching in the classroom or payment of the teacher's sustenance. Many types of equipment, now considered essential, better could be done without.

For me, therefore, the feat is impossible to select so indispensable an item from the composite of total costs, and characterize it as not aiding, contributing to, promoting or sustaining the propagation of beliefs which it is the very end of all to bring about. Unless this can be maintained, and the Court does not maintain it, the aid thus given is outlawed. Payment of transportation is no more, nor is it any the less essential to education, whether religious or secular, than payment for tuitions, for teachers' salaries, for buildings, equipment and necessary materials. Nor is it any the less directly related, in a school giving religious instruction, to the primary religious objective all those essential items of cost are intended to achieve. No rational line can be drawn between payment for such larger, but not more necessary, items and payment for transportation. The only line that can be so drawn is one between more dollars and less. Certainly in this realm such a line can be no valid constitutional measure. . . .

But we are told that the New Jersey statute is valid in its present application because the appropriation is for a public, not a private purpose, namely, the promotion of education, and the majority accept this idea in the conclusion that all we have here is "public welfare legislation." . . .

If the fact alone be determinative that religious schools are engaged in education, thus promoting the general and individual welfare, together with the legislature's decision that the payment of public moneys for their aid makes their work a public function, then I can see no possible basis, except one of dubious legislative policy, for the state's refusal to make full appropriation for support of private, religious schools, just as is done for public instruction. There could not be, on that basis, valid constitutional objection.

Of course paying the cost of transportation promotes the general cause of education and the welfare of the individual. So does paying all other items of educational expense. And obviously, as the majority say, it is much too late to urge that legislation designed to facilitate the opportunities of children to secure a secular education serves no public purpose. Our nationwide system of public education rests on the contrary view, as do all grants in aid of education, public or private, which is not religious in character. . . .

No one conscious of religious values can be unsympathetic toward the burden which our constitutional separation puts on parents who desire religious instruction mixed with secular for their children. They pay taxes for others' children's education, at the same time the added cost of instruction for their own. Nor can one happily see benefits denied to children which others receive, because in conscience they or their parents for them desire a different kind of training others do not demand.

But if those feelings should prevail, there would be an end to our historic constitutional policy and command. No more unjust or discriminatory in fact is it to deny attendants at religious schools the cost of their transportation than it is to deny them tuitions, sustenance for their teachers, or any other educational expense which others receive at public cost. Hardship in fact there is which none can blink. But, for assuring to those who undergo it the greater, the most comprehensive freedom, it is one written by design and firm intent into our basic law.

Of course discrimination in the legal sense does not exist. The child attending the religious school has the same right as any other to attend the public school. But he foregoes exercising it because the same guaranty which assures this freedom forbids the public school or any agency of the state to give or aid him in securing the religious instruction he seeks.

Were he to accept the common school, he would be

the first to protest the teaching there of any creed or faith not his own. And it is precisely for the reason that their atmosphere is wholly secular that children are not sent to public schools under the *Pierce* doctrine. But that is a constitutional necessity, because we have staked the very existence of our country on the faith that complete separation between the state and religion is best for the state and best for religion. Remonstrance, Par. 8, 12.

That policy necessarily entails hardship upon persons who forego the right to educational advantages the state can supply in order to secure others it is precluded from giving. Indeed this may hamper the parent and the child forced by conscience to that choice. But it does not make the state unneutral to withhold what the Constitution forbids it to give. On the contrary it is only by observing the prohibition rigidly that the state can maintain its neutrality and avoid partisanship in the dissensions inevitable when sect opposes sect over demands for public moneys to further religious education, teaching or training in any form or degree, directly or indirectly. Like St. Paul's freedom, religious liberty with a great price must be bought. And for those who exercise it most fully, by insisting upon religious education for their children mixed with secular, by the terms of our Constitution the price is greater than for others.

The problem then cannot be cast in terms of legal discrimination or its absence. This would be true, even though the state in giving aid should treat all religious instruction alike. Thus, if the present statute and its application were shown to apply equally to all religious schools of whatever faith, yet in the light of our tradition it could not stand. For then the adherent of one creed still would pay for the support of another, the childless taxpayer with others more fortunate. Then too there would seem to be no bar to making appropriations for transportation and other expenses of children attending public or other secular schools, after hours in separate places and classes for their exclusively religious instruction. The person who embraces no creed also would be forced to pay for teaching what he does not believe. Again, it was the furnishing of "contributions of money for the propagation of opinions which he disbelieves" that the fathers outlawed. That consequence and effect are not removed by multiplying to all-inclusiveness the sects for which support is exacted. The Constitution requires, not comprehensive identification of state with religion, but complete separation. . . .

3. West Virginia State Board of Education v. Barnette

319 U.S. 624 (1943)

In 1940, in Minersville School District *v.* Gobitis, *310 U.S. 586, the Supreme Court held that "the promotion of national cohesion" through the compulsory flag salute in the public schools is a more important interest than that of religious freedom. Mr. Justice Stone stood alone in dissenting from this decision. When the question came up again in 1943, the Court reversed itself, and ruled the other way by a five-to-three vote. Portions of the majority and dissenting opinions are given below; two other concurring opinions were also written.*

Appeal from the U.S. District Court for the Southern District of West Virginia.

MR. JUSTICE JACKSON delivered the opinion of the Court.

Following the decision by this Court on June 3, 1940, in *Minersville School District* v. *Gobitis,* 310 U.S. 586, the West Virginia legislature amended its statutes to require all schools therein to conduct courses of instruction in history, civics, and in the Constitutions of the United States and of the State "for the purpose of teaching, fostering and perpetuating the ideals, principles and spirit of Americanism, and increasing the knowledge of the organization and machinery of the government." Appellant Board of Education was directed, with advice of the State Superintendent of Schools, to "prescribe the courses of study covering these subjects" for public schools. The Act made it the duty of private, parochial and denominational schools to prescribe courses of study "similar to those required for the public schools."

The Board of Education on January 9, 1942, adopted a resolution containing recitals taken largely from the Court's *Gobitis* opinion and ordering that the salute to the flag become "a regular part of the program of activities in the public schools," that all teachers and pupils "shall be required to participate in the salute honoring the Nation represented by the Flag; provided, however, that refusal to salute the Flag be regarded as an act of insubordination, and shall be dealt with accordingly."

The resolution originally required the "commonly accepted salute to the Flag" which it defined. Objections to the salute as "being too much like Hitler's" were raised by the Parent and Teachers Association, the Boy and Girl Scouts, the Red Cross, and the Federation of Women's Clubs. Some modification appears to have been made in deference to these objections, but no concession was made to Jehovah's Witnesses. What is now required is the "stiff-arm" salute, the saluter to keep the right hand raised with palm turned up while the following is repeated: "I pledge allegiance to the Flag of the United States of America and to the Republic for which it stands; one Nation, indivisible, with liberty and justice for all."

Failure to conform is "insubordination" dealt with by expulsion. Readmission is denied by statute until compliance. Meanwhile the expelled child is "unlawfully absent" and may be proceeded against as a delinquent. His parents or guardians are liable to prosecution, and if convicted are subject to fine not exceeding $50 and jail term not exceeding thirty days.

Appellees, citizens of the United States and of West Virginia, brought suit in the United States District Court for themselves and others similarly situated asking its injunction to restrain enforcement of these laws and regulations against Jehovah's Witnesses. The Witnesses are an unincorporated body teaching that the obligation imposed by law of God is superior to that of laws enacted by temporal government. Their religious beliefs include a literal version of Exodus, Chapter 20, verses 4 and 5, which says: "Thou shalt not make unto thee any graven image, or any likeness of anything that is in heaven above, or that is in the earth beneath, or that is in the water under the earth; thou shalt not bow down thyself to them nor serve them." They consider that the flag is an "image" within this command. For this reason they refuse to salute it.

Children of this faith have been expelled from school and are threatened with exclusion for no other cause. Officials threaten to send them to reformatories maintained for criminally inclined juveniles. Parents of such children have been prosecuted and are threatened with prosecutions for causing delinquency.

The Board of Education moved to dismiss the complaint setting forth these facts and alleging that the law and regulations are an unconstitutional denial of religious freedom, and of freedom of speech, and are invalid under the "due process" and "equal protection" clauses of the Fourteenth Amendment to the Federal Constitution. The cause was submitted on the pleadings to a

District Court of three judges. It restrained enforcement as to the plaintiffs and those of that class. The Board of Education brought the case here by direct appeal.

This case calls upon us to reconsider a precedent decision, as the Court throughout its history often has been required to do. Before turning to the *Gobitis* case, however, it is desirable to notice certain characteristics by which this controversy is distinguished.

The freedom asserted by these appellees does not bring them into collision with rights asserted by any other individual. It is such conflicts which most frequently require intervention of the State to determine where the rights of one end and those of another begin. But the refusal of these persons to participate in the ceremony does not interfere with or deny rights of others to do so. Nor is there any question in this case that their behavior is peaceable and orderly. The sole conflict is between authority and rights of the individual. The State asserts power to condition access to public education on making a prescribed sign and profession and at the same time to coerce attendance by punishing both parent and child. The latter stand on a right of self-determination in matters that touch individual opinion and personal attitude. . . .

There is no doubt that, in connection with the pledges, the flag salute is a form of utterance. Symbolism is a primitive but effective way of communicating ideas. The use of an emblem or flag to symbolize some system, idea, institution, or personality, is a short cut from mind to mind. Causes and nations, political parties, lodges and ecclesiastical groups seek to knit the loyalty of their followings to a flag or banner, a color or design. The State announces rank, function, and authority through

crowns and maces, uniforms and black robes; the church
speaks through the Cross, the Crucifix, the altar and
shrine, and clerical raiment. Symbols of State often con
vey political ideas just as religious symbols come to con
vey theological ones. Associated with many of these sym
bols are appropriate gestures of acceptance or respect:
a salute, a bowed or bared head, a bended knee. A per
son gets from a symbol the meaning he puts into it, and
what is one man's comfort and inspiration is another's
jest and scorn. . . .

It is also to be noted that the compulsory flag salute
and pledge requires affirmation of a belief and an attitude of mind. It is not clear whether the regulation con-
templates that pupils forego any contrary convictions of
their own and become unwilling converts to the prescribed ceremony or whether it will be acceptable if they
simulate assent by words without belief and by a gesture
barren of meaning. It is now a commonplace that censorship or suppression of expression of opinion is tolerated
by our Constitution only when the expression presents a
clear and present danger of action of a kind the State is
empowered to prevent and punish. It would seem that
involuntary affirmation could be commanded only on
even more immediate and urgent grounds than silence.
But here the power of compulsion is invoked without
any allegation that remaining passive during a flag
salute ritual creates a clear and present danger that
would justify an effort even to muffle expression. To sustain the compulsory flag salute we are required to say
that a Bill of Rights which guards the individual's right
to speak his own mind, left it open to public authorities
to compel him to utter what is not in his mind.

Whether the First Amendment to the Constitution
will permit officials to order observance of ritual of this

nature does not depend upon whether as a voluntary exercise we would think it to be good, bad or merely innocuous. Any credo of nationalism is likely to include what some disapprove or to omit what others think essential, and to give off different overtones as it takes on different accents or interpretations. If official power exists to coerce acceptance of any patriotic creed, what it shall contain cannot be decided by courts, but must be largely discretionary with the ordaining authority, whose power to prescribe would no doubt include power to amend. Hence validity of the asserted power to force an American citizen publicly to profess any statement of belief or to engage in any ceremony of assent to one, presents questions of power that must be considered independently of any idea we may have as to the utility of the ceremony in question.

Nor does the issue as we see it turn on one's possession of particular religious views or the sincerity with which they are held. While religion supplies appellees' motive for enduring the discomforts of making the issue in this case, many citizens who do not share these religious views hold such a compulsory rite to infringe constitutional liberty of the individual. It is not necessary to inquire whether nonconformist beliefs will exempt from the duty to salute unless we first find power to make the salute a legal duty.

The *Gobitis* decision, however, *assumed,* as did the argument in that case and in this, that power exists in the State to impose the flag salute discipline upon school children in general. The Court only examined and rejected a claim based on religious beliefs of immunity from an unquestioned general rule. The question which underlies the flag salute controversy is whether such a ceremony so touching matters of opinion and political attitude may be imposed upon the individual by official authority under powers committed to any political organization under our Constitution. We examine rather than assume existence of this power and, against this broader definition of issues in this case, reexamine specific grounds assigned for the *Gobitis* decision.

1. It was said that the flag-salute controversy confronted the Court with "the problem which Lincoln cast in memorable dilemma: 'Must a government of necessity be too *strong* for the liberties of its people, or too *weak* to maintain its own existence?'" and that the answer must be in favor of strength. . . .

We think these issues may be examined free of pressure or restraint growing out of such considerations.

It may be doubted whether Mr. Lincoln would have thought that the strength of government to maintain itself would be impressively vindicated by our confirming power of the State to expel a handful of children from school. Such oversimplification, so handy in political debate, often lacks the precision necessary to postulates of judicial reasoning. If validly applied to this problem, the utterance cited would resolve every issue of power in favor of those in authority and would require us to override every liberty thought to weaken or delay execution of their policies.

Government of limited power need not be anemic government. Assurance that rights are secure tends to diminish fear and jealousy of strong government, and by making us feel safe to live under it makes for its better support. Without promise of a limiting Bill of Rights it is doubtful if our Constitution could have mustered enough strength to enable its ratification. To enforce those rights today is not to choose weak government over strong government. It is only to adhere as a means of strength to individual freedom of mind in preference to officially disciplined uniformity for which history indicates a disappointing and disastrous end.

The subject now before us exemplifies this principle. Free public education, if faithful to the ideal of secular instruction and political neutrality, will not be partisan or enemy of any class, creed, party, or faction. If it is to impose any ideological discipline, however, each party or denomination must seek to control, or failing that, to weaken the influence of the educational system. Observance of the limitations of the Constitution will not weaken government in the field appropriate for its exercise.

2. It was also considered in the *Gobitis* case that functions of educational officers in States, counties and school districts were such that to interfere with their authority "would in effect make us the school board for the country."

The Fourteenth Amendment, as now applied to the States, protects the citizen against the State itself and all of its creatures—Boards of Education not excepted. These have, of course, important, delicate, and highly discretionary functions, but none that they may not perform within the limits of the Bill of Rights. That they are educating the young for citizenship is reason for scrupulous protection of Constitutional freedoms of the individual, if we are not to strangle the free mind at its source and teach youth to discount important principles of our government as mere platitudes.

Such Boards are numerous and their territorial jurisdiction often small. But small and local authority may feel less sense of responsibility to the Constitution, and agencies of publicity may be less vigilant in calling it to account. The action of Congress in making flag observance voluntary and respecting the conscience of the objector in a matter so vital as raising the Army contrasts sharply with these local regulations in matters relatively trivial to the welfare of the nation. There are village tyrants as well as village Hampdens, but none who acts under color of law is beyond reach of the Constitution.

3. The *Gobitis* opinion reasoned that this is a field "where courts possess no marked and certainly no controlling competence," that it is committed to the legislatures as well as the courts to guard cherished liberties and that it is constitutionally appropriate to "fight out the wise use of legislative authority in the forum of public opinion and before legislative assemblies rather than to transfer such a contest to the judicial arena," since all the "effective means of inducing political changes are left free."

The very purpose of a Bill of Rights was to withdraw certain subjects from the vicissitudes of political controversy, to place them beyond the reach of majorities and officials and to establish them as legal principles to be applied by the courts. One's right to life, liberty, and property, to free speech, a free press, freedom of worship and assembly, and other fundamental rights may not be submitted to vote; they depend on the outcome of no elections.

In weighing arguments of the parties it is important to distinguish between the due process clause of the Fourteenth Amendment as an instrument for transmitting the principles of the First Amendment and those cases in which it is applied for its own sake. The test of legislation which collides with the Fourteenth Amendment, because it also collides with the principles of the First, is much more definite than the test when only the Fourteenth is involved. Much of the vagueness of the due process clause disappears when the specific prohibitions of the First become its standard. The right of a State to regulate, for example, a public utility may well include, so far as the due process test is concerned, power to impose all of the restrictions which a legislature may have a "rational basis" for adopting. But freedoms of speech and of press, of assembly, and of worship may not be infringed on such slender grounds. They are susceptible of restriction only to prevent grave and immediate danger to interests which the State may lawfully protect. It is important to note that while it is the Fourteenth Amendment which bears directly upon the State it is the more specific limiting principles of the First Amendment that finally govern this case.

Nor does our duty to apply the Bill of Rights to assertions of official authority depend upon our possession of marked competence in the field where the invasion of rights occurs. True, the task of translating the majestic generalities of the Bill of Rights, conceived as part of the pattern of liberal government in the eighteenth century, into concrete restraints on officials dealing with the problems of the twentieth century, is one to disturb self-confidence. These principles grew in soil which also produced a philosophy that the individual was the center of society, that his liberty was attainable through mere absence of governmental restraints, and that government should be entrusted with few controls and only the mildest supervision over men's affairs. We must transplant these rights to a soil in which the *laissez-faire* concept or principle of noninterference has withered at least as to economic affairs, and social advancements are increasingly sought through closer integration of society and through expanded and strengthened governmental controls. These changed conditions often deprive prec-

edents of reliability and cast us more than we would
choose upon our own judgment. But we act in these
matters not by authority of our competence but by force
of our commissions. We cannot, because of modest esti-
mates of our competence in such specialties as public
education, withhold the judgment that history authenti-
cates as the function of this Court when liberty is infringed.

4. Lastly, and this is the very heart of the *Gobitis*
opinion, it reasons that "National unity is the basis of
national security," that the authorities have "the right to
select appropriate means for its attainment," and hence
reaches the conclusion that such compulsory measures
toward "national unity" are constitutional. Upon the
verity of this assumption depends our answer in this case.

National unity as an end which officials may foster by
persuasion and example is not in question. The problem
is whether under our Constitution compulsion as here
employed is a permissible means for its achievement.

Struggles to coerce uniformity of sentiment in support
of some end thought essential to their time and country
have been waged by many good as well as by evil men.
Nationalism is a relatively recent phenomenon but at
other times and places the ends have been racial or territorial security, support of a dynasty or regime, and particular plans for saving souls. As first and moderate
methods to attain unity have failed, those bent on its
accomplishment must resort to an ever-increasing sever-
ity. As governmental pressure toward unity becomes
greater, so strife becomes more bitter as to whose unity
it shall be. Probably no deeper division of our people
could proceed from any provocation than from finding
it necessary to choose what doctrine and whose program
public educational officials shall compel youth to unite

n embracing. Ultimate futility of such attempts to compel coherence is the lesson of every such effort from the Roman drive to stamp out Christianity as a disturber of its pagan unity, the Inquisition, as a means to religious and dynastic unity, the Siberian exiles as a means to Russian unity, down to the fast failing efforts of our present totalitarian enemies. Those who begin coercive elimination of dissent soon find themselves exterminating dissenters. Compulsory unification of opinion achieves only the unanimity of the graveyard.

It seems trite but necessary to say that the First Amendment to our Constitution was designed to avoid these ends by avoiding these beginnings. There is no mysticism in the American concept of the State or of the nature or origin of its authority. We set up government by consent of the governed, and the Bill of Rights denies those in power any legal opportunity to coerce that consent. Authority here is to be controlled by public opinion, not public opinion by authority.

The case is made difficult not because the principles of its decision are obscure but because the flag involved is our own. Nevertheless, we apply the limitations of the Constitution with no fear that freedom to be intellectually and spiritually diverse or even contrary will disintegrate the social organization. To believe that patriotism will not flourish if patriotic ceremonies are voluntary and spontaneous instead of a compulsory routine is to make an unflattering estimate of the appeal of our institutions to free minds. We can have intellectual individualism and the rich cultural diversities that we owe to exceptional minds only at the price of occasional eccentricity and abnormal attitudes. When they are so harmless to others or to the State as those we deal with here, the price is not too great. But freedom

to differ is not limited to things that do not matter
much. That would be a mere shadow of freedom. The
test of its substance is the right to differ as to things that
touch the heart of the existing order.

If there is any fixed star in our constitutional con-
stellation, it is that no official, high or petty, can prescribe what shall be orthodox in politics, nationalism,
religion, or other matters of opinion or force citizens to
confess by word or act their faith therein. If there are
any circumstances which permit an exception, they do
not now occur to us. . . .

The decision of this Court in *Minersville School District* v. *Gobitis* and the holdings of those few *per curiam*
decisions which preceded and foreshadowed it are overruled, and the judgment enjoining enforcement of the
West Virginia Regulation is *affirmed*. . . .

MR. JUSTICE FRANKFURTER, dissenting.

One who belongs to the most vilified and persecuted
minority in history is not likely to be insensible to the
freedoms guaranteed by our Constitution. Were my
purely personal attitude relevant I should wholeheart-
edly associate myself with the general libertarian views
in the Court's opinion, representing as they do the
thought and action of a lifetime. But as judges we are
neither Jew nor Gentile, neither Catholic nor agnostic.
We owe equal attachment to the Constitution and are
equally bound by our judicial obligations whether we
derive our citizenship from the earliest or the latest im-
migrants to these shores. As a member of this Court I am
not justified in writing my private notions of policy into
the Constitution, no matter how deeply I may cherish
them or how mischievous I may deem their disregard.

he duty of a judge who must decide which of two
laims before the Court shall prevail, that of a State to
nact and enforce laws within its general competence or
hat of an individual to refuse obedience because of the
.emands of his conscience, is not that of the ordinary
•erson. It can never be emphasized too much that one's
•wn opinion about the wisdom or evil of a law should
•e excluded altogether when one is doing one's duty on
he bench. The only opinion of our own even looking
n that direction that is material is our opinion whether
egislators could in reason have enacted such a law. In
he light of all the circumstances, including the history
•f this question in this Court, it would require more
laring than I possess to deny that reasonable legislators
ould have taken the action which is before us for re-
iew. Most unwillingly, therefore, I must differ from my
•rethren with regard to legislation like this. I cannot
•ring my mind to believe that the "liberty" secured by
he Due Process Clause gives this Court authority to
leny to the State of West Virginia the attainment of
hat which we all recognize as a legitimate legislative
:nd, namely, the promotion of good citizenship, by em-
•loyment of the means here chosen. . . .

We are not reviewing merely the action of a local
chool board. The flag salute requirement in this case
:omes before us with the full authority of the State of
West Virginia. We are in fact passing judgment on "the
•ower of the State as a whole." . . . Practically we are
•assing upon the political power of each of the forty-
:ight states. . . .

The constitutional protection of religious freedom
erminated disabilities, it did not create new privileges.
It gave religious equality, not civil immunity. Its essence
s freedom from conformity to religious dogma, not free-

dom from conformity to law because of religious dogm.
Religious loyalties may be exercised without hindranc
from the state, not the state may not exercise that whic
except by leave of religious loyalties is within the domai
of temporal power. Otherwise each individual could se
up his own censor against obedience to laws consc
entiously deemed for the public good by those whos
business it is to make laws. . . .

An act compelling profession of allegiance to a rel
gion, no matter how subtly or tenuously promoted, i
bad. But an act promoting good citizenship and nationa
allegiance is within the domain of governmental au
thority and is therefore to be judged by the same con
siderations of power and of constitutionality as thos
involved in the many claims of immunity from civi
obedience because of religious scruples.

That claims are pressed on behalf of sincere religiou
convictions does not of itself establish their constitu
tional validity. Nor does waving the banner of religiou
freedom relieve us from examining into the power w
are asked to deny the states. Otherwise the doctrine o
separation of church and state, so cardinal in the his
tory of this nation and for the liberty of the people
would mean not the disestablishment of a state churc
but the establishment of all churches and of all religiou
groups. . . .

We are told that symbolism is a dramatic but primi
tive way of communicating ideas. Symbolism is ines
capable. Even the most sophisticated live by symbols
But it is not for this Court to make psychological judg
ments as to the effectiveness of a particular symbol in
inculcating concededly indispensable feelings, particu
larly if the state happens to see fit to utilize the symbol
that represents our heritage and our hopes. And surely

only flippancy could be responsible for the suggestion that constitutional validity of a requirement to salute our flag implies equal validity of a requirement to salute a dictator. The significance of a symbol lies in what it represents. To reject the swastika does not imply rejection of the Cross. And so it bears repetition to say that it mocks reason and denies our whole history to find in the allowance of a requirement to salute our flag on fitting occasions the seeds of sanction for obeisance to a leader. To deny the power to employ educational symbols is to say that the state's educational system may not stimulate the imagination because this may lead to unwise stimulation. . . .

Of course patriotism cannot be enforced by the flag salute. But neither can the liberal spirit be enforced by judicial invalidation of illiberal legislation. Our constant preoccupation with the constitutionality of legislation rather than with its wisdom tends to preoccupation of the American mind with a false value. The tendency of focusing attention on constitutionality is to make constitutionality synonymous with wisdom, to regard a law as all right if it is constitutional. Such an attitude is a great enemy of liberalism. Particularly in legislation affecting freedom of thought and freedom of speech much which should offend a free-spirited society is constitutional. Reliance for the most precious interests of civilization, therefore, must be found outside of their vindication in courts of law. Only a persistent positive translation of the faith of a free society into the convictions and habits and actions of a community is the ultimate reliance against unabated temptations to fetter the human spirit.

4. Illinois ex rel. McCollum v. Board of Education

333 U.S. 203 (1948)

Appeal from the Supreme Court of Illinois.

MR. JUSTICE BLACK delivered the opinion of the Court.

This case relates to the power of a state to utilize its tax-supported public school system in aid of religious instruction insofar as that power may be restricted by the First and Fourteenth Amendments to the Federal Constitution.

The appellant, Vashti McCollum, began this action for mandamus against the Champaign Board of Education in the Circuit Court of Champaign County, Illinois. Her asserted interest was that of a resident and taxpayer of Champaign and of a parent whose child was then enrolled in the Champaign public schools. Illinois has a compulsory education law which, with exceptions, requires parents to send their children, aged seven to sixteen, to its tax-supported public schools where the children are to remain in attendance during the hours when the schools are regularly in session. Parents who violate this law commit a misdemeanor punishable by fine unless the children attend private or parochial schools which meet educational standards fixed by the State. District boards of education are given general supervisory powers over the use of the public school buildings within the school districts. . . .

Appellant's petition for mandamus alleged that religious teachers, employed by private religious groups, were permitted to come weekly into the school buildings during the regular hours set apart for secular teaching, and then and there for a period of thirty minutes substitute their religious teaching for the secular education provided under the compulsory education law. The petitioner charged that this joint public-school religious-group program violated the First and Fourteenth Amendments to the United States Constitution. . . .

Although there are disputes between the parties as to various inferences that may or may not properly be drawn from the evidence concerning the religious program, the following facts are shown by the record without dispute. In 1940 interested members of the Jewish, Roman Catholic, and a few of the Protestant faiths formed a voluntary association called the Champaign Council on Religious Education. They obtained permission from the Board of Education to offer classes in religious instruction to public school pupils in grades four to nine inclusive. Classes were made up of pupils whose parents signed printed cards requesting that their children be permitted to attend; they were held weekly, thirty minutes for the lower grades, forty-five minutes for the higher. The council employed the religious teachers at no expense to the school authorities, but the instructors were subject to the approval and supervision of the superintendent of schools. The classes were taught in three separate religious groups by Protestant teachers, Catholic priests, and a Jewish rabbi, although for the past several years there have apparently been no classes instructed in the Jewish religion. Classes were conducted in the regular classrooms of the school building. Student who did not choose to take the religious instruction were not released from public school duties; they were required to leave their classrooms and go to some other place in the school building for pursuit of their secular studies. On the other hand, students who were released from secular study for the religious instructions were required to be present at the religious classes. Reports of their presence or absence were to be made to their secular teachers.

The foregoing facts, without reference to others that appear in the record, show the use of tax-supported property for religious instruction and the close cooperation between the school authorities and the religious council in promoting religious education. The operation of the State's compulsory education system thus assists and is integrated with the program of religious instruction carried on by separate religious sects. Pupils compelled by law to go to school for secular education are released in part from their legal duty upon the condition that they attend the religious classes. This is beyond all question a utilization of the tax-established and tax-supported public school system to aid religious groups to spread their faith. And it falls squarely under the ban of the First Amendment (made applicable to the States by the Fourteenth) as we interpreted it in *Everson* v. *Board of Education*, 330 U.S. 1. . . .

Recognizing that the Illinois program is barred by the First and Fourteenth Amendments if we adhere to the views expressed both by the majority and the minority in the *Everson* case, counsel for the respondents challenge those views as dicta and urge that we reconsider and repudiate them. They argue that historically the First Amendment was intended to forbid only government preference of one religion over another, not an

mpartial governmental assistance of all religions. In
addition they ask that we distinguish or overrule our
holding in the *Everson* case that the Fourteenth Amendment made the "establishment of religion" clause of the
First Amendment applicable as a prohibition against the
States. After giving full consideration to the arguments
presented we are unable to accept either of these contentions.

To hold that a state cannot consistently with the First
and Fourteenth Amendments utilize its public school system to aid any or all religious faiths or sects in the dissemination of their doctrines and ideals does not, as
counsel urge, manifest a governmental hostility to religion or religious teachings. A manifestation of such hostility would be at war with our national tradition as
embodied in the First Amendment's guaranty of the free
exercise of religion. For the First Amendment rests upon
the premise that both religion and government can best
work to achieve their lofty aims if each is left free from
the other within its respective sphere. Or, as we said in
the *Everson* case, the First Amendment has erected a
wall between Church and State which must be kept high
and impregnable.

Here not only are the State's tax-supported public
school buildings used for the dissemination of religious
doctrines. The State also affords sectarian groups an in-
valuable aid in that it helps to provide pupils for their
religious classes through use of the State's compulsory
public school machinery. This is not separation of
Church and State.

The cause is reversed and remanded to the State Supreme Court for proceedings not inconsistent with this
opinion.

Reversed and remanded.

MR. JUSTICE FRANKFURTER delivered the following opinion, in which MR. JUSTICE JACKSON, MR. JUSTICE
RUTLEDGE, and MR. JUSTICE BURTON join.

We dissented in *Everson* v. *Board of Education,* 330
U.S. 1, because in our view the Constitutional principle
requiring separation of Church and State compelled invalidation of the ordinance sustained by the majority.
Illinois has here authorized the commingling of sectarian
with secular instruction in the public schools. The Constitution of the United States forbids this.

This case, in the light of the *Everson* decision, demonstrates anew that the mere formulation of a relevant
Constitutional principle is the beginning of the solution
of a problem, not its answer. This is so because the
meaning of a spacious conception like that of the separation of Church from State is unfolded as appeal is made
to the principle from case to case. We are all agreed
that the First and the Fourteenth Amendments have a
secular reach far more penetrating in the conduct of
Government than merely to forbid an "established
church." But agreement, in the abstract, that the First
Amendment was designed to erect a "wall of separation
between church and State," does not preclude a clash of
views as to what the wall separates. Involved is not only
the Constitutional principle but the implications of
judicial review in its enforcement. Accommodation of
legislative freedom and Constitutional limitations upon
that freedom cannot be achieved by a mere phrase. We
cannot illuminatingly apply the "wall-of-separation"
metaphor until we have considered the relevant history
of religious education in America, the place of the "released time" movement in that history, and its precise
manifestation in the case before us.

To understand the particular program now before us is a conscientious attempt to accommodate the allowable functions of Government and the special concerns of the Church within the framework of our Constitution and with due regard to the kind of society for which it was designed, we must put this Champaign program of 1940 in its historic setting. Traditionally, organized education in the Western world was Church education. It could hardly be otherwise when the education of children was primarily study of the Word and the ways of God. Even in the Protestant countries, where there was a less close identification of Church and State, the basis of education was largely the Bible, and its chief purpose inculcation of piety. To the extent that the State intervened, it used its authority to further aims of the Church.

The emigrants who came to these shores brought this view of education with them. Colonial schools certainly started with a religious orientation. When the common problems of the early settlers of the Massachusetts Bay Colony revealed the need for common schools, the object was the defeat of "one chief project of that old deluder, Satan, to keep men from the knowledge of the Scriptures." The Laws and Liberties of Massachusetts, 1648 edition (Cambridge 1929) 47.

The evolution of colonial education, largely in the service of religion, into the public school system of today is the story of changing conceptions regarding the American democratic society, of the functions of State-maintained education in such a society, and of the role therein of the free exercise of religion by the people. The modern public school derived from a philosophy of freedom reflected in the First Amendment. It is appropriate to recall that the Remonstrance of James Madison, an event basic in the history of religious liberty, was called forth by a proposal which involved support to religious education. . . . As the momentum for popular education increased and in turn evoked strong claims for State support of religious education, contests not unlike that which in Virginia had produced Madison's Remonstrance appeared in various forms in other States. New York and Massachusetts provide famous chapters in the history that established dissociation of religious teaching from State-maintained schools. In New York, the rise of the common schools led, despite fierce sectarian opposition, to the barring of tax funds to church schools, and later to any school in which sectarian doctrine was taught. In Massachusetts, largely through the efforts of Horace Mann, all sectarian teachings were barred from the common school to save it from being rent by denominational conflict. The upshot of these controversies, often long and fierce, is fairly summarized by saying that long before the Fourteenth Amendment subjected the States to new limitations, the prohibition of furtherance by the State of religious instruction became the guiding principle, in law and feeling, of the American people. . . .

Separation in the field of education, then, was not imposed upon unwilling States by force of superior law. In this respect the Fourteenth Amendment merely reflected a principle then dominant in our national life. To the extent that the Constitution thus made it binding upon the States, the basis of the restriction is the whole experience of our people. Zealous watchfulness against fusion of secular and religious activities by Government itself, through any of its instruments but especially through its educational agencies, was the democratic response of the American community to the particular needs of a young and growing nation, unique in the composition of its people. . . .

It is pertinent to remind that the establishment of this principle of Separation in the field of education was not due to any decline in the religious beliefs of the people. Horace Mann was a devout Christian, and the deep religious feeling of James Madison is stamped upon the Remonstrance. The secular public school did not imply indifference to the basic role of religion in the life of the people, nor rejection of religious education as a means of fostering it. The claims of religion were not minimized by refusing to make the public schools agencies for their assertion. The nonsectarian or secular public school was the means of reconciling freedom in general with religious freedom. The sharp confinement of the public schools to secular education was a recognition of the need of a democratic society to educate its children, insofar as the State undertook to do so, in an atmosphere free from pressures in a realm in which pressures are most resisted and where conflicts are most easily and most bitterly engendered. Designed to serve as perhaps the most powerful agency for promoting cohesion among a heterogeneous democratic people, the public school must keep scrupulously free from entanglement in the strife of sects. The preservation of the community from divisive conflicts, of Government from irreconcilable pressures by religious groups, of religion from censorship and coercion however subtly exercised, requires strict confinement of the State to instruction other than religious, leaving to the individual's church and home, indoctrination in the faith of his choice. . . .

MR. JUSTICE JACKSON, concurring.

I join the opinion of MR. JUSTICE FRANKFURTER, and concur in the result reached by the Court, but with these reservations: I think it is doubtful whether the facts of this case establish jurisdiction in this Court, but in any event that we should place some bounds on the demands for interference with local schools that we are empowered or willing to entertain. I make these reservations a matter of record in view of the number of litigations likely to be started as a result of this decision. . . .

MR. JUSTICE REED, dissenting.

As I am convinced that this interpretation of the First Amendment is erroneous, I feel impelled to express the reasons for my disagreement. By directing attention to the many instances of close association of church and state in American society and by recalling that many of these relations are so much a part of our tradition and culture that they are accepted without more, this dissent may help in an appraisal of the meaning of the clause of the First Amendment concerning the establishment of religion and of the reasons which lead to the approval or disapproval of the judgment below. . . .

I find it difficult to extract from the opinions any conclusion as to what it is in the Champaign plan that is unconstitutional. Is it the use of school buildings for religious instruction; the release of pupils by the schools for religious instruction during school hours; the so-called assistance by teachers in handing out the request cards to pupils, in keeping lists of them for release and records of their attendance; or the action of the principals in arranging an opportunity for the classes and the appearance of the Council's instructors? None of the reversing opinions say whether the purpose of the

Champaign plan for religious instruction during school hours is unconstitutional or whether it is some ingredient used in or omitted from the formula that makes the plan unconstitutional.

From the tenor of the opinions I conclude that their teachings are that any use of a pupil's school time, whether that use is on or off the school grounds, with the necessary school regulations to facilitate attendance, falls under the ban. . . .

Mr. Jefferson, as one of the founders of the University of Virginia, a school which from its establishment in 1819 has been wholly governed, managed and controlled by the State of Virginia, was faced with the same problem that is before this Court today: the question of the constitutional limitation upon religious education in public schools. In his annual report as Rector, to the President and Directors of the Literary Fund, dated October 7, 1822, approved by the Visitors of the University of whom Mr. Madison was one, Mr. Jefferson set forth his views at some length. These suggestions of Mr. Jefferson were adopted and ch. II, § 1, of the Regulations of the University of October 4, 1824, provided that:

Should the religious sects of this State, or any of them, according to the invitation held out to them, establish within, or adjacent to, the precincts of the University, schools for instruction in the religion of their sect, the students of the University will be free, and expected to attend religious worship at the establishment of their respective sects, in the morning, and in time to meet their school in the University at its stated hour.

Thus, the "wall of separation between church and State" that Mr. Jefferson built at the University which he founded did not exclude religious education from that school. The difference between the generality of his statements on the separation of church and state and the specificity of his conclusions on education are considerable. A rule of law should not be drawn from a figure of speech.

Mr. Madison's *Memorial and Remonstrance against Religious Assessments,* relied upon by the dissenting Justices in *Everson,* is not applicable here. Mr. Madison was one of the principal opponents in the Virginia General Assembly of *A Bill Establishing a Provision for Teachers of the Christian Religion.* The monies raised by the taxing section of that bill were to be appropriated "by the Vestries, Elders, or Directors of each religious society, . . . to a provision for a Minister or Teacher of the Gospel of their denomination, or the providing places of divine worship, and to none other use whatsoever. . . ." The conclusive legislative struggle over this act took place in the fall of 1785, before the adoption of the Bill of Rights. The *Remonstrance* had been issued before the General Assembly convened and was instrumental in the final defeat of the act, which died in committee. Throughout the *Remonstrance,* Mr. Madison speaks of the "establishment" sought to be effected by the act. It is clear from its historical setting and its language that the *Remonstrance* was a protest against an effort by Virginia to support Christian sects by taxation. Issues similar to those raised by the instant case were not discussed. Thus, Mr. Madison's approval of Mr. Jefferson's report as Rector gives, in my opinion, a clearer indication of his views on the constitutionality of religious education in public schools than his general statements on a different subject. . . .

It seems clear to me that the "aid" referred to by the

Court in the *Everson* case could not have been those incidental advantages that religious bodies, with other
groups similarly situated, obtain as a by-product of
organized society. This explains the well-known fact
that all churches receive "aid" from government in the
form of freedom from taxation. The *Everson* decision
itself justified the transportation of children to church
schools by New Jersey for safety reasons. It accords with
Cochran v. *Louisiana State Board of Education,* 281
U.S. 370, where this Court upheld a free textbook
statute of Louisiana against a charge that it aided private schools on the ground that the books were for the
education of the children, not to aid religious schools.
Likewise the National School Lunch Act aids all school
children attending tax-exempt schools. In *Bradfield* v.
Roberts, 175 U.S. 291, this Court held proper the payment of money by the Federal Government to build an
addition to a hospital, chartered by individuals who
were members of a Roman Catholic sisterhood, and
operated under the auspices of the Roman Catholic
Church. This was done over the objection that it aided
the establishment of religion. While obviously in these
instances the respective churches, in a certain sense, were
aided, this Court has never held that such "aid" was in
violation of the First or Fourteenth Amendment. . . .

The practices of the federal government offer many
examples of this kind of "aid" by the state to religion.
The Congress of the United States has a chaplain for
each House who daily invokes divine blessings and guidance for the proceedings. The armed forces have com-
missioned chaplains from early days. They conduct the
public services in accordance with the liturgical requirements of their respective faiths, ashore and afloat, employing for the purpose property belonging to the United

States and dedicated to the services of religion. Under the Servicemen's Readjustment Act of 1944, eligible veterans may receive training at government expense for the ministry in denominational schools. The schools of the District of Columbia have opening exercises which "include a reading from the Bible without note or comment, and the Lord's prayer."

In the United States Naval Academy and the United States Military Academy, schools wholly supported and completely controlled by the federal government, there are a number of religious activities. Chaplains are attached to both schools. Attendance at church services on Sunday is compulsory at both the Military and Naval Academies. At West Point the Protestant services are held in the Cadet Chapel, the Catholic in the Catholic Chapel, and the Jewish in the Old Cadet Chapel; at Annapolis only Protestant services are held on the reservation, midshipmen of other religious persuasions attend the churches of the city of Annapolis. These facts indicate that both schools since their earliest beginnings have maintained and enforced a pattern of participation in formal worship. . . .

The prohibition of enactments respecting the establishment of religion does not bar every friendly gesture between church and state. It is not an absolute prohibition against every conceivable situation where the two may work together, any more than the other provisions of the First Amendment—free speech, free press—are absolutes. If abuses occur, such as the use of the instruction hour for sectarian purposes, I have no doubt, in view of the *Ring* case, that Illinois will promptly correct them. If they are of a kind that tend to the establishment of a church or interfere with the free exercise of religion, this Court is open for a review of any erroneous decision. This Court cannot be too cautious in upsetting practices embedded in our society by many years of experience. A state is entitled to have great leeway in its legislation when dealing with the important social problems of its population. A definite violation of legislative limits must be established. The Constitution should not be stretched to forbid national customs in the way courts act to reach arrangements to avoid federal taxation. Devotion to the great principle of religious liberty should not lead us into a rigid interpretation of the constitutional guarantee that conflicts with accepted habits of our people. This is an instance where, for me, the history of past practices is determinative of the meaning of a constitutional clause, not a decorous introduction to the study of its text. The judgment should be affirmed.

5. Zorach v. Clauson

343 U. S. 306 (1952)

Appeal from the Court of Appeals of New York.

MR. JUSTICE DOUGLAS delivered the opinion of the Court.

New York City has a program which permits its public schools to release students during the school day so that they may leave the school buildings and school grounds and go to religious centers for religious instruction or devotional exercises. A student is released on written request of his parents. Those not released stay in the classroom. The churches make weekly reports to the schools, sending a list of children who have been released from public school but who have not reported for religious instruction.

This "released time" program involves neither religious instruction in public school classrooms nor the expenditure of public funds. All costs, including the application blanks, are paid by the religious organizations. The case is therefore unlike *McCollum* v. *Board of Education,* 333 U.S. 203, which involved a "released time" program from Illinois. In that case the classrooms were turned over to religious instructors. We accordingly held that the program violated the First Amendment which (by reason of the Fourteenth Amendment) prohibits the states from establishing religion or prohibiting its free exercise.

Appellants, who are taxpayers and residents of New York City and whose children attend its public schools, challenge the present law, contending it is in essence not different from the one involved in the *McCollum* case. Their argument, stated elaborately in various ways, reduces itself to this: the weight and influence of the school is put behind a program for religious instruction; public school teachers police it, keeping tab on students who are released; the classroom activities come to a halt while the students who are released for religious instruction are on leave; the school is a crutch on which the churches are leaning for support in their religious training; without the cooperation of the schools this "released time" program, like the one in the *McCollum* case, would be futile and ineffective. The New York Court of Appeals sustained the law against this claim of unconstitutionality. . . .

The briefs and arguments are replete with data bearing on the merits of this type of "released time" program. Views *pro* and *con* are expressed, based on practical experience with these programs and with their implications. We do not stop to summarize these materials nor to burden the opinion with an analysis of them. For they involve considerations not germane to the narrow constitutional issue presented. They largely concern the wisdom of the system, its efficiency from an educational point of view, and the political considerations which have motivated its adoption or rejection in some communities. Those matters are of no concern here, since our problem reduces itself to whether New York by this system has either prohibited the "free exercise" of religion or has made a law "respecting an establishment of religion" within the meaning of the First Amendment.

It takes obtuse reasoning to inject any issue of the "free exercise" of religion into the present case. No one is forced to go to the religious classroom and no religious exercise or instruction is brought to the classrooms of the public schools. A student need not take religious instruction. He is left to his own desires as to the manner or time of his religious devotions, if any.

There is a suggestion that the system involves the use of coercion to get public school students into religious classrooms. There is no evidence in the record before us that supports that conclusion. The present record indeed tells us that the school authorities are neutral in this regard and do no more than release students whose parents so request. If in fact coercion were used, if it were established that any one or more teachers were using their office to persuade or force students to take the religious instruction, a wholly different case would be presented. Hence we put aside that claim of coercion both as respects the "free exercise" of religion and "an establishment of religion" within the meaning of the First Amendment.

Moreover, apart from that claim of coercion, we do not see how New York by this type of "released time" program has made a law respecting an establishment of religion within the meaning of the First Amendment. There is much talk of the separation of Church and State in the history of the Bill of Rights and in the decisions clustering around the First Amendment. . . . There cannot be the slightest doubt that the First Amendment reflects the philosophy that Church and State should be separated. And so far as interference with the "free exercise" of religion and "establishment" of religion are concerned, the separation must be complete and unequivocal. The First Amendment within the scope of its coverage permits no exception; the prohibition is absolute. The First Amendment, however, does not say that in every and all respects there shall be a separation of Church and State. Rather, it studiously defines the manner, the specific ways, in which there shall be no concert or union or dependency one on the other. That is the common sense of the matter. Otherwise the state and religion would be aliens to each other—hostile, suspicious, and even unfriendly. Churches could not be required to pay even property taxes. Municipalities would not be permitted to render police or fire protection to religious groups. Policemen who helped parishioners into their places of worship would violate the Constitution. Prayers in our legislative halls; the appeals to the Almighty in the messages of the Chief Executive; the proclamations making Thanksgiving Day a holiday; "so help me God" in our courtroom oaths—these and all other references to the Almighty that run through our laws, our public rituals, our ceremonies would be flouting the First Amendment. A fastidious atheist or agnostic could even object to the supplication with which the Court opens each session: "God save the United States and this Honorable Court."

We would have to press the concept of separation of Church and State to these extremes to condemn the present law on constitutional grounds. The nullification of this law would have wide and profound effects. A Catholic student applies to his teacher for permission to leave the school during hours on a Holy Day of Obligation to attend a mass. A Jewish student asks his teacher for permission to be excused for Yom Kippur. A Protestant wants the afternoon off for a family baptismal ceremony. In each case the teacher requires parental consent in writing. In each case the teacher, in order to make sure the student is not a truant, goes further and requires a report from the priest, the rabbi, or the minister. The teacher in other words cooperates in a religious program to the extent of making it possible for her students to participate in it. Whether she does it occasionally for a few students, regularly for one, or pursuant to a systematized program designed to further the religious needs of all the students does not alter the character of the act.

We are a religious people whose institutions presuppose a Supreme Being. We guarantee the freedom to worship as one chooses. We make room for as wide a variety of beliefs and creeds as the spiritual needs of man deem necessary. We sponsor an attitude on the part of government that shows no partiality to any one group and that lets each flourish according to the zeal of its adherents and the appeal of its dogma. When the state encourages religious instruction or cooperates with religious authorities by adjusting the schedule of public events to sectarian needs, it follows the best of our traditions. For it then respects the religious nature of our people and accommodates the public service to their spiritual needs. To hold that it may not would be to find in the Constitution a requirement that the government show a callous indifference to religious groups. That would be preferring those who believe in no religion over those who do believe. Government may not finance religious groups nor undertake religious instruction nor blend secular and sectarian education nor use secular institutions to force one or some religion on any person. But we find no constitutional requirement which makes it necessary for government to be hostile to religion and to throw its weight against efforts to widen the effective scope of religious influence. The govern-

ment must be neutral when it comes to competition between sects. It may not thrust any sect on any person.
It may not make a religious observance compulsory. It
may not coerce anyone to attend church, to observe a
religious holiday, or to take religious instruction. But it
can close its doors or suspend its operations as to those
who want to repair to their religious sanctuary for worship or instruction. No more than that is undertaken
here.

This program may be unwise and improvident from
an educational or a community viewpoint. . . . Our individual preferences, however, are not the constitutional
standard. The constitutional standard is the separation
of Church and State. The problem, like many problems
in constitutional law, is one of degree. . . .

Affirmed.

Mr. Justice Black, dissenting.

I see no significant difference between the invalid Illinois system and that of New York here sustained.
Except for the use of the school buildings in Illinois,
there is no difference between the systems which I consider even worthy of mention. In the New York program, as in that of Illinois, the school authorities release
some of the children on the condition that they attend
the religious classes, get reports on whether they attend,
and hold the other children in the school building until
the religious hour is over. As we attempted to make
categorically clear, the *McCollum* decision would have
been the same if the religious classes had not been held
in the school buildings. . . .

I am aware that our *McCollum* decision on separation
of Church and State has been subjected to a most search-

ing examination throughout the country. Probably few opinions from this Court in recent years have attracted more attention or stirred wider debate. Our insistence on "a wall between Church and State which must be kept high and impregnable" has seemed to some a correct exposition of the philosophy and a true interpretation of the language of the First Amendment to which we should strictly adhere. With equal conviction and sincerity, others have thought the *McCollum* decision fundamentally wrong and have pledged continuous warfare against it. The opinions in the court below and the briefs here reflect these diverse viewpoints. In dissenting today, I mean to do more than give routine approval to our *McCollum* decision. I mean also to reaffirm my faith in the fundamental philosophy expressed in *McCollum* and *Everson* v. *Board of Education*, 330 U.S. 1. . . .

Here the sole question is whether New York can use its compulsory education laws to help religious sects get attendants presumably too unenthusiastic to go unless moved to do so by the pressure of this state machinery. That this is the plan, purpose, design and consequence of the New York program cannot be denied. The state thus makes religious sects beneficiaries of its power to compel children to attend secular schools. Any use of such coercive power by the state to help or hinder some religious sects or to prefer all religious sects over non-believers or vice versa is just what I think the First Amendment forbids. In considering whether a state has entered this forbidden field the question is not whether it has entered too far but whether it has entered at all. New York is manipulating its compulsory education laws to help religious sects get pupils. This is not separation but combination of Church and State.

The Court's validation of the New York system rests

in part on its statement that Americans are "a religious people whose institutions presuppose a Supreme Being." This was at least as true when the First Amendment was adopted; and it was just as true when eight Justices of this Court invalidated the released time system in *McCollum* on the premise that a state can no more "aid all religions" than it can aid one. It was precisely because Eighteenth Century Americans were a religious people divided into many fighting sects that we were given the constitutional mandate to keep Church and State completely separate. Colonial history had already shown that, here as elsewhere zealous sectarians entrusted with governmental power to further their causes would sometimes torture, maim and kill those they branded "heretics," "atheists" or "agnostics." The First Amendment was therefore to insure that no one powerful sect or combination of sects could use political or governmental power to punish dissenters whom they could not convert to their faith. Now as then, it is only by wholly isolating the state from the religious sphere and compelling it to be completely neutral, that the freedom of each and every denomination and of all nonbelievers can be maintained. It is this neutrality the Court abandons today when it treats New York's coercive system as a program which *merely* "encourages religious instruction or cooperates with religious authorities." The abandonment is all the more dangerous to liberty because of the Court's legal exaltation of the orthodox and its derogation of unbelievers.

Under our system of religious freedom, people have gone to their religious sanctuaries not because they feared the law but because they loved their God. The choice of all has been as free as the choice of those who answered the call to worship moved only by the music of the old Sunday morning church bells. The spiritual mind of man has thus been free to believe, disbelieve, or doubt, without repression, great or small, by the heavy hand of government. Statutes authorizing such repression have been stricken. Before today, our judicial opinions have refrained from drawing invidious distinctions between those who believe in no religion and those who do believe. The First Amendment has lost much if the religious follower and the atheist are no longer to be judicially regarded as entitled to equal justice under the law.

State help to religion injects political and party prejudices into a holy field. It too often substitutes force for prayer, hate for love, and persecution for persuasion. Government should not be allowed, under cover of the soft euphemism of "cooperation," to steal into the sacred area of religious choice.

MR. JUSTICE FRANKFURTER, dissenting.

Of course, a State may provide that the classes in its schools shall be dismissed, for any reason, or no reason, on fixed days, or for special occasions. The essence of this case is that the school system did not "close its doors" and did not "suspend its operations." There is all the difference in the world between letting the children out of school and letting some of them out of school into religious classes. If every one is free to make what use he will of time wholly unconnected from schooling required by law—those who wish sectarian instruction devoting it to that purpose, those who have ethical instruction at home, to that, those who study music, to that—then of course there is no conflict with the Fourteenth Amendment.

The pith of the case is that formalized religious instruction is substituted for other school activity which those who do not participate in the released-time program are compelled to attend. The school system is very much in operation during this kind of released time. If its doors are closed, they are closed upon those students who do not attend the religious instruction, in order to keep them within the school. That is the very thing which raises the constitutional issue. It is not met by disregarding it. Failure to discuss this issue does not take it out of the case. . . .

The deeply divisive controversy aroused by the attempts to secure public school pupils for sectarian instruction would promptly end if the advocates of such instruction were content to have the school "close its doors or suspend its operations"—that is, dismiss classes in their entirety, without discrimination—instead of seeking to use the public schools as the instrument for securing attendence at denominational classes. The unwillingness of the promoters of this movement to dispense with such use of the public schools betrays a surprising want of confidence in the inherent power of the various faiths to draw children to outside sectarian classes—an attitude that hardly reflects the faith of the greatest religious spirits.

Mr. Justice Jackson, dissenting.

This released time program is founded upon a use of the State's power of coercion, which, for me, determines its unconstitutionality. . . .

If public education were taking so much of the pupils' time as to injure the public or the students' welfare by encroaching upon their religious opportunity, simply shortening everyone's school day would facilitate voluntary and optional attendance at Church classes. But that suggestion is rejected upon the ground that if they are made free many students will not go to the Church. Hence, they must be deprived of freedom for this period, with Church attendance put to them as one of the two permissible ways of using it.

The greater effectiveness of this system over voluntary attendance after school hours is due to the truant officer who, if the youngster fails to go to the Church school, dogs him back to the public schoolroom. Here schooling is more or less suspended during the "released time" so that nonreligious attendants will not forge ahead of the churchgoing absentees. But it serves as a temporary jail for a pupil who will not go to Church. It takes more subtlety of mind than I possess to deny that this is governmental constraint in support of religion. It is as unconstitutional, in my view, when exerted by indirection as when exercised forthrightly.

As one whose children, as a matter of free choice, have been sent to privately supported Church schools, I may challenge the Court's suggestion that opposition to this plan can only be antireligious, atheistic, or agnostic. My evangelistic brethren confuse an objection to compulsion with an objection to religion. It is possible to hold a faith with enough confidence to believe that what should be rendered to God does not need to be decided and collected by Caesar.

The day that this country ceases to be free for irreligion it will cease to be free for religion—except for the sect that can win political power. The same epithetical jurisprudence used by the Court today to beat down those who oppose pressuring children into some religion can devise as good epithets tomorrow against those who object to pressuring them into a favored religion. And, after all, if we concede to the State power and wisdom to single out "duly constituted religious" bodies as exclusive alternatives for compulsory secular instruction, it would be logical to also uphold the power and wisdom to choose the true faith among those "duly constituted." We start down a rough road when we begin to mix compulsory public education with compulsory godliness. . . .

The wall which the Court was professing to erect between Church and State has become even more warped and twisted than I expected. Today's judgment will be more interesting to students of psychology and of the judicial processes than to students of constitutional law.

6.   Engel v. Vitale

370 U.S. 421 (1962)

Pursuant to the recommendation of the New York State Board of Regents, which has broad supervisory powers over the State's public school system, the Board of Education of a local school district adopted the following brief, denominationally neutral prayer, to be said by each class in the presence of a teacher at the beginning of each school day:

"Almighty God, we acknowledge our dependence upon Thee, and we beg Thy blessings upon us, our parents, our teachers and our country."

In a suit brought by the parents of several pupils, the New York courts upheld the power of the state to use this Regents' prayer as part of the public school's daily procedure so long as the schools did not compel any pupil to join in the prayer over his or his parents' objection. The United States Supreme Court took the case by the discretionary writ of certiorari, and reversed on the ground that the action of the Board violated that part of the First Amendment which forbids an establishment of religion, as applied to the states by way of the Due Process Clause of the Fourteenth Amendment.

Certiorari to the Court of Appeals of New York.

MR. JUSTICE BLACK delivered the opinion of the Court.

We think that by using its public school system to encourage recitation of the Regents' prayer, the State of New York has adopted a practice wholly inconsistent with the Establishment Clause. There can, of course, be no doubt that New York's program of daily classroom invocation of God's blessings as prescribed in the Regents' prayer is a religious activity. It is a solemn avowal of divine faith and supplication for the blessings of the Almighty. The nature of such a prayer has always been religious, none of the respondents has denied this and the trial court expressly so found. . . .

The petitioners contend among other things that the state laws requiring or permitting use of the Regents' prayer must be struck down as a violation of the Establishment Clause because that prayer was composed by governmental officials as a part of a governmental program to further religious beliefs. For this reason, petitioners argue, the State's use of the Regents' prayer in its public school system breaches the constitutional wall of separation between Church and State. We agree with that contention since we think that the constitutional prohibition against laws respecting an establishment of religion must at least mean that in this country it is no part of the business of government to compose official prayers for any group of the American people to recite as a part of a religious program carried on by government.

It is a matter of history that this very practice of establishing governmentally composed prayers for religious services was one of the reasons which caused many of our early colonists to leave England and seek religious freedom in America. The Book of Common Prayer, which was created under governmental direction and which was approved by Acts of Parliament in 1548 and 1549, set out in minute detail the accepted form and content of prayer and other religious ceremonies to be used in the established, tax-supported Church of England. The controversies over the Book and what should be its content repeatedly threatened to disrupt the peace of that country as the accepted forms of prayer in the established church changed with the views of the particular ruler that happened to be in control at the time. Powerful groups representing some of the varying religious views of the people struggled among themselves to impress their particular views upon the Government and obtain amendments of the Book more suitable to their respective notions of how religious services should be conducted in order that the official religious establishment would advance their particular religious beliefs. Other groups, lacking the necessary political power to influence the Government on the matter, decided to leave England and its established church and seek freedom in America from England's governmentally ordained and supported religion.

It is an unfortunate fact of history that when some of the very groups which had most strenuously opposed the established Church of England found themselves sufficiently in control of colonial governments in this country to write their own prayers into law, they passed laws making their own religion the official religion of their respective colonies. Indeed, as late as the time of the Revolutionary War, there were established churches in at least eight of the thirteen former colonies and established religions in at least four of the other five. But the successful Revolution against English political domination was shortly followed by intense opposition to the

actice of establishing religion by law. This opposition
ystallized rapidly into an effective political force in
irginia where the minority religious groups such as
resbyterians, Lutherans, Quakers and Baptists had
ained such strength that the adherents to the established
piscopal Church were actually a minority themselves. In
785–1786, those opposed to the established Church, led
y James Madison and Thomas Jefferson, who, though
emselves not members of any of these dissenting reli-
ous groups, opposed all religious establishments by law
n grounds of principle, obtained the enactment of the
mous "Virginia Bill for Religious Liberty" by which
ll religious groups were placed on an equal footing so
r as the State was concerned. Similar though less far-
aching legislation was being considered and passed in
ther States.

By the time of the adoption of the Constitution, our
istory shows that there was a widespread awareness
mong many Americans of the dangers of a union of
hurch and State. These people knew, some of them
om bitter personal experience, that one of the greatest
angers to the freedom of the individual to worship in
is own way lay in the Government's placing its official
amp of approval upon one particular kind of prayer or
ne particular form of religious services. They knew the
nguish, hardship and bitter strife that could come when
ealous religious groups struggled with one another to
btain the Government's stamp of approval from each
ing, Queen, or Protector that came to temporary power.
he Constitution was intended to avert a part of this
anger by leaving the government of this country in
e hands of the people rather than in the hands of any
onarch. But this safeguard was not enough. Our Found-
rs were no more willing to let the content of their

prayers and their privilege of praying whenever the
pleased be influenced by the ballot box than they we
to let these vital matters of personal conscience depen
upon the succession of monarchs. The First Amendmer
was added to the Constitution to stand as a guarante
that neither the power nor the prestige of the Feder
Government would be used to control, support or in
fluence the kinds of prayer the American people ca
say—that the people's religions must not be subjected t
the pressures of government for change each time a ne
political administration is elected to office. Under tha
Amendment's prohibition against governmental estab
lishment of religion, as reinforced by the provisions o
the Fourteenth Amendment, government in this country
be it state or federal, is without power to prescribe b
law any particular form of prayer which is to be use
as an official prayer in carrying on any program of go
ernmentally sponsored religious activity.

There can be no doubt that New York's state praye
program officially establishes the religious beliefs em
bodied in the Regents' prayer. The respondents' argu
ment to the contrary, which is largely based upon th
contention that the Regents' prayer is "non-denomina
tional" and the fact that the program, as modified an
approved by state courts, does not require all pupils to
recite the prayer but permits those who wish to do so to
remain silent or be excused from the room, ignores th
essential nature of the program's constitutional defect
Neither the fact that the prayer may be denominationall
neutral nor the fact that its observance on the part o
the students is voluntary can serve to free it from th
limitations of the Establishment Clause, as it might from
the Free Exercise Clause, of the First Amendment, bot
of which are operative against the States by virtue of th

ourteenth Amendment. Although these two clauses may
n certain instances overlap, they forbid two quite dif-
erent kinds of governmental encroachment upon reli-
ious freedom. The Establishment Clause, unlike the Free
Exercise Clause, does not depend upon any showing of
direct governmental compulsion and is violated by the
nactment of laws which establish an official religion
whether those laws operate directly to coerce nonobserv-
ng individuals or not. This is not to say, of course, that
aws officially prescribing a particular form of religious
worship do not involve coercion of such individuals.
When the power, prestige and financial support of government is placed behind a particular religious belief,
he indirect coercive pressure upon religious minorities
o conform to the prevailing officially approved religion
s plain. But the purposes underlying the Establishment
Clause go much further than that. Its first and most immediate purpose rested on the belief that a union of
government and religion tends to destroy government
and to degrade religion. The history of governmentally
established religion, both in England and in this country,
howed that whenever government had allied itself with
one particular form of religion, the inevitable result had
been that it had incurred the hatred, disrespect and even
contempt of those who held contrary beliefs. That same
history showed that many people had lost their respect
for any religion that had relied upon the support of
government to spread its faith. The Establishment Clause
thus stands as an expression of principle on the part of
the Founders of our Constitution that religion is too
personal, too sacred, too holy, to permit its "unhallowed
perversion" by a civil magistrate. Another purpose of the
Establishment Clause rested upon an awareness of the
historical fact that governmentally established religions

and religious persecutions go hand in hand. The Found
ers knew that only a few years after the Book of Com
mon Prayer became the only accepted form of religiou
services in the established Church of England, an Act o
Uniformity was passed to compel all Englishmen to a
tend those services and to make it a criminal offense t
conduct or attend religious gatherings of any othe
kind—a law which was consistently flouted by dissentin
religious groups in England and which contributed t
widespread persecutions of people like John Bunya
who persisted in holding "unlawful [religious] meeting
. . . to the great disturbance and distraction of the goo
subjects of this kingdom. . . ." And they knew that sim
lar persecutions had received the sanction of law in se
eral of the colonies in this country soon after the estab
lishment of official religions in those colonies. It was i
large part to get completely away from this sort of sy
tematic religious persecution that the Founders brough
into being our Nation, our Constitution, and our Bill o
Rights with its prohibition against any governmenta
establishment of religion. The New York laws officiall
prescribing the Regents' prayer are inconsistent wit
both the purposes of the Establishment Clause and wit
the Establishment Clause itself.

It has been argued that to apply the Constitution i
such a way as to prohibit state laws respecting an estab
lishment of religious services in public schools is to indi
cate a hostility toward religion or toward prayer. Nothing
of course, could be more wrong. The history of man i
inseparable from the history of religion. And perhaps i
is not too much to say that since the beginning of tha
history many people have devoutly believed that "Mor
things are wrought by prayer than this world dreams of.'
It was doubtless largely due to men who believed thi

that there grew up a sentiment that caused men to leave the cross-currents of officially established state religions and religious persecution in Europe and come to this country filled with the hope that they could find a place in which they could pray when they pleased to the God of their faith in the language they chose. And there were men of this same faith in the power of prayer who led the fight for adoption of our Constitution and also for our Bill of Rights with the very guarantees of religious freedom that forbid the sort of governmental activity which New York has attempted here. These men knew that the First Amendment, which tried to put an end to governmental control of religion and of prayer, was not written to destroy either. They knew rather that it was written to quiet well-justified fears which nearly all of them felt arising out of an awareness that governments of the past had shackled men's tongues to make them speak only the religious thoughts that government wanted them to speak and to pray only to the God that government wanted them to pray to. It is neither sacrilegious nor antireligious to say that each separate government in this country should stay out of the business of writing or sanctioning official prayers and leave that purely religious function to the people themselves and to those the people choose to look to for religious guidance. . . .

Reversed and remanded.

Mr. Justice Frankfurter took no part in the decision of this case.

Mr. Justice White took no part in the consideration or decision of this case.

Mr. Justice Douglas, concurring.

The point for decision is whether the Government can constitutionally finance a religious exercise. Our system at the federal and state levels is presently honeycombed with such financing. Nevertheless, I think it is an unconstitutional undertaking whatever form it takes. . . .

. . . I cannot say that to authorize this prayer is to establish a religion in the strictly historic meaning of those words. A religion is not established in the usual sense merely by letting those who choose to do so say the prayer that the public school teacher leads. Yet once government finances a religious exercise it inserts a divisive influence into our communities. The New York court said that the prayer given does not conform to all of the tenets of the Jewish, Unitarian, and Ethical Culture groups. One of petitioners is an agnostic. . . .

The First Amendment leaves the Government in a position not of hostility to religion but of neutrality. The philosophy is that the atheist or agnostic—the nonbeliever—is entitled to go his own way. The philosophy is that if government interferes in matters spiritual, it will be a divisive force. The First Amendment teaches that a government neutral in the field of religion better serves all religious interests. . . .

MR. JUSTICE STEWART, dissenting.

With all respect, I think the Court has misapplied a great constitutional principle. I cannot see how an "official religion" is established by letting those who want to say a prayer say it. On the contrary, I think that to deny the wish of these school children to join in reciting this prayer is to deny them the opportunity of sharing in the spiritual heritage of our Nation.

The Court's historical review of the quarrels over the

Book of Common Prayer in England throws no light for me on the issue before us in this case. England had then and has now an established church. Equally unenlightening, I think, is the history of the early establishment and later rejection of an official church in our own States. For we deal here not with the establishment of a state church, which would, of course, be constitutionally impermissible, but with whether school children who want to begin their day by joining in prayer must be prohibited from doing so. Moreover, I think that the Court's task, in this as in all areas of constitutional adjudication, is not responsibly aided by the uncritical invocation of metaphors like the "wall of separation," a phrase nowhere to be found in the Constitution. What is relevant to the issue here is not the history of an established church in sixteenth century England or in eighteenth century America, but the history of the religious traditions of our people, reflected in countless practices of the institutions and officials of our government.

At the opening of each day's Session of this Court we stand, while one of our officials invokes the protection of God. Since the days of John Marshall our Crier has said, "God save the United States and this Honorable Court." Both the Senate and the House of Representatives open their daily Sessions with prayer. Each of our Presidents, from George Washington to John F. Kennedy, has upon assuming his Office asked the protection and help of God.

The Court today says that the state and federal governments are without constitutional power to prescribe any particular form of words to be recited by any group of the American people on any subject touching religion. The third stanza of "The Star-Spangled Banner," made our National Anthem by Act of Congress in 1931, contains these verses:

> "Blest with victory and peace, may
>   the heav'n rescued land
> Praise the Pow'r that hath made and
>   preserved us a nation!
> Then conquer we must, when our
>   cause it is just,
> And this be our motto 'In God is our
>   Trust.' "

In 1954 Congress added a phrase to the Pledge of Allegiance to the Flag so that it now contains the words "one Nation *under God*, indivisible, with liberty and justice for all." In 1952 Congress enacted legislation calling upon the President each year to proclaim a National Day of Prayer. Since 1865 the words "IN GOD WE TRUST" have been impressed on our coins.

Countless similar examples could be listed, but there is no need to belabor the obvious. . . .

I do not believe that this Court, or the Congress, or the President has by the actions and practices I have mentioned established an "official religion" in violation of the Constitution. And I do not believe the State of New York has done so in this case. What each has done has been to recognize and to follow the deeply entrenched and highly cherished spiritual traditions of our Nation —traditions which come down to us from those who almost two hundred years ago avowed their "firm reliance on the Protection of divine Providence" when they proclaimed the freedom and independence of this brave new world.

I dissent.

7. Abington School District v. Schempp

374 U.S. 203 (1963)

This decision involved a joinder of two cases, one from Pennsylvania and one from Maryland, testing the meaning of the "establishment" clause of the First Amendment as applied to the states through the Due Process Clause of the Fourteenth Amendment. The Pennsylvania case dealt with a statute, and the Maryland case with a rule made under statutory authority by the Board of School Commissioners of Baltimore City, which required the reading, without comment, at the beginning of each school day, of verses from the Bible and the recitation by the students, in unison, of the Lord's Prayer. These were prescribed curricular activities applicable to students who are required by law to attend school, and were held in public school buildings under the supervision of and with the participation of the teachers. Upon written request of a parent or guardian a child could be excused from these exercises. Eight Justices agreed that these exercises violated the "establishment" clause of the Constitution, though four of them enlarged upon their views in separate concurring opinions.

Appeal from U.S. District Court for the Eastern District of Pennsylvania.

Certiorari to the Maryland Court of Appeals.

MR. JUSTICE CLARK delivered the opinion of the Court.

It is true that religion has been closely identified with
our history and government. . . . The fact that the
Founding Fathers believed devotedly that there was a
God and that the unalienable rights of man were rooted
in Him is clearly evidenced in their writings, from the
Mayflower Compact to the Constitution itself. This
background is evidenced today in our public life through
the continuance in our oaths of office from the Presidency
to the Alderman of the final supplication, "So help me
God." Likewise each House of the Congress provides
through its Chaplain an opening prayer, and the sessions
of this Court are declared open by the crier in a short
ceremony, the final phrase of which invokes the grace of
God. Again, there are such manifestations in our mili
tary forces, where those of our citizens who are under the
restrictions of military service wish to engage in volun
tary worship. Indeed, only last year an official survey of
the country indicated that 64% of our people have church
membership . . . while less than 3% profess no religion
whatever. . . . It can be truly said, therefore, that today
as in the beginning, our national life reflects a religious
people. . . .

This is not to say, however, that religion has been so
identified with our history and government that religious
freedom is not likewise as strongly imbedded in our pub
lic and private life. Nothing but the most telling of
personal experiences in religious persecution suffered by
our forebears . . . could have planted our belief in lib
erty of religious opinion any more deeply in our heritage
It is true that this liberty frequently was not realized by

he colonists, but this is readily accountable by their close
ies to the Mother Country. However, the views of Madi-
on and Jefferson, preceded by Roger Williams, came to
be incorporated not only in the Federal Constitution but
likewise in those of most of our States. This freedom to
worship was indispensable in a country whose people
came from the four quarters of the earth and brought
with them a diversity of religious opinion. Today author-
ties list 83 separate religious bodies, each with membership exceeding 50,000, existing among our people, as well
as innumerable smaller groups. . . .

First, this Court has decisively settled that the First
Amendment's mandate that "Congress shall make no law
respecting an establishment of religion, or prohibiting
the free exercise thereof" has been made wholly applicable to the States by the Fourteenth Amendment. . . .

Second, this Court has rejected unequivocally the contention that the Establishment Clause forbids only governmental preference of one religion over another. Almost 20 years ago in *Everson* . . . the Court said that
"[n]either a state nor the Federal Government can set up
a church. Neither can pass laws which aid one religion,
aid all religions, or prefer one religion over another. . . ."

While none of the parties to either of these cases has
questioned these basic conclusions of the Court, both of
which have been long established, recognized and consistently reaffirmed, others continue to question their
history, logic and efficacy. Such contentions, in the light
of the consistent interpretation in cases of this Court,
seem entirely untenable and of value only as academic
exercises. . . .

The wholesome "neutrality" of which this Court's
cases speak thus stems from a recognition of the teachings
of history that powerful sects or groups might bring

about a fusion of governmental and religious functior or a concert or dependency of one upon the other to th end that official support of the State or Federal Goverr ment would be placed behind the tenets of one or of a orthodoxies. This the Establishment Clause prohibit And a further reason for neutrality is found in the Fre Exercise Clause, which recognizes the value of religiou training, teaching and observance and, more particularl the right of every person to freely choose his own cours with reference thereto, free of any compulsion from th state. This the Free Exercise Clause guarantees. Thu as we have seen, the two clauses may overlap. As we hav indicated, the Establishment Clause has been directl considered by this Court eight times in the past score o years and, with only one Justice dissenting on the poin it has consistently held that the clause withdrew all leg islative power respecting religious belief or the expres sion thereof. The test may be stated as follows: what ar the purpose and the primary effect of the enactment? I either is the advancement or inhibition of religion ther the enactment exceeds the scope of legislative power a circumscribed by the Constitution. That is to say that t withstand the strictures of the Establishment Claus there must be a secular legislative purpose and a primar effect that neither advances nor inhibits religion. . . The Free Exercise Clause, likewise considered many time here, withdraws from legislative power, state and federal the exertion of any restraint on the free exercise of re ligion. Its purpose is to secure religious liberty in th individual by prohibiting any invasions thereof by civi authority. Hence it is necessary in a free exercise case fo one to show the coercive effect of the enactment as i operates against him in the practice of his religion. The distinction between the two clauses is apparent—a viola tion of the Free Exercise Clause is predicated on coercion while the Establishment Clause violation need not be so attended. . . .

. . . In both cases the laws require religious exercises and such exercises are being conducted in direct violation of the rights of the appellees and petitioners. Nor are these required exercises mitigated by the fact that individual students may absent themselves upon parental request, for that fact furnishes no defense to a claim of unconstitutionality under the Establishment Clause. . . . Further, it is no defense to urge that the religious practices here may be relatively minor encroachments on the First Amendment. The breach of neutrality that is today a trickling stream may all too soon become a raging torrent and, in the words of Madison, "it is proper to take alarm at the first experiment on our liberties." . . .

It is insisted that unless these religious exercises are permitted a "religion of secularism" is established in the schools. We agree of course that the State may not establish a "religion of secularism" in the sense of affirmatively opposing or showing hostility to religion, thus "preferring those who believe in no religion over those who do believe." . . . We do not agree, however, that this decision in any sense has that effect. In addition, it might well be said that one's education is not complete without a study of comparative religion or the history of religion and its relationship to the advancement of civilization. It certainly may be said that the Bible is worthy of study for its literary and historic qualities. Nothing we have said here indicates that such study of the Bible or of religion, when presented objectively as part of a secular program of education, may not be effected consistently with the First Amendment. But the exercises here do not fall into those categories. They are religious exercises, required by the States in violation of the command of the First Amendment that the Government maintain strict neutrality, neither aiding nor opposing religion.

Finally, we cannot accept that the concept of neutrality, which does not permit a State to require a religious exercise even with the consent of the majority of those affected, collides with the majority's right to free exercise of religion. While the Free Exercise Clause clearly prohibits the use of state action to deny the rights of free exercise to *anyone,* it has never meant that a majority could use the machinery of the State to practice its beliefs. Such a contention was effectively answered by Mr. Justice Jackson for the Court in *West Virginia State Board of Education* v. *Barnette.* . . .

"The very purpose of a Bill of Rights was to withdraw certain subjects from the vicissitudes of political controversy, to place them beyond the reach of majorities and officials and to establish them as legal principles to be applied by the courts. One's right to . . . freedom of worship . . . and other fundamental rights may not be submitted to vote; they depend on the outcome of no elections."

The place of religion in our society is an exalted one, achieved through a long tradition of reliance on the home, the church and the inviolable citadel of the individual heart and mind. We have come to recognize through bitter experience that it is not within the power of government to invade that citadel, whether its purpose or effect be to aid or oppose, to advance or retard. In the relationship between man and religion, the State is firmly committed to a position of neutrality. Though the application of that rule requires interpretation of a delicate sort, the rule itself is clearly and concisely stated in the words of the First Amendment. . . .

[The judgment of the federal Court was affirmed and that of the Maryland Court was reversed.]

MR. JUSTICE DOUGLAS, concurring.

In these cases we have no coercive religious exercise aimed at making the students conform. The prayers announced are not compulsory, though some may think they have that indirect effect because the nonconformist student may be induced to participate for fear of being called an "oddball." But that coercion, if it be present, has not been shown; so the vices of the present regimes are different.

These regimes violate the Establishment Clause in two different ways. In each case the State is conducting a religious exercise; and, as the Court holds, that cannot be done without violating the "neutrality" required of the State by the balance of power between individual, church and state that has been struck by the First Amendment. But the Establishment Clause is not limited to precluding the State itself from conducting religious exercises. It also forbids the State to employ its facilities or funds in a way that gives any church, or all churches, greater strength in our society than it would have by relying on its members alone. Thus, the present regimes must fall under that clause for the additional reason that public funds, though small in amount, are being used to promote a religious exercise. Through the mechanism of the State, all of the people are being required to finance a religious exercise that only some of the people want and that violates the sensibilities of others.

The most effective way to establish any institution is to finance it; and this truth is reflected in the appeals by church groups for public funds to finance their religious schools. Financing a church either in its strictly religious activities or in its other activities is equally unconstitutional, as I understand the Establishment Clause. Budgets for one activity may be technically separable from budgets for others. But the institution is an inseparable whole, a living organism, which is strengthened in proselytizing when it is strengthened in any department by contributions from other than its own members.

MR. JUSTICE BRENNAN, concurring.

Americans regard the public schools as a most vital civic institution for the preservation of a democratic system of government. It is therefore understandable that the constitutional prohibitions encounter their severest test when they are sought to be applied in the school classroom. . . . While our institutions reflect a firm conviction that we are a religious people, those institutions by solemn constitutional injunction may not officially involve religion in such a way as to prefer, discriminate against, or oppress, a particular sect or religion. Equally the Constitution enjoins those involvements of religious with secular institutions which (a) serve the essentially religious activities of religious institutions; (b) employ the organs of government for essentially religious purposes; or (c) use essentially religious means to serve governmental ends where secular means would suffice. . . .

A too literal quest for the advice of the Founding Fathers upon the issues of these cases seems to me futile and misdirected for several reasons: First, on our precise problem the historical record is at best ambiguous, and statements can readily be found to support either side of the proposition. The ambiguity of history is understandable if we recall the nature of the problems uppermost in the thinking of the statesmen who fashioned the religious guarantees; they were concerned with far more flagrant intrusions of government into the realm of religion than any that our century has witnessed. While it is clear to me that the Framers meant the Establishment Clause to prohibit more than the creation of an established federal church such as existed in England, I have no doubt that, in their preoccupation with the imminent question of established churches, they gave no distinct consideration to the particular question whether the clause also forbade devotional exercises in public institutions.

Second, the structure of American education has greatly changed since the First Amendment was adopted. In the context of our modern emphasis upon public education available to all citizens, any views of the eighteenth century as to whether the exercises at bar are an "establishment" offer little aid to decision. Education, as the Framers knew it, was in the main confined to private schools more often than not under strictly sectarian supervision. Only gradually did control of education pass largely to public officials. It would, therefore, hardly be significant if the fact was that the nearly universal devotional exercises in the schools of the young Republic did not provoke criticism; even today religious ceremonies in church-supported private schools are constitutionally unobjectionable.

Third, our religious composition makes us a vastly more diverse people than were our forefathers. They knew differences chiefly among Protestant sects. Today the Nation is far more heterogeneous religiously, including as it does substantial minorities not only of Catholics and Jews but as well of those who worship according to no version of the Bible and those who worship no God at all. . . .

Fourth, the American experiment in free public education available to all children has been guided in large measure by the dramatic evolution of the religious diversity among the population which our public schools serve. . . . It is implicit in the history and character of American public education that the public schools serve a uniquely *public* function: the training of American citizens in an atmosphere free of parochial, divisive, or separatist influences of any sort—an atmosphere in which children may assimilate a heritage common to all American groups and religions. . . . This is a heritage neither theistic nor atheistic, but simply civic and patriotic. . . .

Attendance at the public schools has never been compulsory; parents remain morally and constitutionally free to choose the academic environment in which they wish their children to be educated. The relationship of the Establishment Clause of the First Amendment to the public school system is preeminently that of reserving such a choice to the individual parent, rather than vesting it in the majority of voters of each State or school district. The choice which is thus preserved is between a public secular education with its uniquely democratic values, and some form of private or sectarian education, which offers values of its own. In my judgment the First Amendment forbids the State to inhibit that freedom of choice by diminishing the attractiveness of either alternative—either by restricting the liberty of the private schools to inculcate whatever values they wish, or by jeopardizing the freedom of the public schools from private or sectarian pressures. . . .

Daily recital of the Lord's Prayer and the reading of passages of Scripture are quite as clearly breaches of the command of the Establishment Clause as was the daily use of the rather bland Regents' Prayer in the New York public schools. Indeed, I would suppose that, if anything, the Lord's Prayer and the Holy Bible are more clearly sectarian, and the present violations of the First Amendment consequently more serious. But the religious exercises challenged in these cases have a long history. And almost from the beginning, Bible reading and daily prayer in the schools have been the subject of debate, criticism by educators and other public officials, and proscription by courts and legislative councils. . . .

. . . Much has been written about the moral and spiritual values of infusing some religious influence or instruction into the public school classroom. To the extent that only *religious* materials will serve this purpose, it seems to me that the purpose as well as the means is so plainly religious that the exercise is necessarily forbidden by the Establishment Clause. . . .

It has not been shown that readings from the speeches and messages of great Americans, . . . or from the documents of our heritage of liberty, daily recitation of the Pledge of Allegiance, or even the observance of a moment of reverent silence at the opening of class, may not adequately serve the solely secular purposes of the devotional activities without jeopardizing either the religious liberties of any members of the community or the proper degree of separation between the spheres of religion and government. Such substitutes would, I think, be unsatisfactory or inadequate only to the extent that the present activities do in fact serve religious goals. . . .

Both the Baltimore and Abington procedures permit . . . the reading of any of several versions of the Bible, and this flexibility is said to ensure neutrality sufficiently to avoid the constitutional prohibition. One answer, which might be dispositive, is that any version of the Bible is inherently sectarian, else there would be no need to offer a system of rotation or alternation of versions in the first place, that is, to allow different sectarian versions to be used on different days. The sectarian character of the Holy Bible has been at the core of the whole controversy over religious practices in the public schools throughout its long and often bitter history. . . .

The argument contains, however, a more basic flaw. There are persons in every community—often deeply devout—to whom any version of the Judaeo-Christian Bible is offensive. There are others whose reverence for the Holy Scriptures demands private study or reflection and to whom public reading or recitation is sacrilegious. . . .

. . . The availability of excusal or exemption simply has no relevance to the establishment question, if it is once found that these practices are essentially religious exercises designed at least in part to achieve religious aims through the use of public school facilities during the school day.

The more difficult question, however, is whether the availability of excusal for the dissenting child serves to refute challenges to these practices under the Free Exercise Clause. . . . By requiring what is tantamount in the eyes of teachers and schoolmates to a profession of disbelief, or at least of nonconformity, the procedure may well deter those children who do not wish to participate for any reason based upon the dictates of conscience from exercising an indisputably constitutional right to be excused. Thus the excusal provision in its operation subjects them to a cruel dilemma. In consequence, even devout children may well avoid claiming their right and simply continue to participate in exercises distasteful to hem because of an understandable reluctance to be stigmatized as atheists or nonconformists simply on the basis of their request.

Such reluctance to seek exemption seems all the more likely in view of the fact that children are disinclined at this age to step out of line or to flout "peer-group norms." Such is the widely held view of experts who have studied the behaviors and attitudes of children. . . .

These considerations bring me to a final contention of the school officials in these cases: that the invalidation of the exercises at bar permits this Court no alternative but to declare unconstitutional every vestige, however slight, of cooperation or accommodation between religion and government. I cannot accept that contention. . . .

The State must be steadfastly neutral in all matters of faith, and neither favor nor inhibit religion. In my view, government cannot sponsor religious exercises in the public schools without jeopardizing that neutrality. On the other hand, hostility, not neutrality, would characterize the refusal to provide chaplains and places of worship for prisoners and soldiers cut off by the State from all civilian opportunities for public communion, the withholding of draft exemptions for ministers and conscientious objectors, or the denial of the temporary use of an empty public building to a congregation whose place of worship has been destroyed by fire or flood. I do not say that government *must* provide chaplains or draft exemptions, or that the courts should intercede if it fails to do so.

. . . The saying of invocational prayers in legislative chambers, state or federal, and the appointment of legislative chaplains, might well represent no involvements of the kind prohibited by the Establishment Clause. Legislators, federal and state, are mature adults who may presumably absent themselves from such public and ceremonial exercises without incurring any penalty, direct or indirect. . . .

. . . The holding of the Court today plainly does not foreclose teaching *about* the Holy Scriptures or about the differences between religious sects in classes in literature or history. Indeed, whether or not the Bible is involved, it would be impossible to teach meaningfully many subjects in the social sciences or the humanities without some mention of religion. To what extent, and at what points in the curriculum, religious materials should be cited are matters which the courts ought to entrust very largely to the experienced officials who superintend our Nation's public schools. They are experts in such matters, and we are not. . . .

Nothing we hold today questions the propriety of certain tax deductions or exemptions which incidentally benefit churches and religious institutions, along with many secular charities and nonprofit organizations. If religious institutions benefit, it is in spite of rather than because of their religious character. For religious institutions simply share benefits which government makes generally available to educational, charitable, and eleemosynary groups. There is no indication that taxing authorities have used such benefits in any way to subsidize worship or foster belief in God. And as among religious beneficiaries, the tax exemption or deduction can be truly nondiscriminatory, available on equal terms to small as well as large religious bodies, to popular and unpopular sects, and to those organizations which reject as well as those which accept a belief in God. . . . .

MR. JUSTICE GOLDBERG, with whom MR. JUSTICE HARLAN joins, concurring.

The practices here involved do not fall within any sensible or acceptable concept of compelled or permitted accommodation and involve the state so significantly and directly in the realm of the sectarian as to give rise to those very divisive influences and inhibitions of freedom which both religion clauses of the First Amendment preclude. The state has ordained and has utilized its facilities to engage in unmistakably religious exercises—the devotional reading and recitation of the Holy Bible—in a manner having substantial and significant import and impact. That it has selected, rather than written, a particular devotional liturgy seems to me without constitutional import. The pervasive religiosity and direct governmental involvement inhering in the prescription of prayer and Bible reading in the public schools, during and as part of the curricular day, involving young impressionable children whose school attendance is statutorily compelled, and utilizing the prestige, power, and influence of school administration, staff, and authority, cannot realistically be termed simply accommodation, and must fall within the interdiction of the First Amendment. I find nothing in the opinion of the Court which says more than this. And, of course, today's decision does not mean that all incidents of government which import of the religious are therefore and without more banned by the strictures of the Establishment Clause. . . .

MR. JUSTICE STEWART, dissenting.

I think the records in the two cases before us are so fundamentally deficient as to make impossible an informed or responsible determination of the constitutional issues presented. Specifically, I cannot agree that on these records we can say that the Establishment Clause has neces-

sarily been violated. But I think there exist serious ques
tions under both that provision and the Free Exercise
Clause—insofar as each is imbedded in the Fourteenth
Amendment—which require the remand of these cases
for the taking of additional evidence. . . .

. . . Religious exercises are not constitutionally in
valid if they simply reflect differences which exist in the
society from which the school draws its pupils. They be
come constitutionally invalid only if their administration
places the sanction of secular authority behind one or
more particular religious or irreligious beliefs. . . .

Viewed in this light, it seems to me clear that the rec
ords in both of the cases before us are wholly inadequate
to support an informed or responsible decision. Both
cases involve provisions which explicitly permit any stu
dent who wishes, to be excused from participation in the
exercises. There is no evidence in either case as to whether
there would exist any coercion of any kind upon a stu
dent who did not want to participate. . . .

What our Constitution indispensably protects is the
freedom of each of us, be he Jew or Agnostic, Christian or
Atheist, Buddhist or Freethinker, to believe or disbelieve,
to worship or not worship, to pray or keep silent, accord
ing to his own conscience, uncoerced and unrestrained
by government. It is conceivable that these school boards,
or even all school boards, might eventually find it impos
sible to administer a system of religious exercises during
school hours in such a way as to meet this constitutional
standard—in such a way as completely to free from any
kind of official coercion those who do not affirmatively
want to participate. But I think we must not assume that
school boards so lack the qualities of inventiveness and
good will as to make impossible the achievement of that
goal.

8. Board of Education of Central School District v. Allen

392 U.S. 236 (1968)

In 1930, the Supreme Court by unanimous vote upheld the constitutionality of a Louisiana statute which required school books to be furnished by the State Board of Education without charge to all students, whether in public or private schools, rejecting the claim that the statute violated the Fourteenth Amendment because it did not serve a "public purpose," Cochran *v.* Louisiana State Board of Education, *281 U.S. 370. After 1940, however, as the Supreme Court read the freedom of religion and no-establishment clauses of the First Amendment as limiting the states by way of the Fourteenth Amendment, the issue of state aid to religion moved into the complicated area of state-church relations. Thus the textbook question as it came up from New York in 1968 was examined within a framework of ideas not even touched upon in the 1930 decision.*

Appeal from the Court of Appeals of New York.

MR. JUSTICE WHITE delivered the opinion of the Court.

A law of the State of New York requires local public school authorities to lend textbooks free of charge to all students in grades seven through 12; students attending private schools are included. This case presents the question whether this statute is a "law respecting the establishment of religion or prohibiting the free exercise thereof," and so in conflict with the First and Fourteenth Amendments to the Constitution, because it authorizes the loan of textbooks to students attending parochial schools. We hold that the law is not in violation of the Constitution.

Until 1965, § 701 of the Educational Law of the State of New York authorized public school boards to designate textbooks for use in the public schools, to purchase such books with public funds, and to rent or sell the books to public school students. In 1965 the Legislature amended § 701, basing the amendments on findings that the "public welfare and safety require that the state and local communities give assistance to educational programs which are important to our national defense and the general welfare of the state." Beginning with the 1966–1967 school year, local school boards were required to purchase textbooks and lend them without charge "to all children residing in such district who are enrolled in grades seven to twelve of a public or private school which complies with the compulsory education law." The books now loaned are "text-books which are designated for use in any public, elementary or secondary schools of the state or are approved by any boards of education," and which—according to a 1966 amendment—"a pupil is required to use as a text for a semester or more in a particular class in the school he legally attends." . . .

On appeal, the New York Court of Appeals . . . by a . . . 4–3 vote held that § 701 was not in violation of either the State or the Federal Constitution. . . . The Court of Appeals said that the law's purpose was to benefit all school children, regardless of the type of school they attended, and that only textbooks approved by public school authorities could be loaned. It therefore considered § 701 "completely neutral with respect to religion, merely making available secular textbooks at the request of the individual student and asking no question about what school he attends." Section 701, the Court of Appeals concluded, is not a law which "establishes a religion or constitutes the use of public funds to aid religious schools." . . .

Everson v. *Board of Education,* 330 U.S. 1 (1947), is the case decided by this Court that is most nearly in point for today's problem. New Jersey reimbursed parents for expenses incurred in busing their children to parochial schools. . . . The statute was held to be valid even though one of its results was that "children are helped to get to church schools" and "some of the children might not be sent to the church schools if the parents were compelled to pay their children's bus fares out of their own pockets. . . ." As with public provision of police and fire protection, sewage facilities, and streets and sidewalks, payment of bus fares was of some value to the religious school, but was nevertheless not such support of a religious institution as to be a prohibited establishment of religion within the meaning of the First Amendment.

Everson and later cases have shown that the line between state neutrality to religion and state support of religion is not easy to locate. . . . The statute upheld in *Everson* would be considered a law having "a secular legislative purpose and a primary effect that neither advances nor inhibits religion." We reach the same result with respect to the New York law requiring school books to be loaned free of charge to all students in specified grades. The express purpose of § 701 was stated by the New York Legislature to be furtherance of the educational opportunities available to the young. Appellants have shown us nothing about the necessary effects of the statute that is contrary to its stated purpose. The law merely makes available to all children the benefits of a general program to lend school books free of charge. Books are furnished at the request of the pupil and ownership remains, at least technically, in the State. Thus no funds or books are furnished to parochial schools, and the financial benefit is to parents and children, not to schools. Perhaps free books make it more likely that some children choose to attend a sectarian school, but that was true of the state-paid bus fares in *Everson* and does not alone demonstrate an unconstitutional degree of support for a religious institution.

Of course books are different from buses. Most bus rides have no inherent religious significance, while religious books are common. However, the language of § 701 does not authorize the loan of religious books, and the State claims no right to distribute religious literature. Although the books loaned are those required by the parochial school for use in specific courses, each book loaned must be approved by the public school authorities; only secular books may receive approval. The law was construed by the Court of Appeals of New York as "merely making available secular textbooks at the request of the individual student," . . . and the record contains no suggestion that religious books have been loaned. Absent evidence, we cannot assume that school authorities, who constantly face the same problem in selecting textbooks for use in the public schools, are unable to distinguish between secular and religious books or that they will not honestly discharge their duties uner the law. In judging the validity of the statue on his record we must proceed on the assumption that books loaned to students are books that are not unsuitable for use in the public schools because of religious content.

The major reason offered by appellants for distinguishing free textbooks from free bus fares is that books, but not buses, are critical to the teaching process, and in a sectarian school that process is employed to teach religion. However, this Court has long recognized that religious schools pursue two goals, religious instruction and secular education. In the leading case of *Pierce* v. *Society of Sisters,* 268 U.S. 510 (1925), the Court held that although it would not question Oregon's power to compel school attendance or require that the attendance be at an institution meeting State-imposed requirements as to quality and nature of curriculum, Oregon had not shown that its interest in secular education required that all children attend publicly operated schools. A premise of this holding was the view that the State's interest in education would be served sufficiently by reliance on the secular teaching that accompanied religious training in the schools maintained by the Society of Sisters. Since *Pierce,* a substantial body of case law has confirmed the power of the States to insist that attendance at private schools, if it is to satisfy state compulsory-attendance laws, be at institutions which provide minimum hours of instruction, employ teachers of specified training, and cover prescribed subjects of instruction. Indeed, the State's interest in assuring that these standards are being met has been considered a sufficient reason for refusing to accept instruction at home as compliance with compulsory education statutes. These cases were a sensible corollary of *Pierce* v. *Society of Sisters:*

if the State must satisfy its interest in secular education
through the instrument of private schools, it has a
proper interest in the manner in which those schools
perform their secular educational function. Another
corollary was *Cochran* v. *Louisiana State Board of Education,* 281 U.S. 370 (1930), where appellants said that a
statute requiring school books to be furnished without
charge to all students, whether they attended public or
private schools, did not serve a "public purpose," and
so offended the Fourteenth Amendment. Speaking
through Chief Justice Hughes, the Court summarized as
follows its conclusion that Louisiana's interest in the
secular education being provided by private schools made
provision of textbooks to students in those schools a
properly public concern: "[The State's] interest is education, broadly; its method, comprehensive. Individual
interests are aided only as the common interest is safeguarded." . . .

Underlying these cases, and underlying also the legislative judgments that have preceded the court decisions,
has been a recognition that private education has played
and is playing a significant and valuable role in raising
national levels of knowledge, competence, and experience. Americans care about the quality of the secular
education available to their children. They have considered high quality education to be an indispensable
ingredient for achieving the kind of nation, and the
kind of citizenry, that they have desired to create. Considering this attitude, the continued willingness to rely
on private school systems, including parochial systems,
strongly suggests that a wide segment of informed opinion, legislative and otherwise, has found that those
schools do an acceptable job of providing secular education to their students. This judgment is further evidenced

at parochial schools are performing, in addition to
eir sectarian function, the task of secular education.

Against this background of judgment and experience,
nchallenged in the meager record before us in this
se, we cannot agree with appellants either that all
aching in a sectarian school is religious or that the
ocesses of secular and religious training are so inter-
ined that secular textbooks furnished to students by
e public are in fact instrumental in the teaching of
ligion. This case comes to us after summary judgment
itered on the pleadings. Nothing in this record sup-
orts the proposition that all textbooks, whether they
al with mathematics, physics, foreign languages, his-
ry, or literature, are used by the parochial schools to
ach religion. No evidence has been offered about par-
cular schools, particular courses, particular teachers, or
irticular books. We are unable to hold, based solely
a judicial notice, that this statute results in unconstitu-
onal involvement of the State with religious instruc-
on or that § 701, for this or the other reasons urged, is
law respecting the establishment of religion within
ie meaning of the First Amendment. . . .

The judgment is affirmed.

[R. JUSTICE BLACK, dissenting.

believe the New York law held valid is a flat, flagrant,
en violation of the First and Fourteenth Amendments
hich together forbid Congress or state legislatures to
iact any law "respecting an establishment of religion."
or that reason I would reverse the New York Court of
ppeals' judgments. . . .

It is true, of course, that the New York law does not
yet formally adopt or establish a state religion. But

it takes a great stride in that direction and coming even
cast their shadows before them. The same powerfu
sectarian religious propagandists who have succeeded i:
securing passage of the present law to help religiou
schools carry on their sectarian religious purposes ca
and doubtless will continue their propaganda, lookin
toward complete domination and supremacy of thei
particular brand of religion. And it nearly always is b
insidious approaches that the citadels of liberty are mos
successfully attacked. . . .

The First Amendment's bar to establishment of re
ligion must preclude a State from using funds levie
from all of its citizens to purchase books for use by sec
tarian schools, which, although "secular," realisticall
will in some way inevitably tend to propagate the re
ligious views of the favored sect. Books are the most es
sential tool of education since they contain the resource
of knowledge which the educational process is designe
to exploit. In this sense it is not difficult to distinguis
books, which are the heart of any school, from bus fares
which provide a convenient and helpful general publi
transportation service. With respect to the former, stat
financial support actively and directly assists the teachin
and propagation of sectarian religious viewpoints i
clear conflict with the First Amendment's establishmen
bar; with respect to the latter, the State merely provide
a general and nondiscriminatory transportation servic
in no way related to substantive religious views an
beliefs.

This New York law, it may be said by some, make
but a small inroad and does not amount to complet
state establishment of religion. But that is no excus
for upholding it. It requires no prophet to foresee tha
on the argument used to support this law others coul

e upheld providing for state or federal government unds to buy property on which to erect religious school uildings or to erect the buildings themselves, to pay the alaries of the religious school teachers, and finally to ave the sectarian religious groups cease to rely on voluntary contributions of members of their sects while vaiting for the Government to pick up all the bills for he religious schools. . . .

I still subscribe to the belief that tax-raised funds annot constitutionally be used to support religious chools, buy their school books, erect their buildings, pay heir teachers, or pay any other of their maintenance xpenses, even to the extent of one penny. The First Amendment's prohibition against governmental establishment of religion was written on the assumption that tate aid to religion and religious schools generates disord, disharmony, hatred, and strife among our people, nd that any government that supplies such aids is to hat extent a tyranny. And I still believe that the only vay to protect minority religious groups from majority groups in this country is to keep the wall of separation)etween church and state high and impregnable as the First and Fourteenth Amendments provide. The Court's affirmance here bodes nothing but evil to religious peace n this country.

MR. JUSTICE DOUGLAS, dissenting.

The statute on its face empowers each parochial school .o determine for itself which textbooks will be eligible for loans to its students, for the Act provides that the only text which the State may provide is "a book which a pupil is required to use as a text for a semester or more in a particular class in the school he legally attends." . . . This initial and crucial selection is undoubtedly made by the parochial school's principal or its individual instructors, who are, in the case of Roman Catholic schools, normally priests or nuns.

The next step under the Act is an "individual request" for an eligible textbook . . . but the State Education Department has ruled that a pupil may make his request to the local public board of education through a "private school official." Local boards have accordingly provided for those requests to be made by the individual or "by groups or classes." . . .

The role of the local public school board is to decide whether to veto the selection made by the parochial school. This is done by determining first whether the text has been or should be "approved" for use in public schools and second whether the text is "secular," "non-religious," or "nonsectarian." The local boards apparently have broad discretion in exercising this veto power.

Thus the statutory system provides that the parochial school will ask for the books that it wants. Can there be the slightest doubt that the head of the parochial school will select the book or books that best promote its sectarian creed?

If the board of education supinely submits by approving and supplying the sectarian or sectarian-oriented textbooks, the struggle to keep church and state separate has been lost. If the board resists, then the battle-line between church and state will have been drawn and the contest will be on to keep the school board independent or to put it under church domination and control.

Whatever may be said of *Everson,* there is nothing ideological about a bus. There is nothing ideological about a school lunch, nor a public nurse, nor a scholar-

hip. The constitutionality of such public aid to students in parochial schools turns on considerations not
present in this textbook case. The textbook goes to the
very heart of education in a parochial school. It is the
chief, although not solitary, instrumentality for propa-
gating a particular religious creed or faith. How can
we possibly approve such state aid to a religion? A parochial school textbook may contain many, many more
seeds of creed and dogma than a prayer. . . .

Even where the treatment given to a particular topic
in a school textbook is not blatantly sectarian, it will
necessarily have certain shadings that will lead a parochial school to prefer one text over another.

The Crusades, for example, may be taught as a Christian undertaking to "save the Holy Land" from the
Moslem Turks who "became a threat to Christianity
and its holy places," which "they did not treat . . . with
respect" . . . or as essentially a series of wars born out
of political and materialistic motives. . . .

Is the dawn of man to be explained in the words,
"God created man and made man master of the earth"
. . . or in the language of evolution? . . .

Is the slaughter of the Aztecs by Cortes and his en-
tourage to be lamented for its destruction of a New
World culture . . . or forgiven because the Spaniards
"carried the true Faith" to a barbaric people who practiced human sacrifice? . . .

Is Franco's revolution in Spain to be taught as a
crusade against anti-Catholic forces . . . or as an effort
by reactionary elements to regain control of that country? . . .

9. Epperson v. Arkansas

393 U.S. 97 (1968)

Appeal from the Supreme Court of Arkansas.

MR. JUSTICE FORTAS delivered the opinion of the Court

I

This appeal challenges the constitutionality of the "antievolution" statute which the State of Arkansas adopted in 1928 to prohibit the teaching in its public schools and universities of the theory that man evolved from other species of life. The statute was a product of the upsurge of "fundamentalist" religious fervor of the twenties. The Arkansas statute was an adaptation of the famous Tennessee "monkey law" which that State adopted in 1925. The constitutionality of the Tennessee law was upheld by the Tennessee Supreme Court in the celebrated *Scopes* case in 1927.

The Arkansas law makes it unlawful for a teacher in any state-supported school or university "to teach the theory or doctrine that mankind ascended or descended from a lower order of animals," or "to adopt or use in any such institution a textbook that teaches" this theory. Violation is a misdemeanor and subjects the violator to dismissal from his position.

The present case concerns the teaching of biology in a high school in Little Rock. According to the testimony, until the events here in litigation, the official textbook furnished for the high school biology course "did not have a section on the Darwinian Theory." Then, for the academic year 1965–1966, the school administration, on recommendation of the teachers of biology in the school system, adopted and prescribed a textbook which contained a chapter setting forth "the theory about the origin . . . of man from a lower form of animal."

Susan Epperson, a young woman who graduated from Arkansas' school system and then obtained her master's degree in zoology at the University of Illinois, was employed by the Little Rock school system in the fall of 1964 to teach 10th grade biology at Central High School. At the start of the next academic year, 1965, she was confronted by the new textbook (which one surmises from the record was not unwelcome to her). She faced at least a literal dilemma because she was supposed to use the new textbook for classroom instruction and presumably to teach the statutorily condemned chapter; but to do so would be a criminal offense and subject her to dismissal.

She instituted the present action in the Chancery Court of the State, seeking a declaration that the Arkansas statute is void and enjoining the State and the defendant officials of the Little Rock school system from dismissing her for violation of the statute's provisions. . . .

The Chancery Court, in an opinion by Chancellor Murray O. Reed, held that the statute violated the Fourteenth Amendment to the United States Constitution. The court noted that this Amendment encompasses the prohibitions upon state interference with freedom of speech and thought which are contained in the First Amendment. Accordingly, it held that the challenged statute is unconstitutional because, in violation of the First Amendment, it "tends to hinder the quest for knowledge, restrict the freedom to learn, and restrain the freedom to teach." In this perspective, the Act, it held, was an unconstitutional and void restraint upon the freedom of speech guaranteed by the Constitution.

On appeal, the Supreme Court of Arkansas reversed ... It sustained the statute as an exercise of the State's power to specify the curriculum in public schools. It did not address itself to the competing constitutional considerations. . . .

Only Arkansas and Mississippi have such "anti-evolution" or "monkey" laws on their books. There is no record of any prosecutions in Arkansas under its statute. It is possible that the statute is presently more of a curiosity than a vital fact of life in these States. Nevertheless, the present case was brought, the appeal as of right is properly here, and it is our duty to decide the issues presented.

II

At the outset, it is urged upon us that the challenged statute is vague and uncertain and therefore within the condemnation of the Due Process Clause of the Fourteenth Amendment. The contention that the Act is vague and uncertain is supported by the language in the brief opinion of Arkansas' Supreme Court. That court, perhaps reflecting the discomfort which the statute's quixotic prohibition necessarily engenders in the modern mind, stated that it "expresses no opinion" as to whether the Act prohibits "explanation" of the theory of evolution or merely forbids "teaching that the theory is true." Regardless of this uncertainty, the court held that the statute is constitutional.

On the other hand, counsel for the State, in oral argument in this Court, candidly stated that, despite the State Supreme Court's equivocation, Arkansas would interpret the statute "to mean that to make a student aware of the theory . . . just to teach that there was such a theory" would be grounds for dismissal and for prosecution under the statute; and he said "that the Supreme Court of Arkansas' opinion should be interpreted in that manner." He said "If Mrs. Epperson would tell her students that 'Here is Darwin's theory, that man ascended or descended from a lower form of being,' then I think she would be under this statute liable for prosecution."

In any event, we do not rest our decision upon the asserted vagueness of the statute. On either interpretation of its language, Arkansas' statute cannot stand. It is of no moment whether the law is deemed to prohibit mention of Darwin's theory, or to forbid any or all of the infinite varieties of communication embraced within the term "teaching." Under either interpretation, the law must be stricken because of its conflict with the constitutional prohibition of state laws respecting an establishment of religion or prohibiting the free exercise thereof. The overriding fact is that Arkansas' law selects from the body of knowledge a particular segment which it proscribes for the sole reason that it is deemed to conflict with a particular religious doctrine; that is, with a particular interpretation of the Book of Genesis by a particular religious group.

III

The antecedents of today's decision are many and unmistakable. They are rooted in the foundation soil of our Nation. They are fundamental to freedom.

Government in our democracy, state and national, must be neutral in matters of religious theory, doctrine, and practice. It may not be hostile to any religion or to the advocacy of no-religion; and it may not aid, foster, or promote one religion or religious theory against another or even against the militant opposite. The First Amendment mandates governmental neutrality between religion and religion, and between religion and non-religion.

As early as 1872, this Court said: "The law knows no heresy, and is committed to the support of no dogma, the establishment of no sect." . . . This has been the interpretation of the great First Amendment which this Court has applied in the many and subtle problems which the ferment of our national life has presented for decision within the Amendment's broad command.

Judicial interposition in the operation of the public school system of the Nation raises problems requiring care and restraint. Our courts, however, have not failed to apply the First Amendment's mandate in our educational system where essential to safeguard the fundamental values of freedom of speech and inquiry and of belief. By and large, public education in our Nation is committed to the control of state and local authorities. Courts do not and cannot intervene in the resolution of conflicts which arise in the daily operation of school systems and which do not directly and sharply implicate basic constitutional values. On the other hand, "[t]he vigilant protection of constitutional freedoms is nowhere more vital than in the community of American schools." . . .

The earliest cases in this Court on the subject of the impact of constitutional guarantees upon the classroom were decided before the Court expressly applied the specific prohibitions of the First Amendment to the States. But as early as 1923, the Court did not hesitate to condemn under the Due Process Clause "arbitrary" restrictions upon the freedom of teachers to teach and of students to learn. In that year, the Court, in an opinion by JUSTICE MCREYNOLDS, held unconstitutional an Act of the State of Nebraska making it a crime to teach any subject in any language other than English to pupils who had not passed the eighth grade. The State's purpose in enacting the law was to promote civic cohesiveness by encouraging the learning of English and to combat the "baneful effect" of permitting foreigners to rear and educate their children in the language of the parents' native land. The Court recognized these purposes, and it acknowledged the State's power to prescribe the school curriculum, but it held that these were not adequate to support the restriction upon the liberty of teacher and pupil. The challenged statute, it held, unconstitutionally interfered with the right of the individuals, guaranteed by the Due Process Clause, to engage in any of the common occupations of life and to acquire useful knowledge. *Meyer* v. *State of Nebraska,* 262 U.S. 390 (1923). . . .

For purposes of the present case, we need not re-enter the difficult terrain which the Court, in 1923, traversed without apparent misgivings. . . . Today's problem is capable of resolution in the narrower terms of the First Amendment's prohibition of laws respecting an establishment of religion or prohibiting the free exercise thereof.

There is and can be no doubt that the First Amendment does not permit the State to require that teaching and learning must be tailored to the principles or prohibitions of any religious sect or dogma. . . .

While study of religions and of the Bible from a literary and historic viewpoint, presented objectively as part of a secular program of education, need not collide with the First Amendment's prohibition, the State may not adopt programs or practices in its public schools or colleges which "aid or oppose" any religion. . . . This prohibition is absolute. It forbids alike the preference of a religious doctrine or the prohibition of theory which is deemed antagonistic to a particular dogma. As MR. JUSTICE CLARK stated in *Joseph Burstyn, Inc.* v. *Wilson*, "the state has no legitimate interest in protecting any or all religions from views distasteful to them. . . ." 343 U.S. 495, 505 (1952). . . .

The State's undoubted right to prescribe the curriculum for its public schools does not carry with it the right to prohibit, on pain of criminal penalty, the teaching of a scientific theory or doctrine where that prohibition is based upon reasons that violate the First Amendment. It is much too late to argue that the State may impose upon the teachers in its schools any conditions that it chooses, however restrictive they may be of constitutional guarantees. . . .

In the present case, there can be no doubt that Arkansas has sought to prevent its teachers from discussing the theory of evolution because it is contrary to the belief of some that the Book of Genesis must be the exclusive source of doctrine as to the origin of man. No suggestion has been made that Arkansas' law may be justified by considerations of state policy other than the religious views of some of its citizens. It is clear that fundamentalist sectarian conviction was and is the law's reason for existence. Its antecedent, Tennessee's "monkey law," candidly stated its purpose: to make it unlawful "to teach any theory that denies the story of the Divine

Creation of man as taught in the Bible, and to teach instead that man has descended from a lower order of animals." Perhaps the sensational publicity attendant upon the *Scopes* trial induced Arkansas to adopt less explicit language. It eliminated Tennessee's reference to "the story of the Divine Creation of man" as taught in the Bible, but there is no doubt that the motivation for the law was the same: to suppress the teaching of a theory which, it was thought, "denied" the divine creation of man.

Arkansas' law cannot be defended as an act of religious neutrality. Arkansas did not seek to excise from the curricula of its schools and universities all discussion of the origin of man. The law's effort was confined to an attempt to blot out a particular theory because of its supposed conflict with the Biblical account, literally read. Plainly, the law is contrary to the mandate of the First, and in violation of the Fourteenth, Amendment to the Constitution.

The judgment of the Supreme Court of Arkansas is
Reversed.

MR. JUSTICE BLACK, concurring.

I am by no means sure that this case presents a genuinely justiciable case or controversy. Although . . . the statute alleged to be unconstitutional, was passed by the voters of Arkansas in 1928, we are informed that there has never been even a single attempt by the State to enforce it. And the pallid, unenthusiastic, even apologetic defense of the Act presented by the State in this Court indicates that the State would make no attempt to enforce the law should it remain on the books for the next century. Now, nearly 40 years after the law has slumbered on the books as though dead, a teacher alleging fear that the State might arouse from its lethargy and try to punish her has asked for a declaratory judgment holding the law unconstitutional. . . .

But agreeing to consider this as a genuine case or controversy I cannot agree to thrust the Federal Government's long arm the least bit further into state school curriculums than decision of this particular case requires. And the Court, in order to invalidate the Arkansas law as a violation of the First Amendment, has been compelled to give the State's law a broader meaning than the State Supreme Court was willing to give it. The Arkansas Supreme Court's opinion, in its entirety, stated that:

"Upon the principal issue, that of constitutionality, the court holds that Initiated Measure No. 1 of 1928, Ark. Stat. Ann. § 80-1627 and § 80-1628 (Repl. 1960), is a valid exercise of the state's power to specify the curriculum in its public schools. The court expresses no opinion on the question whether the Act prohibits any explanation of the theory of evolution or merely prohibits teaching that the theory is true; the answer not being necessary to a decision in the case, and the issue not having been raised."

It is plain that a state law prohibiting all teaching of human development or biology is constitutionally quite different from a law that compels a teacher to teach as true only one theory of a given doctrine. It would be difficult to make a First Amendment case out of a state law eliminating the subject of higher mathematics, or astronomy, or biology from its curriculum. And for all the Supreme Court of Arkansas has said, this particular Act may prohibit that and nothing else. This Court, however, treats the Arkansas Act as though it made it a misdemeanor to teach or to use a book that teaches that evolution is true. But it is not for this Court to arrogate to itself the power to determine the scope of Arkansas statutes. Since the highest court of Arkansas has deliberately refused to give its statute that meaning, we should not presume to do so.

It seems to me that in this situation the statute is too vague for us to strike it down on any ground but that: vagueness. Under this statute as construed by the Arkansas Supreme Court, a teacher cannot know whether he is forbidden to mention Darwin's theory at all or only free to discuss it as long as he refrains from contending that it is true. It is an established rule that a statute which leaves an ordinary man so doubtful about its meaning that he cannot know when he has violated it denies him the first essential of due process. . . .

The Court, not content to strike down this Arkansas Act on the unchallengeable ground of its plain vagueness, chooses rather to invalidate it as a violation of the Establishment of Religion Clause of the First Amendment. I would not decide this case on such a sweeping ground for the following reasons, among others.

1. In the first place I find it difficult to agree with the Court's statement that "there can be no doubt that Arkansas has sought to prevent its teachers from discussing the theory of evolution because it is contrary to the belief of some that the Book of Genesis must be the exclusive source of the doctrine as to the origin of man." It may be instead that the people's motive was merely that it would be best to remove this controversial subject from its schools; there is no reason I can imagine why a State is without power to withdraw from its curriculum any subject deemed too emotional and controversial for its public schools. . . .

2. A second question that arises for me is whether

this Court's decision forbidding a State to exclude the
subject of evolution from its schools infringes the re
ligious freedom of those who consider evolution an anti
religious doctrine. If the theory is considered anti
religious, as the Court indicates, how can the State be
bound by the Federal Constitution to permit its teachers
to advocate such an "anti-religious" doctrine to school
children? The very cases cited by the Court as support
ing its conclusion hold that the State must be neutral,
not favoring one religious or anti-religious view over
another. The Darwinian theory is said to challenge the
Bible's story of creation; so too have some of those who
believe in the Bible, along with many others, challenged
the Darwinian theory. Since there is no indication that
the literal Biblical doctrine of the origin of man is in
cluded in the curriculum of Arkansas schools, does not
the removal of the subject of evolution leave the State
in a neutral position toward these supposedly competing
religious and anti-religious doctrines? Unless this Court
is prepared simply to write off as pure nonsense the views
of those who consider evolution an anti-religious doc
trine, then this issue presents problems under the Estab
lishment Clause far more troublesome than are discussed
in the Court's opinion.

3. I am also not ready to hold that a person hired to
teach school children takes with him into the classroom
a constitutional right to teach sociological, economic,
political, or religious subjects that the school's managers
do not want discussed. This Court has said that the
rights of free speech "while fundamental in our demo
cratic society, still do not mean that everyone with opin
ions or beliefs to express may address a group at any
public place and at any time." . . . I question whether
it is absolutely certain, as the Court's opinion indicates,
that "academic freedom" permits a teacher to breach his

contractual agreement to teach only the subjects designated by the school authorities who hired him.

Certainly the Darwinian theory, precisely like the
Genesis story of the creation of man, is not above challenge. In fact the Darwinian theory has not merely been
criticized by religionists but by scientists, and perhaps
no scientist would be willing to take an oath and swear
that everything announced in the Darwinian theory is
unquestionably true. The Court, it seems to me, makes
a serious mistake in bypassing the plain, unconstitutional vagueness of this statute in order to reach out and
decide this troublesome, to me, First Amendment question. However wise this Court may be or may become
hereafter, it is doubtful that, sitting in Washington, it
can successfully supervise and censor the curriculum of
every public school in every hamlet and city in the
United States. I doubt that our wisdom is so nearly
infallible. . . .

MR. JUSTICE HARLAN, concurring.

I think it deplorable that this case should have come to
us with such an opaque opinion by the State's highest
court. With all respect, that court's handling of the case
savors of a studied effort to avoid coming to grips with
this anachronistic statute and to "pass the buck" to this
Court. . . .

I concur in so much of the Court's opinion as holds
that the Arkansas statute constitutes an "establishment
of religion" forbidden to the States by the Fourteenth
Amendment. I do not understand, however, why the
Court finds it necessary to explore at length appellants'
contentions that the statute is unconstitutionally vague
and that it interferes with free speech, only to conclude
that these issues need not be decided in this case. In the

process of *not* deciding them, the Court obscures it
otherwise straightforward holding, and opens its opinio
to possible implications from which I am constrained t
disassociate myself.

MR. JUSTICE STEWART, concurring in the result.

The States are most assuredly free "to choose their ow
curriculums for their own schools." A State is entirel
free, for example, to decide that the only foreign lan
guage to be taught in its public school system shall b
Spanish. But would a State be constitutionally free t
punish a teacher for letting his students know that othe
languages are also spoken in the world? I think not.

It is one thing for a State to determine that "the sub
ject of higher mathematics, or astronomy, or biology"
shall or shall not be included in its public school cur
riculum. It is quite another thing for a State to make i
a criminal offense for a public school teacher so much a
to mention the very existence of an entire system of re
spected human thought. That kind of criminal law,]
think, would clearly impinge upon the guarantees o
free communication contained in the First Amendment
and made applicable to the States by the Fourteenth.

The Arkansas Supreme Court has said that the statut
before us may or may not be just such a law. The result
as MR. JUSTICE BLACK points out, is that "a teacher can
not know whether he is forbidden to mention Darwin'
theory at all." Since I believe that no State could con
stitutionally forbid a teacher "to mention Darwin's the
ory at all," and since Arkansas may, or may not, have
done just that, I conclude that the statute before us is
so vague as to be invalid under the Fourteenth Amend
ment. . . .

Part II

EDUCATION AND RACIAL SEGREGATION

10. Sweatt v. Painter

339 U.S. 629 (1950)

Certiorari to the Supreme Court of Texas.

Mr. Chief Justice Vinson delivered the opinion of a
unanimous Court.

This case and *McLaurin* v. *Oklahoma State Regents,*
. . present differing aspects of this general question: To
what extent does the Equal Protection Clause of the
Fourteenth Amendment limit the power of a state to
distinguish between students of different races in professional and graduate education in a state university?
Broader issues have been urged for our consideration,
but we adhere to the principle of deciding constitutional
questions only in the context of the particular case before the Court. We have frequently reiterated that this
Court will decide constitutional questions only when
necessary to the disposition of the case at hand, and that
such decisions will be drawn as narrowly as possible. . . .
Because of this traditional reluctance to extend constitutional interpretations to situations or facts which are not
before the Court, much of the excellent research and detailed argument presented in these cases is unnecessary
to their disposition.

In the instant case, petitioner filed an application for
admission to the University of Texas Law School for the
February, 1946 term. His application was rejected solely

because he is a Negro. Petitioner thereupon brought this suit for mandamus against the appropriate school officials, respondents here, to compel his admission. At that time, there was no law school in Texas which admitted Negroes.

The State trial court recognized that the action of the State in denying petitioner the opportunity to gain a legal education while granting it to others deprived him of the equal protection of the laws guaranteed by the Fourteenth Amendment. The court did not grant the relief requested, however, but continued the case for six months to allow the State to supply substantially equal facilities. At the expiration of the six months, in December, 1946, the court denied the writ on the showing that the authorized university officials had adopted an order calling for the opening of a law school for Negroes the following February. While petitioner's appeal was pending, such a school was made available, but petitioner refused to register therein. The Texas Court of Civil Appeals set aside the trial court's judgment and ordered the cause "remanded generally to the trial court for further proceedings without prejudice to the rights of any party to this suit."

On remand, a hearing was held on the issue of the equality of the educational facilities at the newly established school as compared with the University of Texas Law School. Finding that the new school offered petitioner "privileges, advantages, and opportunities for the study of law substantially equivalent to those offered by the State to white students at the University of Texas," the trial court denied mandamus. The Court of Civil Appeals affirmed. . . .

The University of Texas Law School, from which petitioner was excluded, was staffed by a faculty of sixteen

ull-time and three part-time professors, some of whom
re nationally recognized authorities in their field. Its
tudent body numbered 850. The library contained over
5,000 volumes. Among the other facilities available to
he students were a law review, moot court facilities,
cholarship funds, and Order of the Coif affiliation. The
chool's alumni occupy the most distinguished positions
n the private practice of the law and in the public life
f the State. It may properly be considered one of the
ation's ranking law schools.

The law school for Negroes which was to have opened
n February, 1947, would have had no independent faculty or library. The teaching was to be carried on by
our members of the University of Texas Law School faculty, who were to maintain their offices at the University
f Texas while teaching at both institutions. Few of the
10,000 volumes ordered for the library had arrived; nor
vas there any full-time librarian. The school lacked
accreditation.

Since the trial of this case, respondents report the
opening of a law school at the Texas State University
or Negroes. It is apparently on the road to full accredi-
:ation. It has a faculty of five full-time professors; a stu-
lent body of 23; a library of some 16,500 volumes serv-
iced by a full-time staff; a practice court and legal aid
association; and one alumnus who has become a member
of the Texas Bar.

Whether the University of Texas Law School is compared with the original or the new law school for Negroes, we cannot find substantial equality in the educational opportunities offered white and Negro law students
by the State. In terms of number of the faculty, variety
of courses and opportunity for specialization, size of the
student body, scope of the library, availability of law re-

view and similar activities, the University of Texas Law
School is superior. What is more important, the University of Texas Law School possesses to a far greater
degree those qualities which are incapable of objective
measurement but which make for greatness in a law
school. Such qualities, to name but a few, include reputation of the faculty, experience of the administration,
position and influence of the alumni, standing in the
community, traditions and prestige. It is difficult to believe that one who had a free choice between these law
schools would consider the question close.

Moreover, although the law is a highly learned profession, we are well aware that it is an intensely practical
one. The law school, the proving ground for legal learning and practice, cannot be effective in isolation from
the individuals and institutions with which the law in-
teracts. Few students and no one who has practiced law
would choose to study in an academic vacuum, removed
from the interplay of ideas and the exchange of views
with which the law is concerned. The law school to
which Texas is willing to admit petitioner excludes from
its student body members of the racial groups which
number 85% of the population of the State and include
most of the lawyers, witnesses, jurors, judges, and other
officials with whom petitioner will inevitably be dealing
when he becomes a member of the Texas Bar. With
such a substantial and significant segment of society excluded, we cannot conclude that the education offered
petitioner is substantially equal to that which he would
receive if admitted to the University of Texas Law School.

It may be argued that excluding petitioner from that
school is no different from excluding white students from
the new law school. This contention overlooks realities.
It is unlikely that a member of a group so decisively in

he majority, attending a school with rich traditions and
prestige which only a history of consistently maintained
excellence could command, would claim that the oppor-
unities afforded him for legal education were unequal
o those held open to petitioner. That such a claim, if
made, would be dishonored by the State, is no answer.
"Equal protection of the laws is not achieved through
indiscriminate imposition of inequalities." *Shelley* v.
Kraemer, 334 U.S. 1, 22 (1948).

It is fundamental that these cases concern rights which
are personal and present. This Court has stated unanimously that "The State must provide [legal education]
for [petitioner] in conformity with the equal protection
clause of the Fourteenth Amendment and provide it as
soon as it does for applicants of any other group." *Sipuel*
v. Board of Regents, 332 U.S. 631, 633 (1948). That case
"did not present the issue whether a state might not satisfy the equal protection clause of the Fourteenth Amendment by establishing a separate law school for Negroes."
Fisher v. *Hurst,* 333 U.S. 147, 150 (1948). In *Missouri ex*
rel. Gaines v. *Canada,* 305 U.S. 337, 351 (1938), the Court,
speaking through CHIEF JUSTICE HUGHES, declared that
"petitioner's right was a personal one. It was as an individual that he was entitled to the equal protection of the
laws, and the State was bound to furnish him within its
borders facilities for legal education substantially equal
to those which the State there afforded for persons of the
white race, whether or not other Negroes sought the same
opportunity." These are the only cases in this Court
which present the issue of the constitutional validity of
race distinctions in state-supported graduate and professional education.

In accordance with these cases, petitioner may claim
his full constitutional right: legal education equivalent

to that offered by the State to students of other race
Such education is not available to him in a separate la
school as offered by the State. We cannot, therefor
agree with respondents that the doctrine of *Plessy*
Ferguson, 163 U.S. 537 (1896) requires affirmance of th
judgment below. Nor need we reach petitioner's conten
tion that *Plessy* v. *Ferguson* should be reexamined in th
light of contemporary knowledge respecting the pu
poses of the Fourteenth Amendment and the effects c
racial segregation. . . .

We hold that the Equal Protection Clause of th
Fourteenth Amendment requires that petitioner be ac
mitted to the University of Texas Law School. Th
judgment is reversed and the cause is remanded for pro
ceedings not inconsistent with this opinion.

Reversed.

11. Brown v. Board of Education

347 U.S. 483 (1954)

Appeal from the U.S. District Court for the District of Kansas.

Appeal from the U.S. District Court for the Eastern District of South Carolina.

Appeal from the U.S. District Court for the Eastern District of Virginia.

Certiorari to the Supreme Court of Delaware.

MR. CHIEF JUSTICE WARREN delivered the opinion of a unanimous Court.

These cases come to us from the States of Kansas, South Carolina, Virginia, and Delaware. They are premised on different facts and different local conditions, but a common legal question justifies their consideration together in this consolidated opinion.

In each of the cases, minors of the Negro race, through their legal representatives, seek the aid of the courts in obtaining admission to the public schools of their community on a nonsegregated basis. In each instance, they had been denied admission to schools attended by white children under laws requiring or permitting segregation according to race. This segregation was alleged to deprive the plaintiffs of the equal protection of the law under the Fourteenth Amendment. In each of the case other than the Delaware case, a three-judge federal dis trict court denied relief to the plaintiffs on the so-called "separate but equal" doctrine announced by this Cour in *Plessy* v. *Ferguson,* 163 U.S. 537. Under that doctrine equality of treatment is accorded when the races are pro vided substantially equal facilities, even though these fa cilities be separate. . . .

The plaintiffs contend that segregated public school are not "equal" and cannot be made "equal," and tha hence they are deprived of the equal protection of th laws. Because of the obvious importance of the questio presented, the Court took jurisdiction. Argument wa heard in the 1952 Term, and reargument was heard thi Term on certain questions propounded by the Court.

Reargument was largely devoted to the circumstance surrounding the adoption of the Fourteenth Amendmen in 1868. It covered exhaustively consideration of th Amendment in Congress, ratification by the states, the existing practices in racial segregation, and the views o proponents and opponents of the Amendment. Thi discussion and our own investigation convince us that although these sources cast some light, it is not enougl to resolve the problem with which we are faced. At best they are inconclusive. The most avid proponents of th post-War Amendments undoubtedly intended them t remove all legal distinctions among "all persons born o naturalized in the United States." Their opponents, jus as certainly, were antagonistic to both the letter and th spirit of the Amendments and wished them to have th most limited effect. What others in Congress and the stat legislatures had in mind cannot be determined with an degree of certainty.

An additional reason for the inconclusive nature of
he Amendment's history, with respect to segregated
:hools, is the status of public education at that time. In
he South, the movement toward free common schools,
ipported by general taxation, had not yet taken hold.
ducation of white children was largely in the hands of
rivate groups. Education of Negroes was almost non-
xistent, and practically all of the race were illiterate. In
ict, any education of Negroes was forbidden by law in
ime states. Today, in contrast, many Negroes have
chieved outstanding success in the arts and sciences as
ell as in the business and professional world. It is true
lat public school education at the time of the Amend-
lent had advanced further in the North, but the effect
f the Amendment on Northern States was generally
:nored in the congressional debates. Even in the North,
le conditions of public education did not approximate
lose existing today. The curriculum was usually rudi-
lentary; ungraded schools were common in rural areas;
le school term was but three months a year in many
:ates; and compulsory school attendance was virtually
nknown. As a consequence, it is not surprising that
lere should be so little in the history of the Fourteenth
.mendment relating to its intended effect on public
ducation.

In the first cases in this Court construing the Four-
:enth Amendment, decided shortly after its adoption,
le Court interpreted it as proscribing all state-imposed
iscriminations against the Negro race. The doctrine of
separate but equal" did not make its appearance in
lis Court until 1896 in the case of *Plessy* v. *Ferguson,*
. . involving not education but transportation. Ameri-
an courts have since labored with the doctrine for over
alf a century. In this Court, there have been six cases

involving the "separate but equal" doctrine in the field of public education. In *Cumming* v. *County Board of Education,* 175 U.S. 528, and *Gong Lum* v. *Rice,* 275 U.S. 78, the validity of the doctrine itself was not challenged. In more recent cases, all on the graduate school level, inequality was found in that specific benefits enjoyed by white students were denied to Negro students of the same educational qualifications. *Missouri ex rel Gaines* v. *Canada,* 305 U.S. 337; *Sipuel* v. *Oklahoma,* 332 U.S. 631; *Sweatt* v. *Painter,* 339 U.S. 629; *McLaurin* v. *Oklahoma State Regents,* 339 U.S. 637. In none of these cases was it necessary to reexamine the doctrine to grant relief to the Negro plaintiff. And in *Sweatt* v. *Painter,* . . . the Court expressly reserved decision on the question whether *Plessy* v. *Ferguson* should be held inapplicable to public education.

In the instant cases, that question is directly presented. Here, unlike *Sweatt* v. *Painter,* there are findings below that the Negro and white schools involved have been equalized, or are being equalized, with respect to buildings, curricula, qualifications and salaries of teachers and other "tangible" factors. Our decision, therefore, cannot turn on merely a comparison of these tangible factors in the Negro and white schools involved in each of the cases. We must look instead to the effect of segregation itself on public education.

In approaching this problem, we cannot turn the clock back to 1868 when the Amendment was adopted, or even to 1896 when *Plessy* v. *Ferguson* was written. We must consider public education in the light of its full development and its present place in American life throughout the Nation. Only in this way can it be determined if segregation in public schools deprives these plaintiffs of the equal protection of the laws.

Today, education is perhaps the most important function of state and local governments. Compulsory school attendance laws and the great expenditures for education both demonstrate our recognition of the importance of education to our democratic society. It is required in the performance of our most basic public responsibilities, even service in the armed forces. It is the very foundation of good citizenship. Today it is a principal instrument in awakening the child to cultural values, in preparing him for later professional training, and in helping him to adjust normally to his environment. In these days, it is doubtful that any child may reasonably be expected to succeed in life if he is denied the opportunity of an education. Such an opportunity, where the state has undertaken to provide it, is a right which must be made available to all on equal terms.

We come then to the question presented: Does segregation of children in public schools solely on the basis of race, even though the physical facilities and other "tangible" factors may be equal, deprive the children of the minority group of equal educational opportunities? We believe that it does.

In *Sweatt* v. *Painter*, in finding that a segregated law school for Negroes could not provide them equal educational opportunities, this Court relied in large part on "those qualities which are incapable of objective measurement but which make for greatness in a law school." In *McLaurin* v. *Oklahoma State Regents*, the Court, in requiring that a Negro admitted to a white graduate school be treated like all other students, again resorted to intangible considerations: "his ability to study, to engage in discussions and exchange views with other students, and, in general, to learn his profession." Such considerations apply with added force to children in grade and high schools. To separate them from others of similar age and qualifications solely because of their race generates a feeling of inferiority as to their status in the community that may affect their hearts and minds in a way unlikely ever to be undone. The effect of this separation on their educational opportunities was well stated by a finding in the Kansas case by a court which nevertheless felt compelled to rule against the Negro plaintiffs:

Segregation of white and colored children in public schools has a detrimental effect upon the colored children. The impact is greater when it has the sanction of the law; for the policy of separating the races is usually interpreted as denoting the inferiority of the negro group. A sense of inferiority affects the motivation of a child to learn. Segregation with the sanction of law, therefore, has a tendency to [retard] the educational and mental development of negro children and to deprive them of some of the benefits they would receive in a racial[ly] integrated school system.

Whatever may have been the extent of psychological knowledge at the time of *Plessy* v. *Ferguson,* this finding is amply supported by modern authority.[11] Any language in *Plessy* v. *Ferguson* contrary to this finding is rejected.

We conclude that in the field of public education the doctrine of "separate but equal" has no place. Separate

---

[11] K. B. Clark, *Effect of Prejudice and Discrimination on Personality Development* (Midcentury White House Conference on Children and Youth, 1950); Witmer and Kotinsky, *Personality in the Making* (1952), Chap. 6; Deutscher and Chein, "The Psychological Effects of Enforced Segregation: A Survey of Social Science Opinion," 26 *J. Psychol.* 259 (1948); Chein, "What Are the Psychological Effects of Segregation under Conditions of Equal Facilities?" 3 *Int. J. Opinion and Attitude Res.* 229 (1949); Brameld, *Educational Costs,* in *Discrimination and National Welfare* (MacIver, ed., 1949), 44–48; Frazier, *The Negro in the United States* (1949), 674–681. And see generally Myrdal, *An American Dilemma* (1944).

lucational facilities are inherently unequal. Therefore, e hold that the plaintiffs and others similarly situated r whom the actions have been brought are, by reason : the segregation complained of, deprived of the equal rotection of the laws guaranteed by the Fourteenth mendment. This disposition makes unnecessary any scussion whether such segregation also violates the Due rocess Clause of the Fourteenth Amendment.

Because these are class actions, because of the wide pplicability of this decision, and because of the great riety of local conditions, the formulation of decrees in ese cases presents problems of considerable complexity. n reargument, the consideration of appropriate relief as necessarily subordinated to the primary question— e constitutionality of segregation in public education. e have now announced that such segregation is a de- ial of the equal protection of the laws. In order that e may have the full assistance of the parties in formu- ting decrees, the cases will be restored to the docket, nd the parties are requested to present further argu- ent. . . . The Attorney General of the United States is zain invited to participate. The Attorneys General of e states requiring or permitting segregation in public lucation will also be permitted to appear as *amici riae* upon request to do so. . . .

It is so ordered.

12.   Brown v. Board of Education

349 U.S. 294 (1955)

Appeal from the United States District Court for the Di
trict of Kansas, the United States District Court fo
the Eastern District of South Carolina, and from th
United States District Court for the Eastern Distri
of Virginia.

Certiorari to the United States Court of Appeals for th
District of Columbia Circuit and to the Supreme Cou
of Delaware.

MR. CHIEF JUSTICE WARREN delivered the opinion of
unanimous Court.

These cases were decided on May 17, 1954. The opir
ions of that date, declaring the fundamental principl
that racial discrimination in public education is uncor
stitutional, are incorporated herein by reference. Al
provisions of federal, state, or local law requiring o
permitting such discrimination must yield to this prin
ciple. There remains for consideration the manner i
which relief is to be accorded.

Because these cases arose under different local condi
tions and their disposition will involve a variety of loca
problems, we requested further argument on the ques
tion of relief. In view of the nationwide importance o
the decision, we invited the Attorney General of th

nited States and the Attorneys General of all states re-
uiring or permitting racial discrimination in public
ducation to present their views on that question. The
arties, the United States, and the States of Florida,
orth Carolina, Arkansas, Oklahoma, Maryland, and
exas filed briefs and participated in the oral argument.

These presentations were informative and helpful to
ne Court in its consideration of the complexities arising
rom the transition to a system of public education freed
f racial discrimination. The presentations also demon-
trated that substantial steps to eliminate racial discrimi-
ation in public schools have already been taken. . . .

Full implementation of these constitutional principles
nay require solution of varied local school problems.
chool authorities have the primary responsibility for
lucidating, assessing, and solving these problems; courts
vill have to consider whether the action of school au-
horities constitutes good faith implementation of the
overning constitutional principles. Because of their
roximity to local conditions and the possible need for
urther hearings, the courts which originally heard these
ases can best perform this judicial appraisal. Accord-
ngly, we believe it appropriate to remand the cases to
hose courts.

In fashioning and effectuating the decrees, the courts
vill be guided by equitable principles. Traditionally,
quity has been characterized by a practical flexibility in
haping its remedies and by a facility for adjusting and
econciling public and private needs. These cases call
or the exercise of these traditional attributes of equity
ower. At stake is the personal interest of the plaintiffs
n admission to public schools as soon as practicable on
 nondiscriminatory basis. To effectuate this interest
nay call for elimination of a variety of obstacles in mak-

ing the transition to school systems operated in ac
cordance with the constitutional principles set forth in
our May 17, 1954, decision. Courts of equity may prop
erly take into account the public interest in the elimi
nation of such obstacles in a systematic and effective man
ner. But it should go without saying that the vitality
of these constitutional principles cannot be allowed to
yield simply because of disagreement with them.

While giving weight to these public and private con
siderations, the courts will require that the defendant
make a prompt and reasonable start toward full com
pliance with our May 17, 1954, ruling. Once such a start
has been made, the courts may find that additional time
is necessary to carry out the ruling in an effective man
ner. The burden rests upon the defendants to establish
that such time is necessary in the public interest and is
consistent with good faith compliance at the earliest
practicable date. To that end, the courts may consider
problems related to administration, arising from the
physical condition of the school plant, the school trans
portation system, personnel, revision of school districts
and attendance areas into compact units to achieve a
system of determining admission to the public schools
on a nonracial basis, and revision of local laws and regu
lations which may be necessary in solving the foregoing
problems. They will also consider the adequacy of any
plans the defendants may propose to meet these prob
lems and to effectuate a transition to a racially nondis
criminatory school system. During this period of transi
tion, the courts will retain jurisdiction of these cases.

The judgments below, except that in the Delaware
case, are accordingly reversed and the cases are remanded
to the District Courts to take such proceedings and enter
such orders and decrees consistent with this opinion as are

necessary and proper to admit to public schools on a racially nondiscriminatory basis with all deliberate speed the parties to these cases. The judgment in the Delaware case—ordering the immediate admission of the plaintiffs to schools previously attended only by white children—is affirmed on the basis of the principles stated in our May 17, 1954, opinion, but the case is remanded to the Supreme Court of Delaware for such further proceedings as that Court may deem necessary in light of this opinion.

It is so ordered.

13. Cooper v. Aaron

358 U.S. 1 (1958)

Certiorari to the United States Court of Appeals for the Eighth Circuit.

Opinion of the Court by THE CHIEF JUSTICE, MR. JUSTICE BLACK, MR. JUSTICE FRANKFURTER, MR. JUSTICE DOUGLAS, MR. JUSTICE BURTON, MR. JUSTICE CLARK, MR. JUSTICE HARLAN, MR. JUSTICE BRENNAN, and MR. JUSTICE WHITTAKER.

As this case reaches us it raises questions of the highest importance to the maintenance of our federal system of government. It necessarily involves a claim by the Governor and Legislature of a State that there is no duty on state officials to obey federal court orders resting on this Court's considered interpretation of the United States Constitution. Specifically it involves actions by the Governor and Legislature of Arkansas upon the premise that they are not bound by our holding in *Brown* v. *Board of Education,* 347 U.S. 483. That holding was that the Fourteenth Amendment forbids States to use their governmental powers to bar children on racial grounds from attending schools where there is state participation through any arrangement, management, funds or property. We are urged to uphold a suspension of the Little Rock School Board's plan to do away with segregated public schools in Little Rock until state laws and efforts

) upset and nullify our holding in *Brown* v. *Board of Education* have been further challenged and tested in the courts. We reject these contentions.

The case was argued before us on September 11, 1958. On the following day we unanimously affirmed the judgment of the Court of Appeals for the Eighth Circuit, which had reversed a judgment of the District Court for the Eastern District of Arkansas. The District Court had granted the application of the petitioners, the Little Rock School Board and School Superintendent, to suspend for two and one-half years the operation of the School Board's court-approved desegregation program. In order that the School Board might know, without doubt, its duty in this regard before the opening of school, which had been set for the following Monday, September 15, 1958, we immediately issued the judgment, reserving the expression of our supporting views to a later date. This opinion of all the members of the Court embodies those views.

The following are the facts and circumstances so far as necessary to show how the legal questions are presented.

. .

On May 20, 1954, three days after the first *Brown* opinion, the Little Rock District School Board adopted, and on May 23, 1954, made public, a statement of policy entitled "Supreme Court Decision—Segregation in Public Schools." In this statement the Board recognized that 'It is our responsibility to comply with Federal Constitutional Requirements and we intend to do so when the Supreme Court of the United States outlines the method to be followed."

Thereafter the Board undertook studies of the administrative problems confronting the transition to a desegregated public school system at Little Rock. It in-

structed the Superintendent of Schools to prepare a pla
for desegregation, and approved such a plan on May 2
1955, seven days before the second *Brown* opinion. Th
plan provided for desegregation at the senior high schoo
level (grades 10 through 12) as the first stage. Desegreg
tion at the junior high and elementary levels was to fo
low. It was contemplated that desegregation at the hig
school level would commence in the fall of 1957, and th
expectation was that complete desegregation of the schoo
system would be accomplished by 1963. Following th
adoption of this plan, the Superintendent of Schools di
cussed it with a large number of citizen groups in th
city. As a result of these discussions, the Board reache
the conclusion that "a large majority of the residents" o
Little Rock were of "the belief . . . that the Plan, a
though objectionable in principle," from the point o
view of those supporting segregated schools, "was stil
the best for the interests of all pupils in the District."

Upon challenge by a group of Negro plaintiffs desirin
more rapid completion of the desegregation process, th
District Court upheld the School Board's plan, *Aaron v
Cooper,* 143 F. Supp. 855. The Court of Appeals affirmed
243 F2d 361. Review of that judgment was not sough
here.

While the School Board was thus going forward with
its preparation for desegregating the Little Rock schoo
system, other state authorities, in contrast, were actively
pursuing a program designed to perpetuate in Arkansa
the system of racial segregation which this Court had
held violated the Fourteenth Amendment. First came, i
November 1956, an amendment to the State Constitu
tion flatly commanding the Arkansas General Assembly
to oppose "in every Constitutional manner the Un-consti
tutional desegregation decisions of May 17, 1954 and

fay 31, 1955 of the United States Supreme Court," . . .
nd, through the initiative, a pupil assignment law. . . .
ursuant to this state constitutional command, a law re-
eving school children from compulsory attendance at
acially mixed schools, . . . and a law establishing a
tate Sovereignty Commission, . . . were enacted by the
;eneral Assembly in February 1957.

The School Board and the Superintendent of Schools
evertheless continued with preparations to carry out the
rst stage of the desegregation program. Nine Negro
hildren were scheduled for admission in September 1957
o Central High School, which has more than two thou-
and students. Various administrative measures, designed
o assure the smooth transition of this first stage of de-
egregation, were undertaken.

On September 2, 1957, the day before these Negro
tudents were to enter Central High, the school authori-
ies were met with drastic opposing action on the part
f the Governor of Arkansas who dispatched units of the
Arkansas National Guard to the Central High School
rounds, and placed the school "off limits" to colored
tudents. As found by the District Court in subsequent
roceedings, the Governor's action had not been re-
uested by the school authorities, and was entirely un-
eralded. . . .

The next day, September 3, 1957, the Board petitioned
he District Court for instructions, and the court, after
a hearing, found that the Board's request of the Negro
tudents to stay away from the high school had been
nade because of the stationing of the military guards by
he state authorities. The court determined that this
vas not a reason for departing from the approved plan,
ind ordered the School Board and Superintendent to
roceed with it.

On the morning of the next day, September 4, 195'
the Negro children attempted to enter the high schoo
but, as the District Court later found, units of the Arkan
sas National Guard "acting pursuant to the Governor'
order, stood shoulder to shoulder at the school ground
and thereby forcibly prevented the 9 Negro students . . .
from entering," as they continued to do every school da
during the following three weeks. . . .

That same day, September 4, 1957, the United State
Attorney for the Eastern District of Arkansas was re
quested by the District Court to begin an immediate
investigation in order to fix responsibility for the inter
ference with the orderly implementation of the Distric
Court's direction to carry out the desegregation program
Three days later, September 7, the District Court denied
a petition of the School Board and the Superintenden
of Schools for an order temporarily suspending con
tinuance of the program.

Upon completion of the United States Attorney's in
vestigation, he and the Attorney General of the United
States, at the District Court's request, entered the pro
ceedings and filed a petition on behalf of the United
States, as *amicus curiae*, to enjoin the Governor of Ar
kansas and officers of the Arkansas National Guard from
further attempts to prevent obedience to the court's order.
After hearings on the petition, the District Court found
that the School Board's plan had been obstructed by the
Governor through the use of National Guard troops, and
granted a preliminary injunction on September 20, 1957,
enjoining the Governor and the officers of the Guard
from preventing the attendance of Negro children at
Central High School, and from otherwise obstructing or
interfering with the orders of the court in connection
with the plan. . . . The National Guard was then withdrawn from the school.

The next school day was Monday, September 23, 1957. The Negro children entered the high school that morning under the protection of the Little Rock Police Department and members of the Arkansas State Police. But the officers caused the children to be removed from the school during the morning because they had difficulty controlling a large and demonstrating crowd which had gathered at the high school. . . . On September 25, however, the President of the United States dispatched federal troops to Central High School and admission of the Negro students to the school was thereby effected. Regular army troops continued at the high school until November 27, 1957. They were then replaced by federalized National Guardsmen who remained throughout the balance of the school year. Eight of the Negro students remained in attendance at the school throughout the school year.

We come now to the aspect of the proceedings presently before us. On February 20, 1958, the School Board and the Superintendent of Schools filed a petition in the District Court seeking a postponement of their program for desegregation. Their position in essence was that because of extreme public hostility, which they stated had been engendered largely by the official attitudes and actions of the Governor and the Legislature, the maintenance of a sound educational program at Central High School, with the Negro students in attendance, would be impossible. The Board therefore proposed that the Negro students already admitted to the school be withdrawn and sent to segregated schools, and that all further steps to carry out the Board's desegregation program be postponed for a period later suggested by the Board to be two and one-half years.

After a hearing the District Court granted the relief requested by the Board. . . .

In affirming the judgment of the Court of Appeals which reversed the District Court we have accepted without reservation the position of the School Board, the Superintendent of Schools, and their counsel that they displayed entire good faith in the conduct of these proceedings and in dealing with the unfortunate and distressing sequence of events which has been outlined. We likewise have accepted the findings of the District Court as to the conditions at Central High School during the 1957–1958 school year, and also the findings that the educational progress of all the students, white and colored, of that school has suffered and will continue to suffer if the conditions which prevailed last year are permitted to continue.

The significance of these findings, however, is to be considered in light of the fact, indisputably revealed by the record before us, that the conditions they depict are directly traceable to the actions of legislators and executive officials of the State of Arkansas, taken in their official capacities, which reflect their own determination to resist this Court's decision in the *Brown* case and which have brought about violent resistance to that decision in Arkansas. In its petition for certiorari filed in this Court, the School Board itself describes the situation in this language: "The legislative, executive, and judicial departments of the state government opposed the desegregation of Little Rock schools by enacting laws, calling out troops, making statements villifying [*sic*] federal law and federal courts, and failing to utilize state law enforcement agencies and judicial processes to maintain public peace."

One may well sympathize with the position of the Board in the face of the frustrating conditions which have confronted it, but, regardless of the Board's good faith, the actions of the other state agencies responsible for those conditions compel us to reject the Board's legal position. Had Central High School been under the direct management of the State itself, it could hardly be suggested that those immediately in charge of the school should be heard to assert their own good faith as a legal excuse for delay in implementing the constitutional rights of these respondents, when vindication of those rights was rendered difficult or impossible by the actions of other state officials. The situation here is in no different posture because the members of the School Board and the Superintendent of Schools are local officials; from the point of view of the Fourteenth Amendment, they stand in this litigation as the agents of the State.

The constitutional rights of respondents are not to be sacrificed or yielded to the violence and disorder which have followed upon the actions of the Governor and Legislature. As this Court said some forty-one years ago in a unanimous opinion in a case involving another aspect of racial segregation: "It is urged that this proposed segregation will promote the public peace by preventing race conflicts. Desirable as this is, and important as is the preservation of the public peace, this aim cannot be accomplished by laws or ordinances which deny rights created or protected by the Federal Constitution." *Buchanan* v. *Warley,* 245 U.S. 60, 81. Thus law and order are not here to be preserved by depriving the Negro children of their constitutional rights. The record before us clearly establishes that the growth of the Board's difficulties to a magnitude beyond its unaided power to control is the product of state action. Those difficulties, as counsel for the Board forthrightly conceded on the oral argument in this Court, can also be brought under control by state action.

The controlling legal principles are plain. The com mand of the Fourteenth Amendment is that no "State shall deny to any person within its jurisdiction the equa protection of the laws. "A State acts by its legislative, it executive, or its judicial authorities. It can act in n other way. The constitutional provision, therefore, mus mean that no agency of the State, or of the officers o agents by whom its powers are exerted, shall deny t any person within its jurisdiction the equal protectio of the laws. Whoever, by virtue of public position unde a State government, . . . denies or takes away the equa protection of the laws, violates the constitutional inhibi tion; and as he acts in the name and for the State, and i clothed with the State's power, his act is that of th State. This must be so, or the constitutional prohibitio has no meaning." *Ex parte Virginia*, 100 U.S. 339, 347 Thus the prohibitions of the Fourteenth Amendmen extend to all action of the State denying equal protec tion of the laws; whatever the agency of the State taking the action, . . . or whatever the guise in which it i taken. . . . In short, the constitutional rights of children not to be discriminated against in school admission on grounds of race or color declared by this Court in the *Brown* case can neither be nullified openly and directly by state legislators or state executive or judicial officers, nor nullified indirectly by them through evasive schemes for segregation whether attempted "ingeniously or in genuously." . . .

What has been said, in the light of the facts developed, is enough to dispose of the case. However, we should answer the premise of the actions of the Governor and Legislature that they are not bound by our holding in the *Brown* case. It is necessary only to recall some basic constitutional propositions which are settled doctrine.

Article VI of the Constitution makes the Constitution the "supreme Law of the Land." In 1803, CHIEF JUSTICE MARSHALL, speaking for a unanimous Court, referring to the Constitution as "the fundamental and paramount law of the nation," declared in the notable case of *Marbury* v. *Madison,* 1 Cranch 137, 177, that "It is emphatically the province and duty of the judicial department to say what the law is." This decision declared the basic principle that the federal judiciary is supreme in the exposition of the law of the Constitution, and that principle has ever since been respected by this Court and the Country as a permanent and indispensable feature of our constitutional system. It follows that the interpretation of the Fourteenth Amendment enunciated by this Court in the *Brown* case is the supreme law of the land, and Art. VI of the Constitution makes it of binding effect on the States "any Thing in the Constitution or Laws of any State to the Contrary notwithstanding." Every state legislator and executive and judicial officer is solemnly committed by oath taken pursuant to Art. VI, c1, "to support this Constitution." CHIEF JUSTICE TANEY, speaking for a unanimous Court in 1859, said that this requirement reflected the framers' "anxiety to preserve it [the Constitution] in full force, in all its powers, and to guard against resistance to or evasion of its authority, on the part of a State. . . ." *Ableman* v. *Booth,* 21 How. 506, 524.

No state legislator or executive or judicial officer can war against the Constitution without violating his undertaking to support it. CHIEF JUSTICE MARSHALL spoke for a unanimous Court in saying that: "If the legislatures of the several states may, at will, annul the judgments of the courts of the United States, and destroy the rights acquired under those judgments, the constitu-

tion itself becomes a solemn mockery. . . ." *United State*
v. *Peters,* 5 Cranch 115, 136. A Governor who asserts
power to nullify a federal court order is similarly re
strained. If he had such power, said CHIEF JUSTIC
HUGHES, in 1932, also for a unanimous Court, "it is man
fest that the fiat of a state Governor, and not the Con
stitution of the United States, would be the supreme law
of the land; that the restrictions of the Federal Constitu
tion upon the exercise of state power would be but im
potent phrases." *Sterling* v. *Constantin,* 287 U.S. 378
397–398.

It is, of course, quite true that the responsibility fo
public education is primarily the concern of the States
but it is equally true that such responsibilities, like al
other state activity, must be exercised consistently with
federal constitutional requirements as they apply to
state action. The Constitution created a governmen
dedicated to equal justice under law. The Fourteenth
Amendment embodied and emphasized that ideal. State
support of segregated schools through any arrangement
management, funds, or property cannot be squared with
the Amendment's command that no State shall deny to
any person within its jurisdiction the equal protection
of the laws. The right of a student not to be segregated
on racial grounds in schools so maintained is indeed so
fundamental and pervasive that it is embraced in the
concept of due process of law. *Bolling* v. *Sharpe,* 347
U.S. 497. The basic decision in *Brown* was unanimously
reached by this Court only after the case had been
briefed and twice argued and the issues had been given
the most serious consideration. Since the first *Brown*
opinion three new Justices have come to the Court. They
are at one with the Justices still on the Court who par
ticipated in that basic decision as to its correctness, and

that decision is now unanimously reaffirmed. The principles announced in that decision and the obedience of the States to them, according to the command of the Constitution, are indispensable for the protection of the freedoms guaranteed by our fundamental charter for all of us. Our constitutional idea of equal justice under law is thus made a living truth.

14. Griffin v. County School Board of Prince Edward County

377 U.S. 218 (1964)

Certiorari to the United States Court of Appeals for the Fourth Circuit.

MR. JUSTICE BLACK delivered the opinion of the Court.

This litigation began in 1951 when a group of Negro school children living in Prince Edward County, Virginia, filed a complaint in the United States District Court for the Eastern District of Virginia alleging that they had been denied admission to public schools attended by white children and charging that Virginia laws requiring such school segregation denied complainants the equal protection of the laws in violation of the Fourteenth Amendment. On May 17, 1954, ten years ago, we held that the Virginia segregation laws did deny equal protection. *Brown* v. *Board of Education*, 347 U.S. 483. . . . On May 31, 1955, after reargument on the nature of relief, we remanded this case, along with others heard with it, to the District Courts to enter such orders as "necessary and proper to admit [complainants] to public schools on a racially nondiscriminatory basis with all deliberate speed. . . ." *Brown* v. *Board of Education*, 349 U.S. 294. . . .

Efforts to desegregate Prince Edward County's schools met with resistance. In 1956 Section 141 of the Virginia

Constitution was amended to authorize the General Assembly and local governing bodies to appropriate funds to assist students to go to public or to nonsectarian private schools, in addition to those owned by the State or by the locality. The General Assembly met in special session and enacted legislation to close any public schools where white and colored children were enrolled together, to cut off state funds to such schools, to pay tuition grants to children in nonsectarian private schools, and to extend state retirement benefits to teachers in newly created private schools. The legislation closing mixed schools and cutting off state funds was later invalidated by the Supreme Court of Appeals of Virginia, which held that these laws violated the Virginia Constitution. . . In April 1959 the General Assembly abandoned "massive resistance" to desegregation and turned instead to what was called a "freedom of choice" program. The Assembly repealed the rest of the 1956 legislation, as well as a tuition grant law of January 1959, and enacted a new tuition grant program. At the same time the Assembly repealed Virginia's compulsory attendance laws and instead made school attendance a matter of local option.

In June 1959, the United States Court of Appeals for the Fourth Circuit directed the Federal District Court (1) to enjoin discriminatory practices in Prince Edward County schools, (2) to require the County School Board to take "immediate steps" toward admitting students without regard to race to the white high school "in the school term beginning September 1959," and (3) to require the Board to make plans for admissions to elementary schools without regard to race. . . . Having as early as 1956 resolved that they would not operate public schools "wherein white and colored children are

taught together," the Supervisors of Prince Edwar
County refused to levy any school taxes for the 1959
1960 school year, explaining that they were "confronte
with a court decree which requires the admission c
white and colored children to all the schools of th
county without regard to race or color." As a result, th
county's public schools did not reopen in the fall of 195
and have remained closed ever since, although the publi
schools of every other county in Virginia have continue
to operate under laws governing the State's public schoc
system and to draw funds provided by the State for tha
purpose. A private group, the Prince Edward Schoc
Foundation, was formed to operate private schools fo
white children in Prince Edward County and, havin
built its own school plant, has been in operation eve
since the closing of the public schools. An offer to se
up private schools for colored children in the count
was rejected, the Negroes of Prince Edward preferring t
continue the legal battle for desegregated public school
and colored children were without formal educatio
from 1959 to 1963, when federal, state, and county au
thorities cooperated to have classes conducted for N
groes and whites in school buildings owned by the count
During the 1959–1960 school year the Foundation'
schools for white children were supported entirely b
private contributions, but in 1960 the General Assembl
adopted a new tuition grant program making ever
child, regardless of race, eligible for tuition grants o
$125 or $150 to attend a nonsectarian private school o
a public school outside his locality, and also authorizin
localities to provide their own grants. The Prince Ed
ward Board of Supervisors then passed an ordinanc
providing tuition grants of $100, so that each child at
tending the Prince Edward School Foundation's school

:ceived a total of $225 if in elementary school or $250 in high school. In the 1960–1961 session the major ource of financial support for the Foundation was in the idirect form of these state and county tuition grants, aid to children attending Foundation's schools. At the ame time, the County Board of Supervisors passed an rdinance allowing property tax credits up to 25% for ontributions to any "nonprofit, nonsectarian private chool" in the county.

In 1961 petitioners here filed a supplemental comlaint, adding new parties and seeking to enjoin the espondents from refusing to operate an efficient system f public free schools in Prince Edward County and to njoin payment of public funds to help support private chools which excluded students on account of race. . . . 'or reasons to be stated, we agree with the District Court that, under the circumstances here, closing the 'rince Edward County schools while public schools in all he other counties of Virginia were being maintained enied the petitioners and the class of Negro students hey represent the equal protection of the laws guaraneed by the Fourteenth Amendment. . . .

In *County School Board of Prince Edward County* v. *Griffin,* 204 Va. 650, 133 S.E.2d 565 (1963), the Supreme Court of Appeals of Virginia upheld as valid under state aw the closing of the Prince Edward County public chools, the state and county tuition grants for children vho attend private schools, and the county's tax concesions for those who make contributions to private schools. The same opinion also held that each county had "an opion to operate or not to operate public schools." . . .

Virginia law, as here applied, unquestionably treats he school children of Prince Edward differently from the vay it treats the school children of all other Virginia

counties. Prince Edward children must go to a privat
school or none at all; all other Virginia children can g
to public schools. Closing Prince Edward's schools bear
more heavily on Negro children in Prince Edwar
County since white children there have accredited pr
vate schools which they can attend, while colored chi
dren until very recently have had no available privat
schools, and even the school they now attend is a tempo
rary expedient. Apart from this expedient, the result i
that Prince Edward County school children, if they go t
school in their own county, must go to racially segre
gated schools which, although designated as private, ar
beneficiaries of county and state support.

A State, of course, has a wide discretion in decidin
whether laws shall operate statewide or shall operate onl
in certain counties, the legislature "having in mind th
needs and desires of each." . . . But the record in the pres
ent case could not be clearer that Prince Edward's publi
schools were closed and private schools operated in thei
place with state and county assistance, for one reason
and one reason only: to ensure, through measures taken
by the county and the State, that white and colored
children in Prince Edward County would not, under an
circumstances, go to the same school. Whatever non
racial grounds might support a State's allowing a count
to abandon public schools, the object must be a con
stitutional one, and grounds of race and opposition t
desegregation do not qualify as constitutional.

In *Hall v. St. Helena Parish School Board*, 197 F. Supp
649 (D.C.E.D. La. 1961), a three-judge District Court in
validated a Louisiana statute which provided "a mean
by which public schools under desegregation orders ma
be changed to 'private' schools operated in the same way
in the same buildings, with the same furnishings, with

he same money, and under the same supervision as the
ublic schools." . . . In addition, that statute also pro-
ided that where the public schools were "closed," the
chool board was "charged with responsibility for fur-
ishing free lunches, transportation, and grants-in-aid to
he children attending the 'private' schools." *Ibid.* We
ffirmed the District Court's judgment invalidating the
ouisiana statute as a denial of equal protection. 368
U.S. 515 (1962). While the Louisiana plan and the Vir-
inia plan worked in different ways, it is plain that both
were created to accomplish the same thing: the perpetu-
tion of racial segregation by closing public schools and
perating only segregated schools supported directly or
ndirectly by state or county funds. . . . Either plan
works to deny colored students equal protection of the
aws. Accordingly, we agree with the District Court that
losing the Prince Edward schools and meanwhile con-
ributing to the support of the private segregated white
chools that took their place denied petitioners the equal
protection of the laws.

We come now to the question of the kind of decree
ecessary and appropriate to put an end to the racial dis-
rimination practiced against these petitioners under
uthority of the Virginia laws. That relief needs to be
quick and effective. The parties defendant are the Board
f Supervisors, School Board, Treasurer, and Division
Superintendent of Schools of Prince Edward County, and
he State Board of Education and the State Superin-
endent of Education. All of these have duties which
relate directly or indirectly to the financing, supervision,
or operation of the schools in Prince Edward County.
The Board of Supervisors has the special responsibility
to levy local taxes to operate public schools or to aid
children attending the private schools now functioning

there for white children. The District Court enjoined
the county officials from paying county tuition grants or
giving tax exemptions and from processing applications
for state tuition grants so long as the county's public
schools remained closed. We have no doubt of the power
of the court to give this relief to enforce the discontinu-
ance of the county's racially discriminatory practices. . . .
The injunction against paying tuition grants and giving
tax credits while public schools remain closed is appropriate and necessary since those grants and tax credits have
been essential parts of the county's program, successful
thus far, to deprive petitioners of the same advantages of
a public school education enjoyed by children in every
other part of Virginia. For the same reasons the District
Court may, if necessary to prevent further racial discrimination, require the Supervisors to exercise the power
that is theirs to levy taxes to raise funds adequate to reopen, operate, and maintain without racial discrimination a public school system in Prince Edward County
like that operated in other counties in Virginia.

The District Court held that "the public schools of
Prince Edward County may not be closed to avoid the
effect of the law of the land as interpreted by the Supreme Court, while the Commonwealth of Virginia permits other public schools to remain open at the expense
of the taxpayers." . . . At the same time the court gave
notice that it would later consider an order to accomplish
this purpose if the public schools were not reopened by
September 7, 1962. That day has long passed, and the
schools are still closed. On remand, therefore, the court
may find it necessary to consider further such an order.
An order of this kind is within the court's power if required to assure these petitioners that their constitutional rights will no longer be denied them. The time

for mere "deliberate speed" has run out, and that phrase can no longer justify denying these Prince Edward County school children their constitutional rights to an education equal to that afforded by the public schools in the other parts of Virginia.

The judgment of the Court of Appeals is reversed, the judgment of the District Court is affirmed, and the cause is remanded to the District Court with directions to enter a decree which will guarantee that these petitioners will get the kind of education that is given in the State's public schools. . . .

15. Green v. School Board of
New Kent County

391 U.S. 430 (1968)

That the two Brown *decisions and* Cooper v. Aaron *did
not solve the problem of racial segregation in the public
schools quickly became apparent in the years that followed. Since methods of direct resistance were declared
unconstitutional, the strategy of those who sought to
avoid racial integration in the public schools shifted to
various sophisticated devices, such as pupil placement
"freedom-of-choice," "free-transfer," and zoning. In the*
Green *case, and in a companion case decided the same
day,* Raney v. Board of Education of the Gould School
District, *391 U.S. 443, coming up from Arkansas, a unanimous Court ruled that a "freedom-of-choice" plan which
did not actually result in substantial racial integration
did not satisfy the mandate of the Constitution. On the
same day, the Court also invalidated, in* Monroe v. Commissioners of Jackson, Tennessee, *391 U.S. 450, a "free-
transfer" plan which, after three years of operation, did
not in fact accomplish very much in the direction of cre-
ating a racially nondiscriminatory school system.*

Certiorari to the United States Court of Appeals for the
   Fourth Circuit.

1R. JUSTICE BRENNAN delivered the opinion of a unanimous Court.

'etitioners brought this action in March 1965 seeking injunctive relief against respondent's continued maintenance of an alleged racially segregated school system. Iew Kent County is a rural county in Eastern Virginia. bout one-half of its population of some 4,500 are Neroes. There is no residential segregation in the county; ersons of both races reside throughout. The school ystem has only two schools, the New Kent school on the ast side of the county and the George W. Watkins chool on the west side. In a memorandum filed May 17, 966, the District Court found that the "school system erves approximately 1,300 pupils, of which 740 are Iegro and 550 are White. The School Board operates ne white combined elementary and high school [New .ent], and one Negro combined elementary and high chool [George W. Watkins]. There are no attendance ones. Each school serves the entire county." The record ndicates that 21 school buses—11 serving the Watkins chool and 10 serving the New Kent school—travel overapping routes throughout the county to transport upils to and from the two schools.

The segregated system was initially established and 1aintained under the compulsion of Virginia constituional and statutory provisions mandating racial segregaion in public education. . . . The respondent School oard continued the segregated operation of the system fter the *Brown* decisions, presumably on the authority f several statutes enacted by Virginia in resistance to hose decisions. Some of these statutes were held to be nconstitutional on their face or as applied. One statute, he Pupil Placement Act (1964), not repealed until 1966,

divested local boards of authority to assign children
particular schools and placed that authority in a Sta
Pupil Placement Board. Under that Act children we
each year automatically reassigned to the school prev
ously attended unless upon their application the Sta
Board assigned them to another school; students seekin
enrollment for the first time were also assigned at th
discretion of the State Board. To September 1964, n
Negro pupil had applied for admission to the New Ke
school under this statute and no white pupil had applie
for admission to the Watkins school.

The School Board initially sought dismissal of th
suit on the ground that petitioners had failed to app
to the State Board for assignment to New Kent schoo
However, on August 2, 1965, five months after the su
was brought, respondent School Board, in order to r
main eligible for federal financial aid, adopted a "fre
dom-of-choice" plan for desegregating the schools. Und
that plan, each pupil except those entering the first an
eighth grades, may annually choose between the Ne
Kent and Watkins schools and pupils not making
choice are assigned to the school previously attende
first and eighth grade pupils must affirmatively choose
school. . . .

The pattern of separate "white" and "Negro" schoo
in the New Kent County school system established und
compulsion of state laws is precisely the pattern of segr
gation to which *Brown I* and *Brown II* were particularl
addressed, and which *Brown I* declared unconstitutio
ally denied Negro school children equal protection
the laws. Racial identification of the system's schoo
was complete, extending not just to the composition
student bodies at the two schools but to every facet
school operations—faculty, staff, transportation, extr

urricular activities and facilities. In short, the State, cting through the local school board and school officials, rganized and operated a dual system, part "white" and art "Negro."

It was such dual systems that 14 years ago *Brown I* eld unconstitutional and a year later *Brown II* held 1ust be abolished; school boards operating such school ystems were *required* by *Brown II* "to effectuate a tran- tion to a racially nondiscriminatory school system. . . ." t is of course true that for the time immediately after *rown II* the concern was with making an initial break 1 a long-established pattern of excluding Negro children rom schools attended by white children. The principal ocus was on obtaining for those Negro children coura- eous enough to break with tradition a place in the white" schools. . . . Under *Brown II* that immediate oal was only the first step, however. The transition to unitary, nonracial system of public education was and s the ultimate end to be brought about; it was because f the "complexities arising from the transition to a ystem of public education freed of racial discrimination" hat we provided for "all deliberate speed" in the imple- 1entation of the principles of *Brown I*. . . .

It is against this background that 13 years after *Brown I* commanded the abolition of dual systems we must 1easure the effectiveness of respondent School Board's freedom-of-choice" plan to achieve that end. The chool Board contends that it has fully discharged its bligation by adopting a plan by which every student, egardless of race, may "freely" choose the school he will ttend. The Board attempts to cast the issue in its broad- st form by arguing that its "freedom-of-choice" plan nay be faulted only by reading the Fourteenth Amend- nent as universally requiring "compulsory integration,"

a reading it insists the wording of the Amendment wil
not support. But that argument ignores the thrust c
Brown II. In the light of the command of that case
what is involved here is the question whether the Board
has achieved the "racially nondiscriminatory school sys
tem" *Brown II* held must be effectuated in order to rem
edy the established unconstitutional deficiencies of it
segregated system. In the context of the state-imposed
segregated pattern of long standing, the fact that in 196,
the Board opened the doors of the former "white" schoo
to Negro children and of the "Negro" school to whit
children merely begins, not ends, our inquiry whethe
the Board has taken steps adequate to abolish its dual
segregated system. *Brown II* was a call for the dis
mantling of well-entrenched dual systems tempered by a
awareness that complex and multifaceted problem
would arise which would require time and flexibility fo
a successful resolution. School boards such as the re
spondent then operating state-compelled dual system
were nevertheless clearly charged with the affirmative
duty to take whatever steps might be necessary to conver
to a unitary system in which racial discrimination would
be eliminated root and branch. . . . The constitutiona
rights of Negro school children articulated in *Brown*
permit no less than this; and it was to this end tha
Brown II commanded school boards to bend their efforts

In determining whether respondent School Board me
that command by adopting its "freedom-of-choice" plan
it is relevant that this first step did not come until som
11 years after *Brown I* was decided and 10 years afte
Brown II directed the making of a "prompt and reason
able start." This deliberate perpetuation of the uncon
stitutional dual system can only have compounded th
harm of such a system. Such delays are no longe

olerable, for "the governing constitutional principles no onger hear the imprint of newly enunciated doctrine." . . Moreover, a plan that at this late date fails to provide meaningful assurance of prompt and effective lisestablishment of a dual system is also intolerable. "The time for mere 'deliberate speed' has run out;" . . . "the context in which we must interpret and apply this anguage [of *Brown II*] to plans for desegregation has been significantly altered." . . . The burden on a school board today is to come forward with a plan that promises realistically to work, and promises realistically to work *now*.

The obligation of the district courts, as it always has been, is to assess the effectiveness of a proposed plan in achieving desegregation. There is no universal answer o complex problems of desegregation; there is obviously no one plan that will do the job in every case. The matter must be assessed in light of the circumstances present and the options available in each instance. It is incumbent upon the school board to establish that its proposed plan promises meaningful and immediate progress toward disestablishing state-imposed segregation. It is incumbent upon the district court to weigh that claim in light of the facts at hand and in light of any alternatives which may be shown as feasible and more promising in their effectiveness. Where the court finds the board to be acting in good faith and the proposed plan to have real prospects for dismantling the state-imposed dual system "at the earliest practicable date," then the plan may be said to provide effective relief. Of course, the availability to the board of other more promising courses of action may indicate a lack of good faith; and at the least it places a heavy burden upon the board to explain its preference for an apparently less effective method.

Moreover, whatever plan is adopted will require evaluation in practice, and the court should retain jurisdiction
until it is clear that state-imposed segregation has been
completely removed. . . .

We do not hold that "freedom of choice" can have no
place in such a plan. We do not hold that a "freedom-of-
choice" plan might of itself be unconstitutional, although that argument has been urged upon us. Rather,
all we decide today is that in desegregating a dual system
a plan utilizing "freedom of choice" is not an end in
itself. . . .

Although the general experience under "freedom of
choice" to date has been such as to indicate its ineffec-
tiveness as a tool of desegregation, there may well be
instances in which it can serve as an effective device.
Where it offers real promise of aiding a desegregation
program to effectuate conversion of a state-imposed dual
system to a unitary, nonracial system there might be no
objection to allowing such a device to prove itself in
operation. On the other hand, if there are reasonably
available other ways, such for illustration as zoning,
promising speedier and more effective conversion to a
unitary, nonracial school system, "freedom of choice"
must be held unacceptable.

The New Kent School Board's "freedom-of-choice"
plan cannot be accepted as a sufficient step to "effectuate
a transition" to a unitary system. In three years of operation not a single white child has chosen to attend
Watkins school and although 115 Negro children enrolled in New Kent school in 1967 (up from 35 in 1965
and 111 in 1966) 85% of the Negro children in the system still attend the all-Negro Watkins school. In other
words, the school system remains a dual system. Rather
than further the dismantling of the dual system, the plan

as operated simply to burden children and their par-
its with a responsibility which *Brown II* placed
quarely on the School Board. The Board must be re-
uired to formulate a new plan and, in light of other
ourses which appear open to the Board, such as zoning,
shion steps which promise realistically to convert
romptly to a system without a "white" school and a
Negro" school, but just schools.

. . . The case is remanded to the District Court for
arther proceedings consistent with this opinion. . . .

Part III

ACADEMIC FREEDOM

16. Wieman v. Updegraff

344 U.S. 183 (1952)

Appeal from the Supreme Court of Oklahoma.

Mr. Justice Clark delivered the opinion of the Court.

This is an appeal from a decision of the Supreme Court of Oklahoma upholding the validity of a loyalty oath prescribed by Oklahoma statute for all state officers and employees. . . . Appellants, employed by the state as members of the faculty and staff of Oklahoma Agricultural and Mechanical College, failed, within the thirty days permitted, to take the oath required by the Act. . . . Their objections centered largely on the following clauses of the oath:

". . . That I am not affiliated directly or indirectly . . . with any foreign political agency, party, organization or Government, or with any agency, party, organization, association, or group whatever which has been officially determined by the United States Attorney General or other authorized agency of the United States to be a communist front or subversive organization; . . . that I will take up arms in the defense of the United States in time of War, or National Emergency, if necessary; that within the five (5) years immediately preceding the taking of this oath (or affirmation) I have not been a member of . . . any agency, party, organization, association, or group whatever which has been officially determined by the United States Attorney General c other authorized public agency of the United States t be a communist front or subversive organization. . . .

The purpose of the Act, we are told, "was to mak loyalty a qualification to hold public office or b employed by the State." . . . During periods of intern; tional stress, the extent of legislation with such obje; tives accentuates our traditional concern about the rela tion of government to the individual in a free societ The perennial problem of defining that relationshi becomes acute when disloyalty is screened by ideologic; patterns and techniques of disguise that make it difficul to identify. Democratic government is not powerless t meet this threat, but it must do so without infringin, the freedoms that are the ultimate values of all demo cratic living. In the adoption of such means as it be lieves effective, the legislature is therefore confronte; with the problem of balancing its interest in nationa security with the often conflicting constitutional right of the individual. . . .

We are thus brought to the question . . . whethe the Due Process Clause permits a state, in attempting t bar disloyal individuals from its employ, to exclude per sons solely on the basis of organizational membership regardless of their knowledge concerning the organiza tions to which they had belonged. For, under the statut before us, the fact of membership alone disqualifies. I the rule be expressed as a presumption of disloyalty, it i a conclusive one.

But membership may be innocent. A state servan may have joined a proscribed organization unaware o its activities and purposes. In recent years, many com pletely loyal persons have severed organizational tie; after learning for the first time of the character of group;

o which they had belonged. . . . At the time of affilia-
ion, a group itself may be innocent, only later coming
under the influence of those who would turn it toward
illegitimate ends. Conversely, an organization formerly
subversive and therefore designated as such may have
subsequently freed itself from the influences which orig-
nally led to its listing.

There can be no dispute about the consequences vis-
ted upon a person excluded from public employment
on disloyalty grounds. In the view of the community,
the stain is a deep one; indeed, it has become a badge of
infamy. Especially is this so in time of cold war and
hot emotions when "each man begins to eye his neighbor
as a possible enemy." Yet under the Oklahoma Act, the
fact of association alone determines disloyalty and disqualification; it matters not whether association existed
innocently or knowingly. To thus inhibit individual
freedom of movement is to stifle the flow of democratic
expression and controversy at one of its chief sources.
. . Indiscriminate classification of innocent with knowing activity must fall as an assertion of arbitrary power.
The oath offends due process. . . .

We need not pause to consider whether an abstract
right to public employment exists. It is sufficient to say
that constitutional protection does extend to the public
servant whose exclusion pursuant to a statute is patently
arbitrary or discriminatory. . . .

Reversed.

Mr. Justice Black, concurring.

The Oklahoma oath statute is but one manifestation of
a national network of laws aimed at coercing and controlling the minds of men. Test oaths are notorious

tools of tyranny. When used to shackle the mind the
are, or at least they should be, unspeakably odious to
free people. Test oaths are made still more dangerou
when combined with bills of attainder which like th
Oklahoma statute impose pains and penalties for pas
lawful associations and utterances.

Governments need and have ample power to punis
treasonable acts. But it does not follow that they mu
have a further power to punish thought and speech a
distinguished from acts. Our own free society shoul
never forget that laws which stigmatize and penaliz
thought and speech of the unorthodox have a way o
reaching, ensnaring and silencing many more peopl
than at first intended. We must have freedom of speec
for all or we will in the long run have it for none bu
the cringing and the craven. And I cannot too often re
peat my belief that the right to speak on matters of pub
lic concern must be wholly free or eventually be wholl
lost. . . .

MR. JUSTICE FRANKFURTER, whom MR. JUSTICE DOUGLA
joins, concurring.

By limiting the power of the States to interfere wit
freedom of speech and freedom of inquiry and freedor
of association, the Fourteenth Amendment protects a
persons, no matter what their calling. But, in view o
the nature of the teacher's relation to the effective ex
ercise of the rights which are safeguarded by the Bill o
Rights and by the Fourteenth Amendment, inhibition o
freedom of thought, and of action upon thought, in th
case of teachers brings the safeguards of those amenc
ments vividly into operation. Such unwarranted inhib
tion upon the free spirit of teachers affects not only thos

ho, like the appellants, are immediately before the
ourt. It has an unmistakable tendency to chill that free
lay of the spirit which all teachers ought especially to
ultivate and practice; it makes for caution and timidity
i their associations by potential teachers. . . .

That our democracy ultimately rests on public opin-
on is a platitude of speech but not a commonplace in
ction. Public opinion is the ultimate reliance of our
ociety only if it be disciplined and responsible. It can
e disciplined and responsible only if habits of open-
nindedness and of critical inquiry are acquired in the
ormative years of our citizens. The process of education
as naturally enough been the basis of hope for the
erdurance of our democracy on the part of all our great
eaders, from Thomas Jefferson onwards.

To regard teachers—in our entire educational system,
rom the primary grades to the university—as the priests
f our democracy is therefore not to indulge in hyper-
ole. It is the special task of teachers to foster those hab-
ts of open-mindedness and critical inquiry which alone
nake for responsible citizens, who, in turn, make pos-
ible an enlightened and effective public opinion. Teach-
rs must fulfill their function by precept and prac-
ice, by the very atmosphere which they generate; they
nust be exemplars of open-mindedness and free inquiry.
They cannot carry out their noble task if the conditions
or the practice of a responsible and critical mind are
lenied to them. They must have the freedom of respon-
ible inquiry, by thought and action, into the meaning
f social and economic ideas, into the checkered history
f social and economic dogma. They must be free to
ift evanescent doctrine, qualified by time and circum-
tance, from that restless, enduring process of extending
he bounds of understanding and wisdom, to assure

which the freedoms of thought, of speech, of inquiry, (
worship are guaranteed by the Constitution of th
United States against infraction by National or Stat
government.

The functions of educational institutions in our na
tional life and the conditions under which alone the
can adequately perform them are at the basis of thes
limitations upon State and National power. . . .

17. Beilan v. Board of Education of Philadelphia

357 U.S. 399 (1958)

Herman A. Beilan, who had been a teacher for twenty-two years in the Philadelphia public school system, refused to answer questions put to him by the Superintendent of Schools regarding alleged past Communist activities. Pursuant to the provisions of the Pennsylvania Public School Code dealing with dismissal proceedings, Beilan was given a formal hearing before the Board of Public Education on the charge that his refusal to answer his Superintendent's questions constituted "incompetency." By a vote of 14 to one, the Board found that the charge of incompetency had been sustained and discharged Beilan from employment as a teacher. In a companion case, Lerner v. Casey, 357 U.S. 468 (1958), the Court reviewed the discharge of a subway conductor in the New York City Transit System under the New York Security Risk Law. The conductor had refused to answer a question put to him by his employer as to his membership in the Communist Party, and this was held to be evidence of doubtful trust and reliability. Three Justices dissented in both cases.

Certiorari to the Supreme Court of Pennsylvania.

MR. JUSTICE BURTON delivered the opinion of the Court

By engaging in teaching in the public schools, petitioner did not give up his right to freedom of belief, speech or association. He did, however, undertake obligations of frankness, candor and cooperation in answering inquiries made of him by his employing Board examining into his fitness to serve it as a public school teacher.

"A teacher works in a sensitive area in a schoolroom. There he shapes the attitude of young minds towards the society in which they live. In this, the state has a vital concern. It must preserve the integrity of the schools. That the school authorities have the right and the duty to screen the officials, teachers, and employees as to their fitness to maintain the integrity of the schools as a part of ordered society, cannot be doubted." *Adler* v. *Board of Education,* 342 U.S. 485, 493. As this Court stated in *Garner* v. *Board of Public Works,* 341 U.S. 716, 720, "We think that a municipal employer is not disabled because it is an agency of the State from inquiring of its employees as to matters that may prove relevant to their fitness and suitability for the public service."

The question asked of petitioner by his Superintendent was relevant to the issue of petitioner's fitness and suitability to serve as a teacher. Petitioner is not in a position to challenge his dismissal merely because of the remoteness in time of the 1944 activities. It was apparent from the circumstances of the two interviews that the Superintendent had other questions to ask. Petitioner's refusal to answer was not based on the remoteness of his 1944 activities. He made it clear that he would not answer any question of the same type as the one asked. Petitioner blocked from the beginning any inquiry into is Communist activities, however relevant to his present oyalty. The Board based its dismissal upon petitioner's efusal to answer any inquiry about his relevant activi-ies—not upon those activities themselves. It took care o charge petitioner with incompetency, and not with lisloyalty. It found him insubordinate and lacking in rankness and candor—it made no finding as to his oyalty.

We find no requirement in the Federal Constitution hat a teacher's classroom conduct be the sole basis for letermining his fitness. Fitness for teaching depends on ι broad range of factors. The Pennsylvania tenure pro-ision specifies several disqualifying grounds, including mmorality, intemperance, cruelty, mental derangement ιnd persistent and willful violation of the school laws, ιs well as "incompetency." However, the Pennsylvania tatute, unlike those of many other States, contains no :atch-all phrase, such as "conduct unbecoming a teacher," o cover disqualifying conduct not included within the nore specific provisions. Consequently, the Pennsylvania :ourts have given "incompetency" a broad interpreta-ion. . . .

In the instant case, the Pennsylvania Supreme Court ιas held that "incompetency" includes petitioner's 'deliberate and insubordinate refusal to answer the ques-ions of his administrative superior in a vitally impor-:ant matter pertaining to his fitness." . . . This interpre-:ation is not inconsistent with the Federal Constitution.

Petitioner complains that he was denied due process because he was not sufficiently warned of the conse-quences of his refusal to answer his Superintendent. The record, however, shows that the Superintendent, in his second interview, specifically warned petitioner that his refusal to answer "was a very serious and a very impor-

tant matter and that failure to answer the questio
might lead to his dismissal." That was sufficient warnin
to petitioner that his refusal to answer might jeopardi
his employment. Furthermore, at petitioner's reque
his Superintendent gave him ample opportunity to co
sult counsel. There was no element of surprise. . . .

Affirmed.

Mr. Chief Justice Warren, dissenting.

I believe the facts of record . . . compel the conclusio
that Beilan's plea of the Fifth Amendment before a sul
committee of the House Committee on Un-America
Activities was so inextricably involved in the Board
decision to discharge him that the validity of the Board
action cannot be sustained without consideration of th
ground. The clearest indication of this is the fact tha
for 13 months following petitioner's refusal to an
swer the Superintendent's questions, he was retained a
a school teacher and continually rated "satisfactory," ye
five days after his appearance before the House subcon
mittee petitioner was suspended. Since a plea of th
Fifth Amendment before a congressional committee i
an invalid basis for discharge from public employmen
Slochower v. *Board of Higher Education*, 350 U.S. 551
I would reverse the judgment approving the petitioner
dismissal. . . .

Mr. Justice Douglas, with whom Mr. Justice Blac
concurs, dissenting.

Among the liberties of the citizens that are guaran
teed by the Fourteenth Amendment are those containe
in the First Amendment. . . . These include the right t
believe what one chooses, the right to differ from hi

neighbor, the right to pick and choose the political philosophy that he likes best, the right to associate with whomever he chooses, the right to join the groups he prefers, the privilege of selecting his own path to salvation. . . .

We deal here only with a matter of belief. We have no evidence in either case that the employee in question ever committed a crime, ever moved in treasonable opposition against this country. The only mark against them—if it can be called such—is a refusal to answer questions concerning Communist Party membership. This is said to give rise to doubts concerning the competence of the teacher in the *Beilan* case and doubts as to the trustworthiness and reliability of the subway conductor in the *Lerner* case.

Our legal system is premised on the theory that every person is innocent until he is proved guilty. In this country we have, however, been moving away from that concept. We have been generating the belief that anyone who remains silent when interrogated about his unpopular beliefs or affiliations is guilty. I would allow no inference of wrongdoing to flow from the invocation of any constitutional right. I would not let that principle bow to popular passions. For all we know we are dealing here with citizens who are wholly innocent of any wrongful action. That must indeed be our premise. When we make the contrary assumption, we part radically with our tradition.

If it be said that we deal not with guilt or innocence but with frankness, the answer is the same. There are areas where government may not probe. Private citizens, private clubs, private groups may make such deductions and reach such conclusions as they choose from the failure of a citizen to disclose his beliefs, his philosophy, his associates. But government has no business penalizing a citizen merely for his beliefs or associations. . . .

If we break with tradition and let the government penalize these citizens for their beliefs and associations, the most we can assume from their failure to answer is that they were Communists. Yet, as we said in *Wieman v. Updegraff*, 344 U.S. 183, 190, membership in the Communist Party "may be innocent." The member may have thought that the Communist movement would develop in the parliamentary tradition here, or he may not have been aware of any unlawful aim, or knowing it, may have embraced only the socialist philosophy of the group, not any political tactics of violence and terror. Many join associations, societies, and fraternities with less than full endorsement of all their aims.

We compound error in these decisions. We not only impute wrongdoing to those who invoke their constitutional rights. We go further and impute the worst possible motives to them. . . .

In sum, we have here only a bare refusal to testify, and the Court holds that sufficient to show that these employees are unfit to hold their public posts. That makes qualification for public office turn solely on a matter of belief—a notion very much at war with the Bill of Rights.

When we make the belief of the citizen the basis of government action, we move toward the concept of *total security*. Yet *total security* is possible only in a totalitarian regime—the kind of system we profess to combat.

MR. JUSTICE BRENNAN, dissenting.

This Court refuses to pierce the transparent denials that each of these employees was publicly branded disloyal. The Court holds that we are bound by the definition of state law pronounced by the States' high courts that the dismissals were for unreliability and incompetency. Of course, we accept state law as the high court of a State pronounces it, but certainly our duty to secure to the individual the safeguards, embodied in due process, against a State's arbitrary exercise of power is no less when the state courts refuse to recognize what has in fact occurred. . . . In my view the judgments in both cases must be reversed because each petitioner has been branded a disloyal American without the due process of law required of the States by the Fourteenth Amendment. . . .

I might agree that the Due Process Clause imposes no restraint against dismissal of a teacher who refuses to answer his superior's questions asked in the privacy of his office and related to the teacher's fitness to continue in his position.

But in reality Beilan was not dismissed by the Pennsylvania school authorities upon that ground. The question whether he had been an officer in the Communist Party in 1944 was first asked of Beilan by the Superintendent at a private interview on June 25, 1952. Beilan did not refuse at that time to answer but asked permission to consult counsel. The Superintendent summoned him again on October 14, 1952, and it was on that date that Beilan advised the Superintendent that he declined to answer that or similar questions. The Superintendent had told Beilan at the first interview that the question was asked because the Superintendent had information which reflected on Beilan's loyalty. Almost fourteen months elapsed before Beilan was suspended and the charges preferred which led to his dismissal. In that interval Beilan's superiors had twice rated him in the high satisfactory range of competency. Had the authorities seriously regarded Beilan as incompetent because of his refusal to answer the Superintendent's question they would hardly have waited so long before suspending him. The record is clear that proceedings were actually initiated not because of that refusal to answer but because on November 18, 1953, Beilan asserted the privilege against self-incrimination under the Fifth Amendment when interrogated at a publicly televised hearing held in Philadelphia by a Subcommittee of the Committee on Un-American Activities of the House of Representatives. Beilan testified at that hearing that he was not then a member of the Communist Party and had never advocated the overthrow of the Government by force or violence but pleaded the protection of the Fifth Amendment when asked questions directed to past party membership and activities. Five days later, on November 23, 1953, the Superintendent notified Beilan that he had been rated "unsatisfactory" because he had refused to answer the Superintendent's question and also because "you invoked the Fifth Amendment of the Federal Constitution" when questioned as to "past associations with organizations of doubtful loyalty" by the Subcommittee. The opinion on Beilan's administrative appeal which sustained his dismissal by the Board of Education makes it clear that the authorities viewed Beilan's invocation of the Fifth Amendment before the Subcommittee as an admission of disloyalty. . . .

18. Shelton v. Tucker

364 U.S. 479 (1960)

Appeal from the U.S. District Court for the Eastern
   District of Arkansas.

Certiorari to the Supreme Court of Arkansas.

MR. JUSTICE STEWART delivered the opinion of the Court.

An Arkansas statute compels every teacher, as a condition of employment in a state-supported school or college, to file annually an affidavit listing without limitation every organization to which he has belonged or
regularly contributed within the preceding five years.
. . .
   The statute in question is Act 10 of the Second
Extraordinary Session of the Arkansas General Assembly
of 1958. . . .
   Teachers there are hired on a year-to-year basis. They
are not covered by a civil service system, and they have
no job security beyond the end of each school year. The
closest approach to tenure is a statutory provision for
the automatic renewal of a teacher's contract if he is not
notified within ten days after the end of a school year
that the contract has not been renewed. . . .
   The plaintiffs in the Federal District Court (appellants here) were B. T. Shelton, a teacher employed in
the Little Rock Public School System, suing for himself

and others similarly situated, together with the Arkansas
Teachers Association and its Executive Secretary, suing
for the benefit of members of the Association. Shelton
had been employed in the Little Rock Special School
District for twenty-five years. In the spring of 1959 he
was notified that, before he could be employed for the
1959–1960 school year, he must file the affidavit required
by Act 10, listing all his organizational connections over
the previous five years. He declined to file the affidavit,
and his contract for the ensuing school year was not
renewed. At the trial the evidence showed that he was
not a member of the Communist Party or of any organization advocating the overthrow of the Government by
force, and that he was a member of the National Association for the Advancement of Colored People. The court
upheld Act 10, finding the information it required was
"relevant," and relying on the several decisions of this
Court. . . .

The plaintiffs in the state court proceedings (petitioners here) were Max Carr, an associate professor at the
University of Arkansas, and Ernest T. Gephardt, a
teacher at Central High School in Little Rock, each
suing for himself and others similarly situated. Each
refused to execute and file the affidavit required by Act
10. Carr executed an affirmation in which he listed his
membership in professional organizations, denied ever
having been a member of any subversive organization,
and offered to answer any questions which the University
authorities might constitutionally ask touching upon his
qualifications as a teacher. Gephardt filed an affidavit
stating that he had never belonged to a subversive organization, disclosing his membership in the Arkansas
Education Association and the American Legion, and
also offering to answer any questions which the school

uthorities might constitutionally ask touching upon his qualifications as a teacher. Both were advised that their failure to comply with the requirements of Act 10 would make impossible their re-employment as teachers for the following school year. The Supreme Court of Arkansas upheld the constitutionality of Act 10, on its face and as applied to the petitioners. . . .

There can be no doubt of the right of a State to investigate the competence and fitness of those whom it hires to teach in its schools, as this Court before now has had occasion to recognize. . . .

It is not disputed that to compel a teacher to disclose his every associational tie is to impair that teacher's right of free association, a right closely allied to freedom of speech and a right which, like free speech, lies at the foundation of a free society. . . . Such interference with personal freedom is conspicuously accented when the teacher serves at the absolute will of those to whom the disclosure must be made—those who any year can terminate the teacher's employment without bringing charges, without notice, without a hearing, without affording an opportunity to explain.

The statute does not provide that the information it requires be kept confidential. Each school board is left free to deal with the information as it wishes. The record contains evidence to indicate that fear of public disclosure is neither theoretical nor groundless. Even if there were no disclosure to the general public the pressure upon a teacher to avoid any ties which might displease those who control his professional destiny would be constant and heavy. Public exposure, bringing with it the possibility of public pressures upon school boards to discharge teachers who belong to unpopular or minority organizations, would simply operate to widen and aggravate the impairment of constitutional liberty

The vigilant protection of constitutional freedoms i
nowhere more vital than in the community of American
schools. . . .

The question to be decided here is not whether the
State of Arkansas can ask certain of its teachers about al
their organizational relationships. It is not whether the
State can ask all of its teachers about certain of their
associational ties. It is not whether teachers can be asked
how many organizations they belong to, or how much
time they spend in organizational activity. The question
is whether the State can ask every one of its teachers to
disclose every single organization with which he has been
associated over a five-year period. The scope of the inquiry required by Act 10 is completely unlimited. The
statute requires a teacher to reveal the church to which
he belongs, or to which he has given financial support.
It requires him to disclose his political party, and every
political organization to which he may have contributed
over a five-year period. It requires him to list, without
number, every conceivable kind of associational tie—
social, professional, political, avocational, or religious.
Many such relationships could have no possible bearing
upon the teacher's occupational competence or fitness.

In a series of decisions this Court has held that, even
though the governmental purpose be legitimate and substantial, that purpose cannot be pursued by means that
broadly stifle fundamental personal liberties when the
end can be more narrowly achieved. The breadth of
legislative abridgment must be viewed in the light of
less drastic means for achieving the same basic purpose.
. . .

The unlimited and indiscriminate sweep of the statute
now before us brings it within the ban of our prior

cases. The statute's comprehensive interference with associational freedom goes far beyond what might be justified in the exercise of the State's legitimate inquiry into the fitness and competency of its teachers. The judgments in both cases must be reversed. . . .

MR. JUSTICE FRANKFURTER, dissenting.

As one who has strong views against crude intrusions by the state into the atmosphere of creative freedom in which alone the spirit and mind of a teacher can fruitfully function, I may find displeasure with the Arkansas legislation now under review. But in maintaining the distinction between private views and constitutional restrictions, I am constrained to find that it does not exceed the permissible range of state action limited by the Fourteenth Amendment. . . .

. . . The statute challenged in the present cases involves neither administrative discretion to censor nor vague, overreaching tests of criminal responsibility. . . .

If I dissent from the Court's disposition in these cases, it is not that I put a low value on academic freedom. . . . It is because that very freedom, in its most creative reaches, is dependent in no small part upon the careful and discriminating selection of teachers. This process of selection is an intricate affair, a matter of fine judgment, and if it is to be informed, it must be based upon a comprehensive range of information. I am unable to say, on the face of this statute, that Arkansas could not reasonably find that the information which the statute requires —and which may not be otherwise acquired than by asking the question which it asks—is germane to that selection. Nor, on this record, can I attribute to the State a purpose to employ the enactment as a device for the accomplishment of what is constitutionally forbidden. Of course, if the information gathered by the required affidavits is used to further a scheme of terminating the employment of teachers solely because of their membership in unpopular organizations, that use will run afoul of the Fourteenth Amendment. It will be time enough, if such use is made, to hold the application of the statute unconstitutional. . . .

MR. JUSTICE HARLAN, whom MR. JUSTICE FRANKFURTER, MR. JUSTICE CLARK, and MR. JUSTICE WHITAKER join, dissenting.

It must be emphasized that neither of these cases actually presents an issue of racial discrimination. The statute on its face applies to *all* Arkansas teachers irrespective of race, and there is no showing that it has been discriminatorily administered. . . .

It is surely indisputable that a State has the right to choose its teachers on the basis of fitness. And I think it equally clear, as the Court appears to recognize, that information about a teacher's associations may be useful to school authorities in determining the moral, professional, and social qualifications of the teacher, as well as in determining the type of service for which he will be best suited in the educational system. . . .

Finally, I need hardly say that if it turns out that this statute is abused, either by an unwarranted publicizing of the required associational disclosures or otherwise, we would have a different kind of case than those presently before us. . . . All that is now here is the validity of the statute on its face, and I am unable to agree that in this posture of things the enactment can be said to be unconstitutional.

I would affirm in both cases.

19. Cramp v. Board of Public Instruction of Orange County, Florida

368 U.S. 278 (1961)

Appeal from the Supreme Court of Florida.

MR. JUSTICE STEWART delivered the opinion of a unanimous Court.

A Florida statute requires each employee of the State or its subdivisions to execute a written oath in which he must swear that, among other things, he has never lent his "aid, support, advice, counsel or influence to the Communist Party." Failure to subscribe to this oath results under the law in the employee's immediate discharge.

After the applicant had been employed for more than nine years as a public school teacher in Orange County, Florida, it was discovered in 1959 that he had never been required to execute this statutory oath. When requested to do so he refused. . . .

The issue to be decided . . . is whether a State can constitutionally compel those in its service to swear that they have never "knowingly lent their aid, support, advice, counsel, or influence to the Communist Party." More precisely, can Florida consistently with the Due Process Clause of the Fourteenth Amendment force an employee either to take such an oath, at the risk of subsequent prosecution for perjury, or face immediate dismissal from public service?

The provision of the oath here in question, it is to be noted, says nothing of advocacy of violent overthrow of state or federal government. It says nothing of membership or affiliation with the Communist Party, past or present. The provision is completely lacking in these or any other terms susceptible of objective measurement. Those who take this oath must swear, rather, that they have not in the unending past ever knowingly lent their "aid," or "support," or "advice," or "counsel" or "influence" to the Communist Party. What do these phrases mean? In the not too distant past Communist Party candidates appeared regularly and legally on the ballot in many state and local elections. Elsewhere the Communist Party has on occasion endorsed or supported candidates nominated by others. Could one who had ever cast his vote for such a candidate safely subscribe to this legislative oath? Could a lawyer who had ever represented the Communist Party or its members swear with either confidence or honesty that he had never knowingly lent his "counsel" to the Party? Could a journalist who had ever defended the constitutional rights of the Communist Party conscientiously take an oath that he had never lent the Party his "support"? Indeed, could anyone honestly subscribe to this oath who had ever supported any cause with contemporaneous knowledge that the Communist Party also supported it?

The very absurdity of these possibilities brings into focus the extraordinary ambiguity of the statutory language. With such vagaries in mind, it is not unrealistic to suggest that the compulsion of this oath provision might weigh most heavily upon those whose conscien-

ious scruples were the most sensitive. While it is perhaps fanciful to suppose that a perjury prosecution
would ever be instituted for past conduct of the kind
suggested, it requires no strain of the imagination to
envision the possibility of prosecution for other types of
equally guiltless knowing behaviour. It would be blink-
ing reality not to acknowledge that there are some
among us always ready to affix a Communist label upon
those whose ideas they violently oppose. And experience
teaches that prosecutors too are human.

We think this case demonstrably falls within the com-
pass of those decisions of the Court which hold that
'. . . a statute which either forbids or requires the doing of an act in terms so vague that men of common intelligence must necessarily guess at its meaning and differ as to its application, violates the first essential of
due process of law." . . . "No one may be required at
peril of life, liberty or property to speculate as to the
meaning of penal statutes. All are entitled to be informed as to what the State commands or forbids." . . .
"Words which are vague and fluid . . . may be as much
of a trap for the innocent as the ancient laws of Calig-
ula." . . .

The vice of unconstitutional vagueness is further aggravated where, as here, the statute in question operates
to inhibit the exercise of individual freedoms affirmatively protected by the Constitution. . . .

As in *Wieman* v. *Updegraff,* we are not concerned
here with the question "whether an abstract right to
public employment exists." . . . Nor do we question the
power of a State to safeguard the public service from disloyalty. . . . It is enough for the present case to reaffirm

"that constitutional protection does extend to the publi
servant whose exclusion pursuant to a statute is patentl
arbitrary or discriminatory." . . . "The fact . . . that
person is not compelled to hold public office canno
possibly be an excuse for barring him from office b
state-imposed criteria forbidden by the Constitution. . . .

Reversed.

20.   Keyishian v. Board of Regents of the University of the State of New York

385 U.S. 589 (1967)

Under a section of the Civil Service Law of New York any member of an organization advocating the overthrow of government by force, violence, or any unlawful means is ineligible for employment in any public school. To implement this law the legislature adopted the Feinberg Law in 1949. The preamble of this law made elaborate findings that members of subversive groups, particularly of the Communist Party and its affiliated organizations, have been infiltrating into public school employment, to the grave detriment of education. It then provided that the Board of Regents, which has charge of the public school system of the state, shall, after full notice and hearing, make a listing of organizations which it finds advocate, advise, teach, or embrace the doctrine that the government should be overthrown by force, violence, or any other unlawful means. The statute then authorized the Board of Regents to provide, by rule, that membership in any listed organization, after notice and hearing, "shall constitute prima-facie evidence for disqualification for appointment to or retention in any office or position in the school system." Dividing six to three, the Supreme Court upheld the constitutionality of the Feinberg Law in Adler v. Board of Education of New York, 342 *U.S.* 485 *(1952). But in 1967 the Court reopened*

the question, on petition of several professors at the Uni-
versity of Buffalo; it held that the vagueness issue had
not been adjudicated in Adler, and that Adler must be
overruled as inconsistent with decisions made since then.

Appeal from the U.S. District Court for the Western
    District of New York.

MR. JUSTICE BRENNAN delivered the opinion of the Court.

Appellants in this case timely asserted below the unconstitutionality of all these sections on grounds of vagueness and that question is now properly before us for
decision. Moreover, to the extent that *Adler* sustained
the provision of the Feinberg Law constituting membership in an organization advocating forceful overthrow of
government a ground for disqualification, pertinent constitutional doctrines have since rejected the premises
upon which that conclusion rested. *Adler* is therefore
not dispositive of the constitutional issues we must decide in this case. . . .

    Section 3021 requires removal for "treasonable or
seditious" utterances or acts. The 1958 amendment to
§ 105 of the Civil Service Law, now subdivision 3 of that
section, added such utterances or acts as a ground for
removal under that law also. The same wording is used in
both statutes—that "the utterance of any treasonable or
seditious word or words or the doing of any treasonable
or seditious act or acts" shall be ground for removal. But
there is a vital difference between the two laws. Section
3021 does not define the terms "treasonable or seditious"
as used in that section; in contrast, subdivision 3 of § 105
of the Civil Service Law provides that the terms "treasonable word or act" shall mean "treason" as defined in the

enal Law and the terms "seditious word or act" shall
1ean "criminal anarchy" as defined in the Penal Law.

Our experience under the Sedition Act of 1798, . . .
1ught us that dangers fatal to First Amendment free-
oms inhere in the word "seditious." . . . And the word
treasonable," if left undefined, is no less dangerously
ncertain. Thus it becomes important whether, despite
he omission of a similar reference to the Penal Law in §
021, the words as used in that section are to be read as
1eaning only what they mean in subdivision 3 of § 105.
)r are they to be read more broadly and to constitute ut-
erances or acts "seditious" and "treasonable" which
vould not be so regarded for the purposes of § 105?

Even assuming that "treasonable" and "seditious" in
3021 and § 105, subd. 3, have the same meaning, the
1ncertainty is hardly removed. The definition of "trea-
onable" in the Penal Law presents no particular prob-
em. The difficulty centers upon the meaning of "sedi-
ious." Subdivision 3 equates the term "seditious" with
criminal anarchy" as defined in the Penal Law. Is the
eference only to Penal Law § 160, defining criminal
narchy as "the doctrine that organized government
hould be overthrown by force or violence, or by assas-
ination of the executive head or of any of the executive
fficials of government, or by any unlawful means"? But
hat section ends with the sentence "The advocacy of
uch doctrine either by word of mouth or writing is a
elony." Does that sentence draw into § 105, Penal Law
; 161, proscribing "advocacy of criminal anarchy"? If so,
he possible scope of "seditious" utterances or acts has
irtually no limit. For under Penal Law § 161, one com-
1its the felony of advocating criminal anarchy if he
. . . publicly displays any book . . . containing or ad-
ocating, advising or teaching the doctrine that organ-

ized government should be overthrown by force, violence
or any unlawful means." Does the teacher who carries a
copy of the Communist Manifesto on a public street
thereby advocate criminal anarchy? It is no answer to
say that the statute would not be applied in such a case.
We cannot gainsay the potential effect of this obscure
wording on "those with a conscientious and scrupulous
regard for such undertakings." . . . Even were it certain
that the definition referred to in § 105 was solely Penal
Law § 160, the scope of § 105 still remains indefinite.
The teacher cannot know the extent, if any, to which a
"seditious" utterance must transcend mere statement
about abstract doctrine, the extent to which it must be
intended to and tend to indoctrinate or incite to action
in furtherance of the defined doctrine. The crucial consideration is that no teacher can know just where the line
is drawn between "seditious" and nonseditious utterances
and acts.

Other provisions of § 105 also have the same defect of
vagueness. Subdivision 1(a) of § 105 bars employment
of any person who "by word of mouth or writing wilfully
and deliberately advocates, advises or teaches the doctrine" of forceful overthrow of government. This provision is plainly susceptible of sweeping and improper
application. It may well prohibit the employment of
one who merely advocates the doctrine in the abstract
without any attempt to indoctrinate others, or incite
others to action in furtherance of unlawful aims. . . .
And in prohibiting "advising" the "doctrine" of unlawful overthrow does the statute prohibit mere "advising" of the existence of the doctrine, or advising another to support the doctrine? Since "advocacy" of the
doctrine of forceful overthrow is separately prohibited,

ed the person "teaching" or "advising" this doctrine
mself "advocate" it? Does the teacher who informs his
ass about the precepts of Marxism or the Declaration of
dependence violate this prohibition?

Similar uncertainty arises as to the application of
bdivision 1(b) of § 105. That subsection requires the
squalification of an employee involved with the dis-
ibution of written material "containing or advocating,
lvising or teaching the doctrine" of forceful overthrow,
d who himself "advocates, advises, teaches, or em-
aces the duty, necessity or propriety of adopting the
)ctrine contained therein." Here again, mere advocacy
abstract doctrine is apparently included. And does
e prohibition of distribution of matter "containing"
e doctrine bar histories of the evolution of Marxist
)ctrine or tracing the background of the French, Amer-
an, or Russian revolutions? The additional require-
ent, that the person participating in distribution of
e material be one who "advocates, advises, teaches,
· embraces the duty, necessity or propriety of adopting
e doctrine" of forceful overthrow, does not alleviate
e uncertainty in the scope of the section, but exacer-
ates it. Like the language of § 105, subd. 1(a), this lan-
1age may reasonably be construed to cover mere ex-
:ession of belief. For example, does the university
brarian who recommends the reading of such materials
ereby "advocate . . . the . . . propriety of adopting
e doctrine contained therein"?

We do not have the benefit of a judicial gloss by the
ew York courts enlightening us as to the scope of this
mplicated plan. In light of the intricate administra-
ve machinery for its enforcement, this is not surprising.
he very intricacy of the plan and the uncertainty as to

the scope of its proscriptions make it a highly efficie
in terrorem mechanism. It would be a bold teacher wh
would not stay as far as possible from utterances or ac
which might jeopardize his living by enmeshing him
this intricate machinery. The uncertainty as to the u
terances and acts proscribed increases that caution
"those who believe that written law means what it says
. . . The result must be to stifle "that free play of tl
spirit which all teachers ought especially to cultiva
and practice. . . ." That probability is enhanced by th
provisions requiring an annual review of every teache
to determine whether any utterance or act of his, insid
the classroom or out, came within the sanctions of tl
laws. . . .

There can be no doubt of the legitimacy of Ne
York's interest in protecting its education system fro
subversion. But "even though the governmental purpo
be legitimate and substantial, that purpose cannot
pursued by means that broadly stifle fundamental pe
sonal liberties when the end can be more narrowl
achieved." . . .

Our Nation is deeply committed to safeguarding ac
demic freedom, which is of transcendent value to all
us and not merely to the teachers concerned. That free
dom is therefore a special concern of the First Amen
ment, which does not tolerate laws that cast a pall
orthodoxy over the classroom. "The vigilant protectio
of constitutional freedoms is nowhere more vital tha
in the community of American schools." . . . The clas
room is peculiarly the "marketplace of ideas." The N
tion's future depends upon leaders trained through wid
exposure to that robust exchange of ideas which discove
truth "out of a multitude of tongues, [rather] tha
through any kind of authoritative selection." . . . I

veezy v. *New Hampshire,* 354 U.S. 234, 250, . . . we
id:

"The essentiality of freedom in the community of
merican universities is almost self-evident. No one
ould underestimate the vital role in a democracy that
played by those who guide and train our youth. To
pose any strait jacket upon the intellectual leaders in
ur colleges and universities would imperil the future of
ur Nation. No field of education is so thoroughly com-
ehended by man that new discoveries cannot yet be
ade. Particularly is that true in the social sciences,
here few, if any, principles are accepted as absolutes.
holarship cannot flourish in an atmosphere of suspi-
on and distrust. Teachers and students must always
main free to inquire, to study and to evaluate, to gain
w maturity and understanding; otherwise our civili-
tion will stagnate and die."

We emphasize once again that "[p]recision of regula-
on must be the touchstone in an area so closely touch-
g our most precious freedoms." . . . New York's compli-
ted and intricate scheme plainly violates that standard.
hen one must guess what conduct or utterance may
se him his position, one necessarily will "steer far
ider of the unlawful zone. . . ." The danger of that
illing effect upon the exercise of vital First Amend-
ent rights must be guarded against by sensitive tools
hich clearly inform teachers what is being proscribed.
. .

The regulatory maze created by New York is wholly
cking in "terms susceptible of objective measurement."
. . Vagueness of wording is aggravated by prolixity
d profusion of statutes, regulations, and administrative
achinery, and by manifold cross-references to inter-
lated enactments and rules. . . .

Appellants have also challenged the constitutionali of the discrete provisions of subdivision 1(c) of § 1 and subdivision 2 of the Feinberg Law, which mal Communist Party membership, as such, prima-facie e dence of disqualification. . . .

Here again constitutional doctrine has develope since *Adler*. Mere knowing membership without a sp cific intent to further the unlawful aims of an organiz tion is not a constitutionally adequate basis for exclusio from such positions as those held by appellants.

In *Elfbrandt* v. *Russell*, 384 U.S. 11, we said, "Tho who join an organization but do not share its unlawf purposes and who do not participate in its unlawf activities surely pose no threat, either as citizens or public employees." . . . We there struck down a stat torily required oath binding the state employee not become a member of the Communist Party with know edge of its unlawful purpose, on threat of discharg and perjury prosecution if the oath were violated. W found that "[a]ny lingering doubt that proscription mere knowing membership, without any showing 'specific intent,' would run afoul of the Constitution wa set at rest by our decision in *Aptheker* v. *Secretary State*, 378 U.S. 500." . . . In *Aptheker* we held tha Party membership, without knowledge of the Party's ur lawful purposes *and* specific intent to further its unlaw ful aims, could not constitutionally warrant deprivatio of the right to travel abroad. . . .

These limitations clearly apply to a provision, lik § 105, subd. 1(c), which blankets all state employees, re gardless of the "sensitivity" of their positions. But eve the Feinberg Law provision, applicable primarily to a tivities of teachers, who have captive audiences of youn minds, are subject to these limitations in favor of freedom of expression and association; the stifling effect on the academic mind from curtailing freedom of association in such manner is manifest, and has been documented in recent studies. *Elfbrandt* and *Aptheker* state the governing standard: legislation which sanctions membership unaccompanied by specific intent to further the unlawful goals of the organization or which is not active membership violates constitutional limitations.

Measured against this standard, both Civil Service Law § 105, subd. 1(c), and Education Law § 3022, subd. 2, sweep overbroadly into association which may not be proscribed. The presumption of disqualification arising from proof of mere membership may be rebutted, but only by (a) a denial of membership, (b) a denial that the organization advocates the overthrow of government by force, or (c) a denial that the teacher has knowledge of such advocacy. . . . Thus proof of nonactive membership or a showing of the absence of intent to further unlawful aims will not rebut the presumption and defeat dismissal. This is emphasized in official administrative interpretations. . . .

Thus § 105, subd. 1(c), and § 3022, subd. 2, suffer from impermissible "overbreadth." . . . They seek to bar employment both for association which legitimately may be proscribed and for association which may not be proscribed consistently with First Amendment rights. Where statutes have an overbroad sweep, just as where they are vague, "the hazard of loss or substantial impairment of those previous rights may be critical," . . . since those covered by the statute are bound to limit their behavior to that which is unquestionably safe. . . .

The judgment of the District Court is reversed. . . .

MR. JUSTICE CLARK with whom MR. JUSTICE HARLAN
MR. JUSTICE STEWART, and MR. JUSTICE WHITE joir
dissenting.

It is clear that the Feinberg Law, in which this Cour
found "no constitutional infirmity" in 1952, has bee:
given its death blow today. Just as the majority her
finds that there "can be no doubt of the legitimacy o
New York's interest in protecting its education syster.
from subversion" there can also be no doubt that "th
be-all and end-all" of New York's effort is here. And
regardless of its correctness, neither New York nor th
several States that have followed the teaching of *Adle*
v. *Board of Education,* . . . for some 15 years, can eve
put the pieces together again. No court has ever reached
out so far to destroy so much with so little. . . .

This Court has again and again, since at least 1951
approved procedures either identical or at the least simi
lar to the ones the Court condemns today. . . .

The majority makes much over the horribles tha
might arise from subdivision 1(*b*) of § 105 which con
demns the printing, publishing, selling, etc., of matter
containing such doctrine. But the majority fails to state
that this action is condemned only *when and if* the
teacher also personally advocates, advises, teaches, etc.
the necessity or propriety of adopting such doctrine
This places this subdivision on the same footing as 1(*a*).
And the same is true of subdivision 1(*c*) where a teacher
organizes, helps to organize or becomes a member of an
organization which teaches or advocates such doctrine,
for *scienter* would also be a necessary ingredient under
our opinion in *Garner, supra.* Moreover, membership is
only prima-facie evidence of disqualification and could
be rebutted, leaving the burden of proof on the State.

urthermore, all of these procedures are protected by an lversary hearing with full judicial review.

In the light of these considerations the strained and nbelievable suppositions that the majority poses could ardly occur. . . . Where there is doubt as to one's in-nt or the nature of his activities we cannot assume that le administrative boards will not give him full protec-on. Furthermore, the courts always sit to make cer-in that this is done.

The majority says that the Feinberg Law is bad be-iuse it has an "overbroad sweep." I regret to say—and do so with deference—that the majority has by its roadside swept away one of our most precious rights, amely, the right of self-preservation. Our public edu-ational system is the genius of our democracy. The iinds of our youth are developed there and the char-cter of that development will determine the future of ur land. Indeed, our very existence depends upon it. 'he issue here is a very narrow one. It is not freedom f speech, freedom of thought, freedom of press, freedom f assembly, or of association, even in the Communist 'arty. It is simply this: May the State provide that one ho, after a hearing with full judicial review, is found o have wilfully and deliberately advocated, advised, or aught that our Government should be overthrown by orce or violence or other unlawful means; or to have ilfully and deliberately printed, published, etc., any ook or paper that so advocated *and to have personally* dvocated such doctrine himself; or to have wilfully and leliberately become a member of an organization that dvocates such doctrine, is prima-facie disqualified from eaching in its university? My answer, in keeping with ll of our cases up until today, is "Yes"!

I dissent.

21. Pickering v. Board of Education of Township High School

391 U.S. 563 (1968)

Appeal from the Supreme Court of Illinois.

MR. JUSTICE MARSHALL delivered the opinion of the Court.

Appellant Marvin L. Pickering, a teacher in Township High School District 205, Will County, Illinois, was dismissed from his position by the appellee Board of Education for sending a letter to a local newspaper in connection with a recently proposed tax increase that was critical of the way in which the Board and the district superintendent of schools had handled past proposals to raise new revenue for the schools. Appellant's dismissal resulted from a determination by the Board, after a full hearing, that the publication of the letter was "detrimental to the efficient operation and administration of the schools of the district." . . .

Appellant's claim that his writing of the letter was protected by the First and Fourteenth Amendments was rejected. Appellant then sought review of the Board's action in the Circuit Court of Will County, which affirmed his dismissal on the ground that the determination that appellant's letter was detrimental to the interests of the school system was supported by substantial evidence and that the interests of the schools overrode

ppellant's First Amendment rights. On appeal, the
upreme Court of Illinois, two Justices dissenting, af-
rmed the judgment of the Circuit Court. . . .

In February of 1961 the appellee Board of Education
sked the voters of the school district to approve a bond
sue to raise $4,875,000 to erect two new schools. The
roposal was defeated. Then, in December of 1961, the
oard submitted another bond proposal to the voters
hich called for the raising of $5,500,000 to build two
ew schools. This second proposal passed and the schools
ere built with the money raised by the bond sales. In
Iay of 1964 a proposed increase in the tax rate to be
sed for educational purposes was submitted to the voters
y the Board and was defeated. Finally, on September
9, 1964, a second proposal to increase the tax rate was
ubmitted by the Board and was likewise defeated. It
vas in connection with this last proposal of the School
Board that appellant wrote the letter to the editor . . .
hat resulted in his dismissal.

Prior to the vote on the second tax increase proposal
variety of articles attributed to the District 205 Teach-
rs' Organization appeared in the local paper. These
rticles urged passage of the tax increase and stated that
ailure to pass the increase would result in a decline in
he quality of education afforded children in the dis-
rict's schools. A letter from the superintendent of
chools making the same point was published in the
aper two days before the election and submitted to the
oters in mimeographed form the following day. It was
n response to the foregoing material, together with the
ailure of the tax increase to pass, that appellant sub-
nitted the letter in question to the editor of the local
aper.

The letter constituted, basically, an attack on the

School Board's handling of the 1961 bond issue proposa and its subsequent allocation of financial resources b tween the schools' educational and athletic program It also charged the superintendent of schools with a tempting to prevent teachers in the district from oppo ing or criticizing the proposed bond issue.

The Board dismissed Pickering for writing and pu lishing the letter. Pursuant to Illinois law, the Boar was then required to hold a hearing on the dismissa At the hearing the Board charged that numerous state ments in the letter were false and that the publicatio of the statements unjustifiably impugned the "motive honesty, integrity, truthfulness, responsibility and com petence" of both the Board and the school administra tion. The Board also charged that the false statement damaged the professional reputations of its members an of the school administrators, would be disruptive o faculty discipline, and would tend to foment "contro versy, conflict and dissension" among teachers, adminis trators, the Board of Education, and the residents of th district. Testimony was introduced from a variety of wit nesses on the truth or falsity of the particular statement in the letter with which the Board took issue. Th Board found the statements to be false as charged. N evidence was introduced at any point in the proceeding as to the effect of the publication of the letter on th community as a whole or on the administration of th school system in particular, and no specific findings alon these lines were made.

The Illinois courts reviewed the proceedings solel to determine whether the Board's findings were sup ported by substantial evidence and whether, on th facts as found, the Board could reasonably conclude that appellant's publication of the letter was "detrimental to he best interests of the schools." Pickering's claim that his letter was protected by the First Amendment was rejected on the ground that his acceptance of a teaching position in the public schools obliged him to refrain from making statements about the operation of the schools "which in the absence of such position he would have an undoubted right to engage in." . . .

To the extent that the Illinois Supreme Court's opinion may be read to suggest that teachers may constitutionally be compelled to relinquish the First Amendment rights they would otherwise enjoy as citizens to comment on matters of public interest in connection with the operation of the public schools in which they work, it proceeds on a premise that has been unequivocally rejected in numerous prior decisions of this Court. . . . At the same time it cannot be gainsaid that the State has interests as an employer in regulating the speech of its employees that differ significantly from those it possesses in connection with regulation of the speech of the citizenry in general. The problem in any case is to arrive at a balance between the interests of the teacher, as a citizen, in commenting upon matters of public concern and the interest of the State, as an employer, in promoting the efficiency of the public services it performs through its employees.

The Board contends that "the teacher by virtue of his public employment has a duty of loyalty to support his superiors in attaining the generally accepted goals of education and that, if he must speak out publicly, he should do so factually and accurately, commensurate with his education and experience." Appellant, on the other hand, argues that the test applicable to defamatory statements directed against public officials by persons having no occupational relationship with them, namely, that statements to be legally actionable must be made "with knowledge that [they were] . . . false or with reckless disregard of whether [they were] . . . false or not," *New York Times Co.* v. *Sullivan*, 376 U.S. 254, 280 (1964), should also be applied to public statements made by teachers. Because of the enormous variety of fact situations in which critical statements by teachers and other public employees may be thought by their superiors, against whom the statements are directed, to furnish grounds for dismissal, we do not deem it either appropriate or feasible to attempt to lay down a general standard against which all such statements may be judged. However, in the course of evaluating the conflicting claims of First Amendment protection and the need for orderly school administration in the context of this case, we shall indicate some of the general lines along which an analysis of the controlling interests should run.

An examination of the statements in appellant's letter objected to by the Board reveals that they, like the letter as a whole, consist essentially of criticism of the Board's allocation of school funds between educational and athletic programs, and of both the Board's and the superintendent's methods of informing, or preventing the informing of, the district's taxpayers of the real reasons why additional tax revenues were being sought for the schools. The statements are in no way directed towards any person with whom appellant would normally be in contact in the course of his daily work as a teacher. Thus no question of maintaining either discipline by immediate superiors or harmony among coworkers is presented here. Appellant's employment relationships with the Board and, to a somewhat lesser extent, with the superintendent are not the kind of close working rela-

ionships for which it can persuasively be claimed that
personal loyalty and confidence are necessary to their
proper functioning. Accordingly, to the extent that the
Board's position here can be taken to suggest that even
comments on matters of public concern that are substan-
ially correct, . . . may furnish grounds for dismissal if
they are sufficiently critical in tone, we unequivocally
reject it.

We next consider the statements in appellant's letter
which we agree to be false. The Board's original charges
included allegations that the publication of the letter
damaged the professional reputations of the Board and
the superintendent and would foment controversy and
conflict among the Board, teachers, administrators, and
the residents of the district. However, no evidence to
support these allegations was introduced at the hearing.
So far as the record reveals, Pickering's letter was greeted
by everyone but its main target, the Board, with massive
apathy and total disbelief. The Board must, therefore,
have decided, perhaps by analogy with the law of libel,
that the statements were *per se* harmful to the operation
of the schools.

However, the only way in which the Board could conclude, absent any evidence of the actual effect of the
letter, that the statements contained therein were *per se*
detrimental to the interest of the schools was to equate
the Board members' own interests with that of the
schools. Certainly an accusation that too much money is
being spent on athletics by the administrators of the
school system (which is precisely the import of that
portion of appellant's letter containing the statements
that we have found to be false, . . .) cannot reasonably
be regarded as *per se* detrimental to the district's schools.
Such an accusation reflects rather a difference of opinion

between Pickering and the Board as to the preferabl
manner of operating the school system, a difference c
opinion that clearly concerns an issue of general publi
interest.

In addition, the fact that particular illustrations c
the Board's claimed undesirable emphasis on athleti
programs are false would not normally have any neces
sary impact on the actual operation of the schools, be
yond its tendency to anger the Board. For example
Pickering's letter was written after the defeat at the pol
of the second proposed tax increase. It could, therefore
have had no effect on the ability of the school distric
to raise necessary revenue, since there was no showin
that there was any proposal to increase taxes pendin
when the letter was written.

More importantly, the question whether a school sys
tem requires additional funds is a matter of legitimat
public concern on which the judgment of the school ad
ministration, including the School Board, cannot, in ;
society that leaves such questions to popular vote, be
taken as conclusive. On such a question free and open
debate is vital to informed decision making by the elec
torate. Teachers are, as a class, the members of a com
munity most likely to have informed and definite opin
ions as to how funds allotted to the operation of the
schools should be spent. Accordingly, it is essential tha
they be able to speak out freely on such questions with
out fear of retaliatory dismissal.

In addition, the amounts expended on athletics which
Pickering reported erroneously were matters of public
record on which his position as a teacher in the district
did not qualify him to speak with any greater authority
than any other taxpayer. The Board could easily have

rebutted appellant's errors by publishing the accurate figures itself, either via a letter to the same newspaper or otherwise. We are thus not presented with a situation in which a teacher has carelessly made false statements about matters so closely related to the day-to-day operations of the schools that any harmful impact on the public would be difficult to counter because of the teacher's presumed greater access to the real facts. Accordingly, we have no occasion to consider at this time whether under such circumstances a school board could reasonably require that a teacher make substantial efforts to verify the accuracy of his charges before publishing them.

What we do have before us is a case in which a teacher has made erroneous public statements upon issues then currently the subject of public attention, which are critical of his ultimate employer but which are neither shown nor can be presumed to have in any way either impeded the teacher's proper performance of his daily duties in the classroom or to have interfered with the regular operation of the schools generally. In these circumstances we conclude that the interest of the school administration in limiting teachers' opportunities to contribute to public debate is not significantly greater than its interest in limiting a similar contribution by any member of the general public.

The public interest in having free and unhindered debate on matters of public importance—the core value of the Free Speech Clause of the First Amendment—is so great that it has been held that a State cannot authorize the recovery of damages by a public official for defamatory statements directed at him except when such statements are shown to have been made either with

knowledge of their falsity or with reckless disregard fc
their truth or falsity. *New York Times Co.* v. *Sulliva*
376 U.S. 254 (1964). . . . It is therefore perfectly clea
that, were appellant a member of the general public, th
State's power to afford the appellee Board of Educatio
or its members any legal right to sue him for writing th
letter at issue here would be limited by the requiremen
that the letter be judged by the standard laid down i
New York Times.

This Court has also indicated, in more general terms
that statements by public officials on matters of publi
concern must be accorded First Amendment protectio
despite the fact that the statements are directed at thei
nominal superiors. . . .

While criminal sanctions and damage awards have .
somewhat different impact on the exercise of the righ
to freedom of speech from dismissal from employment, i
is apparent that the threat of dismissal from public em
ployment is nonetheless a potent means of inhibitin
speech. We have already noted our disinclination t
make an across-the-board equation of dismissal from
public employment for remarks critical of superior
with awarding damages in a libel suit by a public officia
for similar criticism. However, in a case such as th
present one, in which the fact of employment is onl
tangentially and insubstantially involved in the subjec
matter of the public communication made by a teacher
we conclude that it is necessary to regard the teache
as the member of the general public he seeks to be.

In sum, we hold that, in a case such as this, absent
proof of false statements knowingly or recklessly made
by him, a teacher's exercise of his right to speak on issues
of public importance may not furnish the basis for his

dismissal from public employment. Since no such show-ing has been made in this case regarding appellant's let-ter, . . . his dismissal for writing it cannot be upheld and the judgment of the Illinois Supreme Court must, accordingly, be reversed and the case remanded for fur-ther proceedings not inconsistent with this opinion.

22. Barenblatt v. United States

360 U.S. 109 (1959)

*Barenblatt had been a graduate student and teaching
fellow at the University of Michigan from 1947 to 1950,
and an instructor in psychology at Vassar College from
1950 until shortly before his appearance before a Subcommittee of the House Committee on Un-American
Activities. The Subcommittee was engaged in an inquiry
concerning alleged Communist infiltration into the field
of education. Barenblatt refused to answer questions regarding present or past membership in the Communist
Party or in affiliated organizations. He expressly dis-
claimed reliance upon the Self-Incrimination Clause of
the Fifth Amendment, relying mainly upon the First
Amendment guaranty of freedom of speech, religion and
association. Convicted of contempt of Congress, he
brought his appeal to the Supreme Court. The Court
affirmed the conviction below, holding (1) that the statutory charter of authority of the Committee was not unconstitutionally vague, and that the House of Representatives had never regarded the field of education as being
outside the Committee's authority; (2) that the petitioner
had been properly apprised of the pertinency of the Subcommittee's questions to the subject matter of the inquiry; and (3) that First Amendment rights were not infringed. Portions of the opinion dealing only with the
third issue are reproduced here.*

Certiorari to the U.S. Court of Appeals for the District of Columbia.

MR. JUSTICE HARLAN delivered the opinion of the Court.

In the present case congressional efforts to learn the extent of a nation-wide, indeed world-wide, problem have brought one of its investigating committees into the field of education. Of course, broadly viewed, inquiries cannot be made into the teaching that is pursued in any of our educational institutions. When academic teaching-freedom and its corollary learning-freedom, so essential to the well-being of the Nation, are claimed, this Court will always be on the alert against intrusion by Congress into this constitutionally protected domain. But this does not mean that the Congress is precluded from interrogating a witness merely because he is a teacher. An educational institution is not a constitutional sanctuary from inquiry into matters that may otherwise be within the constitutional legislative domain merely for the reason that inquiry is made of someone within its walls. . . .

The Court's past cases establish sure guides to decision. Undeniably, the First Amendment in some circumstances protects an individual from being compelled to disclose his associational relationships. However, the protections of the First Amendment, unlike a proper claim of the privilege against self-incrimination under the Fifth Amendment, do not afford a witness the right to resist inquiry in all circumstances. Where First Amendment rights are asserted to bar governmental interrogation resolution of the issue always involves a balancing by the courts of the competing private and public interests at stake in the particular circumstances shown. . . .

The first question is whether this investigation was related to a valid legislative purpose, for Congress may not constitutionally require an individual to disclose his political relationships or other private affairs except in relation to such a purpose. . . .

That Congress has wide power to legislate in the field of Communist activity in this Country, and to conduct appropriate investigations in aid thereof, is hardly debatable. The existence of such power has never been questioned by this Court, and it is sufficient to say, without particularization, that Congress has enacted or considered in this field a wide range of legislative measures, not a few of which have stemmed from recommendations of the very Committee whose actions have been drawn in question here. In the last analysis this power rests on the right of self-preservation, "the ultimate value of any society." . . . Justification for its exercise in turn rests on the long and widely accepted view that the tenets of the Communist Party include the ultimate overthrow of the Government of the United States by force and violence, a view which has been given formal expression by the Congress.

On these premises, this Court in its constitutional adjudications has consistently refused to view the Communist Party as an ordinary political party, and has upheld federal legislation aimed at the Communist problem which in a different context would certainly have raised constitutional issues of the gravest character. . . . On the same premises this Court has upheld under the Fourteenth Amendment state legislation requiring those occupying or seeking public office to disclaim knowing membership in any organization advocating overthrow of the Government by force and violence, which legisla-

ion none can avoid seeing was aimed at membership in the Communist Party. . . . Similarly, in other areas, this Court has recognized the close nexus between the Communist Party and violent overthrow of government. . . . To suggest that because the Communist Party may also sponsor peaceable political reforms the constitutional issues before us should now be judged as if that Party were just an ordinary political party from the standpoint of national security, is to ask this Court to blind itself to world affairs which have determined the whole course of our national policy since the close of World War II.
. .

We think that investigatory power in this domain is not to be denied Congress solely because the field of education is involved. Nothing in the prevailing opinions in *Sweezy* v. *State of New Hampshire* . . . stands for a contrary view. The vice existing there was that the questioning of Sweezy, who had not been shown ever to have been connected with the Communist Party, as to the contents of a lecture he had given at the University of New Hampshire, and as to his connections with the Progressive Party, then on the ballot as a normal political party in some 26 States, was too far removed from the premises on which the constitutionality of the State's investigation had to depend to withstand attack under the Fourteenth Amendment. . . . This is a very different thing from inquiring into the extent to which the Communist Party has succeeded in infiltrating into our universities, or elsewhere, persons and groups committed to furthering the objective of overthrow. . . . Indeed we do not understand petitioner here to suggest that Congress in no circumstances may inquire into Communist activity in the field of education. Rather, his position is in effect that this particular investigation was aimed not at the revolutionary aspects but at the theoretical class-room discussion of communism.

In our opinion this position rests on a too constricted view of the nature of the investigatory process, and i not supported by a fair assessment of the record before us. An investigation of advocacy of or preparation for overthrow certainly embraces the right to identify a witness as a member of the Communist Party, . . . and to inquire into the various manifestations of the Party's tenets. The strict requirements of a prosecution under the Smith Act . . . are not the measure of the permissible scope of a congressional investigation into "overthrow," for of necessity the investigatory process must proceed step by step. Nor can it fairly be concluded that this investigation was directed at controlling what is being taught at our universities rather than at overthrow. The statement of the Subcommittee Chairman at the opening of the investigation evinces no such intention, and so far as this record reveals nothing thereafter transpired which would justify our holding that the thrust of the investigation later changed. The record discloses considerable testimony concerning the foreign domination and revolutionary purposes and efforts of the Communist Party. That there was also testimony on the abstract philosophical level does not detract from the dominant theme of this investigation—Communist infiltration furthering the alleged ultimate purpose of overthrow. And certainly the conclusion would not be justified that the questioning of petitioner would have exceeded permissible bounds had he not shut off the Subcommittee at the threshold.

Nor can we accept the further contention that this investigation should not be deemed to have been in furtherance of a legislative purpose because the true objective of the Committee and of the Congress was purely "exposure." So long as Congress acts in pursuance of its constitutional power, the Judiciary lacks authority to intervene on the basis of the motives which spurred the exercise of that power.

Affirmed.

Mr. Justice Black, with whom the Chief Justice and Mr. Justice Douglas concur, dissenting.

The First Amendment says in no equivocal language that Congress shall pass no law abridging freedom of speech, press, assembly or petition. The activities of this Committee, authorized by Congress, do precisely that, through exposure, obloquy and public scorn. . . . The Court does not really deny this fact but relies on a combination of three reasons for permitting the infringement: (A) The notion that despite the First Amendment's command Congress can abridge speech and association if this Court decides that the governmental interest in abridging speech is greater than an individual's interest in exercising that freedom; (B) the Government's right to "preserve itself"; (C) the fact that the Committee is only after Communists or suspected Communists in this investigation.

(A) I do not agree that laws directly abridging First Amendment freedoms can be justified by a congressional or judicial balancing process. . . .

To apply the Court's balancing test under such circumstances is to read the First Amendment to say "Congress shall pass no law abridging freedom of speech, press, assembly and petition, unless Congress and the Supreme Court reach the joint conclusion that on balance the interests of the Government in stifling these freedoms is greater than the interest of the people in having them exercised." This is closely akin to the notion that neither the First Amendment nor any other provision of the Bill of Rights should be enforced unless the Court believes it is *reasonable* to do so. Not only does this violate the genius of our *written* Constitution, but it runs expressly counter to the injunction to Court and Congress made by Madison when he introduced the Bill of Rights. . . .

But even assuming what I cannot assume, that some balancing is proper in this case, I feel that the Court after stating the test ignores it completely. At most it balances the right of the Government to preserve itself, against Barenblatt's right to refrain from revealing Communist affiliations. Such a balance, however, mistakes the factors to be weighed. In the first place, it completely leaves out the real interest in Barenblatt's silence, the interest of the people as a whole in being able to join organizations, advocate causes and make political "mistakes" without later being subjected to governmental penalties for having dared to think for themselves. It is this right, the right to err politically, which keeps us strong as a Nation. For no number of laws against communism can have as much effect as the personal conviction which comes from having heard its arguments and rejected them, or from having once accepted its tenets and later recognized their worthlessness. Instead, the obloquy which results from investigations such as this not only stifles "mistakes" but prevents all but the most courageous from hazarding any views which might at some later time become disfavored. This result, whose importance cannot be overestimated, is doubly crucial when it affects the universities, on which we must largely rely for the experimentation and development of new ideas essential to our country's welfare. It is these interests of society, rather than Barenblatt's own right to silence, which I think the Court should put on the balance against the demands of the Government, if any balancing process is to be tolerated. Instead they are not mentioned, while on the other side the demands of the Government are vastly overstated and called "self preservation." It is admitted that this Committee can only seek information for the purpose of suggesting laws, and that Congress' power to make laws in the realm of speech and association is quite limited, even on the Court's test. Its interest in making such laws in the field of education, primarily a state function, is clearly narrower still. Yet the Court styles this attenuated interest self-preservation and allows it to overcome the need our country has to let us all think, speak, and associate politically as we like and without fear of reprisal. . . .

(B) Moreover, I cannot agree with the Court's notion that First Amendment freedoms must be abridged in order to "preserve" our country. That notion rests on the unarticulated premise that this Nation's security hangs upon its power to punish people because of what they think, speak or write about, or because of those with whom they associate for political purposes. The Government, in its brief, virtually admits this position when it speaks of the "communication of unlawful ideas." I challenge this premise, and deny that ideas can be proscribed under our Constitution. I agree that despotic governments cannot exist without stifling the voice of opposition to their oppressive practices. The First

Amendment means to me, however, that the only constitutional way our Government can preserve itself is to leave its people the fullest possible freedom to praise, criticize or discuss, as they see fit, all governmental policies and to suggest, if they desire, that even its most fundamental postulates are bad and should be changed. . . . On that premise this land was created, and on that premise it has grown to greatness. Our Constitution assumes that the common sense of the people and their attachment to our country will enable them, after free discussion, to withstand ideas that are wrong. To say that our patriotism must be protected against false ideas by means other than these is, I think, to make a baseless charge. . . .

(C)   The Court implies, however, that the ordinary rules and requirements of the Constitution do not apply because the Committee is merely after Communists and they do not constitute a political party but only a criminal gang. . . .

No matter how often or how quickly we repeat the claim that the Communist Party is not a political party, we cannot outlaw it, as a group, without endangering the liberty of all of us. The reason is not hard to find, for mixed among those aims of communism which are illegal are perfectly normal political and social goals. And muddled with its revolutionary tenets is a drive to achieve power through the ballot, if it can be done. These things necessarily make it a political party whatever other, illegal, aims it may have. . . .

The fact is that once we allow any group which has some political aims or ideas to be driven from the ballot and from the battle for men's minds because some of its members are bad and some of its tenets are illegal, no group is safe. . . .

MR. JUSTICE BRENNAN, dissenting.

would reverse this conviction. It is sufficient that I state my complete agreement with my Brother BLACK that no purpose for the investigation of Barenblatt is revealed by the record except exposure purely for the sake of exposure. This is not a purpose to which Barenblatt's rights under the First Amendment can validly be subordinated. An investigation in which the processes of law-making and law-evaluating are submerged entirely in exposure of individual behavior—in adjudication, of a sort, through the exposure process—is outside the constitutional pale of congressional inquiry. . . .

23. Board of Regents of State Colleges v. Roth

408 U.S. 564 (1972)

On June 29, 1972, the Supreme Court decided two cases which raised important issues regarding tenure and reappointment rights of college professors. Perry v. Sundermann, 408 U.S. 593, involved the nonreappointment of a college teacher who had been employed in the Texas state college system for ten years at three different institutions, of which four years were served at the last institution on the basis of one-year contracts. The college had no formal tenure system, but Sundermann claimed that he had an "expectancy" of employment because the college actually had a de facto tenure system. Since he claimed that his nonretention infringed upon his right to free speech, the Court held that he was entitled to a hearing on the issue of whether he had tenure. The companion case, however, involved an assistant professor who had been employed by contract for a fixed term of one academic year. As he was nontenured, the college took the position that the only procedural right Roth had was the right to due notice, which he was given, but Roth alleged that his nonretention was in violation of freedom of speech. By a six-to-two vote the Court ruled against Roth in a holding which took a very narrow view of the due process rights of nontenured professors.

Certiorari to the Court of Appeals for the Seventh Circuit.

MR. JUSTICE STEWART delivered the opinion of the Court.

In 1968 the respondent, David Roth, was hired for his first teaching job as assistant professor of political science at Wisconsin State University–Oshkosh. He was hired for a fixed term of one academic year. The notice of his faculty appointment specified that his employment would begin on September 1, 1968, and would end on June 30, 1969. The respondent completed that term. But he was informed that he would not be rehired for the next academic year.

The respondent had no tenure rights to continued employment. Under Wisconsin statutory law a state university teacher can acquire tenure as a "permanent" employee only after four years of year-to-year employment. Having acquired tenure, a teacher is entitled to continued employment "during efficiency and good behavior." A relatively new teacher without tenure, however, is under Wisconsin law entitled to nothing beyond his one-year appointment. There are no statutory or administrative standards defining eligibility for re-employment. State law thus clearly leaves the decision whether to rehire a nontenured teacher for another year to the unfettered discretion of university officials.

The procedural protection afforded a Wisconsin State University teacher before he is separated from the University corresponds to his job security. As a matter of statutory law, a tenured teacher cannot be "discharged except for cause upon written charges" and pursuant to certain procedures. A nontenured teacher, similarly, is protected to some extent *during* his one-year term. Rules promulgated by the Board of Regents provide that a nontenured teacher "dismissed" before the end of the year may have some opportunity for review of the "dismissal." But the Rules provide no real protection for a nontenured teacher who simply is not re-employed for the next year. He must be informed by February 1 "concerning retention or non-retention for the ensuing year." But "no reason for non-retention need be given. No review or appeal is provided in such case."

In conformance with these Rules, the President of Wisconsin State University–Oshkosh informed the respondent before February 1, 1969, that he would not be rehired for the 1969–1970 academic year. He gave the respondent no reason for the decision and no opportunity to challenge it at any sort of hearing. . . .

The requirements of procedural due process apply only to the deprivation of interests encompassed by the Fourteenth Amendment's protection of liberty and property. When protected interests are implicated, the right to some kind of prior hearing is paramount. But the range of interests protected by procedural due process is not infinite. . . .

Yet, while the Court has eschewed rigid or formalistic limitations on the protection of procedural due process, it has at the same time observed certain boundaries. For the words "liberty" and "property" in the Due Process Clause of the Fourteenth Amendment must be given some meaning.

"While this Court has not attempted to define with exactness the liberty . . . guaranteed [by the Fourteenth Amendment], the term has received much consideration and some of the included things have been definitely stated. Without doubt, it denotes not merely freedom from bodily restraint but also the right of the individual to contract, to engage in any of the common occupations of life, to acquire useful knowledge, to marry, establish a home and bring up children, to worship God according to the dictates of his own conscience, and generally to enjoy those privileges long recognized . . . as essential to the orderly pursuit of happiness by free men." . . . In a Constitution for a free people, there can be no doubt that the meaning of "liberty" must be broad indeed. . . .

There might be cases in which a State refused to re-employ a person under such circumstances that interests in liberty would be implicated. But this is not such a case.

The State, in declining to rehire the respondent, did not make any charge against him that might seriously damage his standing and associations in his community. It did not base the nonrenewal of his contract on a charge, for example, that he had been guilty of dishonesty, or immorality. Had it done so, this would be a different case. For "[w]here a person's good name, reputation, honor, or integrity is at stake because of what the government is doing to him, notice and an opportunity to be heard are essential." . . . In such a case, due process would accord an opportunity to refute the charge before University officials. In the present case, however, there is no suggestion whatever that the respondent's interest in his "good name, reputation, honor, or integrity" is at stake.

Similarly, there is no suggestion that the State, in declining to re-employ the respondent, imposed on him a stigma or other disability that foreclosed his freedom to take advantage of other employment opportunities. The State, for example, did not invoke any regulations to bar the respondent from all other public employment in state universities. Had it done so, this, again, would be a different case. . . .

It stretches the concept too far to suggest that a person

is deprived of "liberty" when he simply is not rehired in one job but remains as free as before to seek another. . .

The Fourteenth Amendment's procedural protection of property is a safeguard of the security of interests that a person has already acquired in specific benefits. These interests—property interests—may take many forms.

Thus, the Court has held that a person receiving welfare benefits under statutory and administrative standards defining eligibility for them has an interest in continued receipt of those benefits that is safeguarded by procedural due process. . . . Similarly, in the area of public employment, the Court has held that a public college professor dismissed from an office held under tenure provisions, . . . and college professors and staff members dismissed during the terms of their contracts, . . . have interests in continued employment that are safeguarded by due process. . . .

To have a property interest in a benefit, a person clearly must have more than an abstract need or desire for it. He must have more than a unilateral expectation of it. He must, instead, have a legitimate claim of entitlement to it. It is a purpose of the ancient institution of property to protect those claims upon which people rely in their daily lives, reliance that must not be arbitrarily undermined. It is a purpose of the constitutional right to a hearing to provide an opportunity for a person to vindicate those claims.

Property interests, of course, are not created by the Constitution. Rather, they are created and their dimensions are defined by existing rules or understandings that stem from an independent source such as state law—rules or understandings that secure certain benefits and that support claims of entitlement to those benefits. . . .

Just as the welfare recipients' "property" interest in

elfare payments was created and defined by statutory :rms, so the respondent's "property" interest in employ- ient at Wisconsin State University–Oshkosh was created nd defined by the terms of his appointment. Those :rms secured his interest in employment up to June 30, 969. But the important fact in this case is that they pecifically provided that the respondent's employment /as to terminate on June 30. They did not provide for ontract renewal absent "sufficient cause." Indeed, they 1ade no provision for renewal whatsoever.

Thus, the terms of the respondent's appointment se- ured absolutely no interest in re-employment for the ext year. They supported absolutely no possible claim f entitlement to re-employment. Nor, significantly, was here any state statute or University rule or policy that ecured his interest in re-employment or that created any egitimate claim to it. In these circumstances, the re- pondent surely had an abstract concern in being rehired, ut he did not have a *property* interest sufficient to re- uire the University authorities to give him a hearing /hen they declined to renew his contract of employ- nent. . . .

MR. JUSTICE POWELL took no part in the decision of this case.

MR. CHIEF JUSTICE BURGER filed a concurring opinion.

MR. JUSTICE DOUGLAS, dissenting.

Though Roth was rated by the faculty as an excellent eacher, he had publicly criticized the administration for uspending an entire group of 94 black students without letermining individual guilt. He also criticized the uni- ersity's regime as being authoritarian and autocratic.

He used his classroom to discuss what was being do
about the black episode; and one day, instead of meeti
his class, he went to the meeting of the Board of R
gents. . . .

No more direct assault on academic freedom can
imagined than for the school authorities to be allowed
discharge a teacher because of his or her philosophic
political, or ideological beliefs. The same may well
true of private schools, if through the device of financi
or other umbilical cords they become instrumentalities
the State. . . .

When a violation of First Amendment rights is allege
the reasons for dismissal or for nonrenewal of an emplo
ment contract must be examined to see if the reaso
given are only a cloak for activity or attitudes protecte
by the Constitution. . . .

If this nonrenewal implicated the First Amendmen
then Roth was deprived of constitutional rights becau
his employment was conditioned on a surrender of Fir
Amendment rights; and apart from the First Amen
ment, he was denied due process when he received r
notice and hearing of the adverse action contemplate
against him. Without a statement of the reasons for th
discharge and an opportunity to rebut those reasons-
both of which were refused by petitioners—there is n
means short of a lawsuit to safeguard the right not to k
discharged for the exercise of First Amendment guara
tees. . . .

MR. JUSTICE MARSHALL, dissenting.

In my view, every citizen who applies for a governmer
job is entitled to it unless the government can establis
some reason for denying the employment. This is th
"property" right that I believe is protected by the Fou

teenth Amendment and that cannot be denied "without due process of law." And it is also liberty—liberty to work—which is the "very essence of the personal freedom and opportunity" secured by the Fourteenth Amendment.

This Court has often had occasion to note that the denial of public employment is a serious blow to any citizen. . . .

Employment is one of the greatest, if not the greatest, benefits that governments offer in modern-day life. When something as valuable as the opportunity to work is at stake, the government may not reward some citizens and not others without demonstrating that its actions are fair and equitable. And it is procedural due process that is our fundamental guarantee of fairness, our protection against arbitrary, capricious, and unreasonable government action. . . .

It may be argued that to provide procedural due process to all public employees or prospective employees would place an intolerable burden on the machinery of government. . . . The short answer to that argument is that it is not burdensome to give reasons when reasons exist. Whenever an application for employment is denied, an employee is discharged, or a decision not to rehire an employee is made, there should be some reason for the decision. It can scarcely be argued that government would be crippled by a requirement that the reason be communicated to the person most directly affected by the government's action.

Where there are numerous applicants for jobs, it is likely that few will choose to demand reasons for not being hired. But, if the demand for reasons is exceptionally great, summary procedures can be devised that would provide fair and adequate information to all persons. As long as the government has a good reason for its actions

it need not fear disclosure. It is only where the gove
ment acts improperly that procedural due process
truly burdensome. And that is precisely when it is m
necessary.

It might also be argued that to require a hearing a
a statement of reasons is to require a useless act, becau
a government bent on denying employment to one
more persons will do so regardless of the procedu
hurdles that are placed in its path. Perhaps this is
but a requirement of procedural regularity at le
renders arbitrary action more difficult. Moreover, prop
procedures will surely eliminate some of the arbitrarin
that results, not from malice, but from innocent err
"Experience teaches . . . that the affording of pro
dural safeguards, which by their nature serve to illun
nate the underlying facts, in itself often operates to p
vent erroneous decisions on the merits from occu
ring." . . .

Part IV

THE RIGHTS OF STUDENTS

24. Tinker v. Des Moines Independent Community School District

393 U.S. 503 (1969)

Three students attending a public high school in Des Moines, as part of a plan formulated by a group of adults and students, wore black armbands to school to demonstrate their objections to American participation in the Vietnam War. They were aware of the fact that a few days earlier the school authorities had adopted a regulation that any student wearing an armband to school would be asked to remove it, and on refusal would be suspended until the rule was complied with. The suspended students filed an action in the U.S. District Court under § 1983 of Title 42 of the U.S. Code, which authorizes lawsuits in federal courts for damages or other relief against persons who, acting under color of state law, deny any person a federal right. After an evidentiary hearing, the district court dismissed the complaint, upholding the constitutionality of the action of the school authorities. Dividing seven to two, the Supreme Court reversed.

Certiorari to the Court of Appeals for the Eighth Circuit.

Mr. Justice Fortas delivered the opinion of the Court.

The District Court recognized that the wearing of an armband for the purpose of expressing certain views is

the type of symbolic act that is within the Free Spee
Clause of the First Amendment. . . . As we shall discus
the wearing of armbands in the circumstances of th
case was entirely divorced from actually or potential
disruptive conduct by those participating in it. It w:
closely akin to "pure speech" which, we have repeated
held, is entitled to comprehensive protection under tl
First Amendment. . . .

First Amendment rights, applied in light of the speci:
characteristics of the school environment, are availab.
to teachers and students. It can hardly be argued tha
either students or teachers shed their constitution:
rights to freedom of speech or expression at the schoo
house gate. This has been the unmistakable holding
this Court for almost 50 years. . . .

The problem posed by the present case does not rela
to regulation of the length of skirts or the type of clotl
ing, to hair style, or deportment. . . . It does not concer
aggressive, disruptive action or even group demonstr:
tions. Our problem involves direct, primary Firs
Amendment rights akin to "pure speech."

The school officials banned and sought to punish pet
tioners for a silent, passive expression of opinion, ur
accompanied by any disorder or disturbance on the par
of petitioners. There is here no evidence whatever c
petitioners' interference, actual or nascent, with th
schools' work or of collision with the rights of othe
students to be secure and to be let alone. Accordingly
this case does not concern speech or action that intrude
upon the work of the schools or the rights of other stu
dents.

Only a few of the 18,000 students in the school systen
wore the black armbands. Only five students were sus
pended for wearing them. There is no indication tha

1e work of the schools or any class was disrupted. Out-
.de the classrooms, a few students made hostile remarks
ɔ the children wearing armbands, but there were no
hreats or acts of violence on school premises.

The District Court concluded that the action of the
chool authorities was reasonable because it was based
pon their fear of a disturbance from the wearing of the
rmbands. But, in our system, undifferentiated fear or
pprehension of disturbance is not enough to overcome
he right to freedom of expression. Any departure from
bsolute regimentation may cause trouble. Any variation
rom the majority's opinion may inspire fear. Any word
poken, in class, in the lunchroom, or on the campus, that
leviates from the views of another person may start an
rgument or cause a disturbance. But our Constitution
ays we must take this risk, . . . and our history says that
t is this sort of hazardous freedom—this kind of open-
ιess—that is the basis of our national strength and of
he independence and vigor of the Americans who grow
ιp and live in this relatively permissive, often disputa-
ious, society.

In order for the State in the person of school officials
ɔ justify prohibition of a particular expression of opin-
on, it must be able to show that its action was caused by
iomething more than a mere desire to avoid the discom-
ort and unpleasantness that always accompany an un-
ɔopular viewpoint. Certainly where there is no finding
ιnd no showing that engaging in the forbidden conduct
would "materially and substantially interfere with the
requirements of appropriate discipline in the operation
ɔf the school," the prohibition cannot be sustained. . . .

In the present case, the District Court made no such
finding, and our independent examination of the record
fails to yield evidence that the school authorities had

reason to anticipate that the wearing of the armban
would substantially interfere with the work of the scho
or impinge upon the rights of other students. Even a
official memorandum prepared after the suspension th
listed the reasons for the ban on wearing the armban
made no reference to the anticipation of such disruptio

On the contrary, the action of the school authoriti
appears to have been based upon an urgent wish to avoi
the controversy which might result from the expressio
even by the silent symbol of armbands, of opposition t
this Nation's part in the conflagration in Vietnam. . .

It is also relevant that the school authorities did n
purport to prohibit the wearing of all symbols of politic
or controversial significance. The record shows that stu
dents in some of the schools wore buttons relating t
national political campaigns, and some even wore th
Iron Cross, traditionally a symbol of Nazism. The orde
prohibiting the wearing of armbands did not extend t
these. Instead, a particular symbol—black armband
worn to exhibit opposition to this Nation's involvemen
in Vietnam—was singled out for prohibition. Clearl
the prohibition of expression of one particular opinio
at least without evidence that it is necessary to avoi
material and substantial interference with schoolwork o
discipline, is not constitutionally permissible.

In our system, state-operated schools may not be er
claves of totalitarianism. School officials do not posses
absolute authority over their students. Students in schoo
as well as out of school are "persons" under our Consti
tution. They are possessed of fundamental rights whic
the State must respect, just as they themselves mus
respect their obligations to the State. In our system
students may not be regarded as closed-circuit recipient
of only that which the State chooses to communicate

They may not be confined to the expression of those sentiments that are officially approved. In the absence of a specific showing of constitutionally valid reasons to regulate their speech, students are entitled to freedom of expression of their views. . . .

The principal use to which the schools are dedicated is to accommodate students during prescribed hours for the purpose of certain types of activities. Among those activities is personal intercommunication among the students. This is not only an inevitable part of the process of attending school; it is also an important part of the educational process. A student's rights, therefore, do not embrace merely the classroom hours. When he is in the cafeteria, or on the playing field, or on the campus during the authorized hours, he may express his opinions, even on controversial subjects like the conflict in Vietnam, if he does so without "materially and substantially interfer[ing] with the requirements of appropriate discipline in the operation of the school" and without colliding with the rights of others. . . . But conduct by the student, in class or out of it, which for any reason—whether it stems from time, place, or type of behavior—materially disrupts classwork or involves substantial disorder or invasion of the rights of others is, of course, not immunized by the constitutional guarantee of freedom of speech. . . .

Mr. Justice Black, dissenting.

The Court's holding in this case ushers in what I deem to be an entirely new era in which the power to control pupils by the elected "officials of state-supported public schools . . ." in the United States is in ultimate effect transferred to the Supreme Court. . . .

As I read the Court's opinion it relies upon the follow
ing grounds for holding unconstitutional the judgmen
of the Des Moines school officials and the two court
below. First, the Court concludes that the wearing c
armbands is "symbolic speech" which is "akin to 'pur
speech' " and therefore protected by the First and Fou
teenth Amendments. Secondly, the Court decides tha
the public schools are an appropriate place to exercis
"symbolic speech" as long as normal school functions ar
not "unreasonably" disrupted. Finally, the Court arrc
gates to itself, rather than to the State's elected official
charged with running the schools, the decision as t
which school disciplinary regulations are "reasonable."

Assuming that the Court is correct in holding that the
conduct of wearing armbands for the purpose of convey
ing political ideas is protected by the First Amendment
. . . the crucial remaining questions are whether stu
dents and teachers may use the schools at their whim a
a platform for the exercise of free speech—"symbolic" o
"pure"—and whether the courts will allocate to them
selves the function of deciding how the pupils' schoo
day will be spent. While I have always believed tha
under the First and Fourteenth Amendments neither the
State nor the Federal Government has any authority to
regulate or censor the content of speech, I have neve
believed that any person has a right to give speeches o
engage in demonstrations where he pleases and when he
pleases. . . .

While the record does not show that any of these arm
band students shouted, used profane language, or were
violent in any manner, detailed testimony by some of
them shows their armbands caused comments, warnings
by other students, the poking of fun at them, and a
warning by an older football player that other, nonpro-

sting students had better let them alone. There is also vidence that a teacher of mathematics had his lesson eriod practically "wrecked" chiefly by disputes with 1ary Beth Tinker, who wore her armband for her demonstration." Even a casual reading of the record 1ows that this armband did divert students' minds from 1eir regular lessions, and that talk, comments, etc., made ohn Tinker "self-conscious" in attending school with is armband. While the absence of obscene remarks or oisterous and loud disorder perhaps justifies the Court's tatement that the few armband students did not actually disrupt" the classwork, I think the record overwhelmngly shows that the armbands did exactly what the lected school officials and principals foresaw they would, hat is, took the students' minds off their classwork and iverted them to thoughts about the highly emotional ubject of the Vietnam war. And I repeat that if the time as come when pupils of state-supported schools, kinderartens, grammar schools, or high schools can defy and lout orders of school officials to keep their minds on their wn schoolwork, it is the beginning of a new revolutionry era of permissiveness in this country fostered by the udiciary. . . .

The truth is that a teacher of kindergarten, grammar chool, or high school pupils no more carries into a school vith him a complete right to freedom of speech and xpression than an anti-Catholic or anti-Semite carries vith him a complete freedom of speech and religion into 1 Catholic church or Jewish synagogue. Nor does a erson carry with him into the United States Senate or House, or into the Supreme Court, or any other court, a omplete constitutional right to go into those places conrary to their rules and speak his mind on any subject he leases. It is a myth to say that any person has a constitu-

tional right to say what he pleases, where he pleases, an
when he pleases. Our Court has decided precisely th
opposite. . . .

In my view, teachers in state-controlled public school
are hired to teach there. . . . Certainly a teacher is no
paid to go into school and teach subjects the State doe
not hire him to teach as a part of its selected curriculum
Nor are public school students sent to the schools a
public expense to broadcast political or any other view
to educate and inform the public. The original idea o
schools, which I do not believe is yet abandoned a
worthless or out of date, was that children had not ye
reached the point of experience and wisdom which en
abled them to teach all of their elders. It may be that the
Nation has outworn the old-fashioned slogan that "chil
dren are to be seen not heard," but one may, I hope, be
permitted to harbor the thought that taxpayers send
children to school on the premise that at their age they
need to learn, not teach. . . .

Change has been said to be truly the law of life but
sometimes the old and the tried and true are worth
holding. The schools of this Nation have undoubtedly
contributed to giving us tranquility and to making us a
more law-abiding people. Uncontrolled and uncontrolla-
ble liberty is an enemy to domestic peace. We cannot
close our eyes to the fact that some of the country's
greatest problems are crimes committed by the youth, too
many of school age. School discipline, like parental discipline, is an integral and important part of training our
children to be good citizens—to be better citizens. Here
a very small number of students have crisply and sum-
marily refused to obey a school order designed to give
pupils who want to learn the opportunity to do so.
One does not need to be a prophet or the son of a

rophet to know that after the Court's holding today
ome students in Iowa schools and indeed in all schools
vill be ready, able, and willing to defy their teachers on
ractically all orders. This is the more unfortunate for
he schools since groups of students all over the land are
lready running loose, conducting break-ins, sit-ins, lie-
ns, and smash-ins. Many of these student groups, as is
ll too familiar to all who read the newspapers and watch
he television news programs, have already engaged in
ioting, property seizures, and destruction. They have
icketed schools to force students not to cross their picket
ines and have too often violently attacked earnest but
rightened students who wanted an education that the
ickets did not want them to get. Students engaged in
uch activities are apparently confident that they know
ar more about how to operate public school systems than
lo their parents, teachers, and elected school officials. It
s no answer to say that the particular students here have
lot yet reached such high points in their demands to
ttend classes in order to exercise their political pressures.
Turned loose with lawsuits for damages and injunctions
against their teachers as they are here, it is nothing but
wishful thinking to imagine that young, immature students will not soon believe it is their right to control the
schools rather than the right of the States that collect the
taxes to hire the teachers for the benefit of the pupils.
This case, therefore, wholly without constitutional reasons in my judgment, subjects all the public schools in
the country to the whims and caprices of their loudest-
mouthed, but maybe not their brightest, students. I, for
one, am not fully persuaded that school pupils are wise
enough, even with this Court's expert help from Washington, to run the 23,390 public school systems in our
50 States. I wish, therefore, wholly to disclaim any pur-

pose on my part to hold that the Federal Constitution compels the teachers, parents, and elected school officials to surrender control of the American public school system to public school students. . . .

MR. JUSTICE HARLAN, dissenting.

I certainly agree that state public school authorities in the discharge of their responsibilities are not wholly exempt from the requirements of the Fourteenth Amendment respecting the freedoms of expression and association. At the same time I am reluctant to believe that there is any disagreement between the majority and myself on the proposition that school officials should be accorded the widest authority in maintaining discipline and good order in their institutions. To translate that proposition into a workable constitutional rule, I would, in cases like this, cast upon those complaining the burden of showing that a particular school measure was motivated by other than legitimate school concerns—for example, a desire to prohibit the expression of an unpopular point of view, while permitting expression of the dominant opinion.

Finding nothing in this record which impugns the good faith of respondents in promulgating the armband regulation, I would affirm the judgment below.

25. Healy v. James

408 U.S. 169 (1972)

A group of students desiring to form a local chapter of Students for a Democratic Society (SDS) applied to the authorities of Central Connecticut State College, a state-supported institution, for official recognition. The application was made at a time of widespread campus unrest throughout the country, involving such activities as civil disobedience, the seizure of buildings, vandalism, arson, the looting of files, and SDS chapters were widely regarded as "a catalytic force." President James refused to grant these students the recognition they sought on the grounds that their philosophy was contrary to the policies of the school, that their asserted independence of the national SDS was doubtful, and that they openly repudiated academic freedom. Denial of recognition was a serious matter, since it meant that this group of students could not put announcements in the student newspaper, use the campus bulletin boards, or meet in campus facilities. When the student group applied to a federal district court for injunctive and declaratory relief, the court held that President James had to give the students a hearing. The president gave them a hearing and then reaffirmed his decision to deny recognition. Thereupon the district court dismissed the petition, and the court of appeals affirmed. By unanimous vote, the Supreme Court reversed and remanded for reconsideration on the basis of considerations spelled out in its opinion.

Certiorari to the Court of Appeals for the Second Circuit.

MR. JUSTICE POWELL delivered the opinion of the Court.

As the case involves delicate issues concerning the academic community, we approach our task with special caution, recognizing the mutual interest of students, faculty members, and administrators in an environment free from disruptive interference with the educational process. We also are mindful of the equally significant interest in the widest latitude for free expression and debate consonant with the maintenance of order. Where these interests appear to compete the First Amendment, made binding on the States by the Fourteenth Amendment, strikes the required balance. . . .

At the outset we note that state colleges and universities are not enclaves immune from the sweep of the First Amendment. "It can hardly be argued that either students or teachers shed their constitutional rights to freedom of speech or expression at the schoolhouse gate." . . . Of course, as Mr. Justice Fortas made clear in *Tinker,* First Amendment rights must always be applied "in light of the special characteristics of the . . . environment" in the particular case. . . . And, where state-operated educational institutions are involved, this Court has long recognized "the need for affirming the comprehensive authority of the States and of school officials, consistent with fundamental constitutional safeguards, to prescribe and control conduct in the schools." . . . Yet, the precedents of this Court leave no room for the view that, because of the acknowledged need for order, First Amendment protections should apply with less force on college campuses than in the community at large. Quite to the contrary, "[t]he vigilant protection of constitutional freedoms is nowhere more vital than in the

community of American schools." . . . The college classroom with its surrounding environs is peculiarly the
"marketplace of ideas," and we break no new constitutional ground in reaffirming this Nation's dedication to
safeguarding academic freedom. . . .

Among the rights protected by the First Amendment is
the right of individuals to associate to further their personal beliefs. While the freedom of association is not
explicitly set out in the Amendment, it has long been
held to be implicit in the freedoms of speech, assembly,
and petition. . . . There can be no doubt that denial of
official recognition, without justification, to college organizations burdens or abridges that associational right.
The primary impediment to free association flowing
from nonrecognition is the denial of use of campus facilities for meetings and other appropriate purposes. The
practical effect of nonrecognition was demonstrated in
this case when, several days after the President's decision
was announced, petitioners were not allowed to hold a
meeting in the campus coffee shop because they were not
an approved group.

Petitioners' associational interests also were circumscribed by the denial of the use of campus bulletin boards
and the school newspaper. If an organization is to remain a viable entity in a campus community in which
new students enter on a regular basis, it must possess the
means of communicating with these students. Moreover,
the organization's ability to participate in the intellectual
give and take of campus debate, and to pursue its stated
purposes, is limited by denial of access to the customary
media for communicating with the administration, faculty members, and other students. Such impediments
cannot be viewed as insubstantial. . . .

We do not agree with the characterization by the courts

below of the consequences of nonrecognition. . . . In this case, the group's possible ability to exist outside the campus community does not ameliorate significantly the disabilities imposed by the President's action. We are not free to disregard the practical realities. MR. JUSTICE STEWART has made the salient point: "Freedoms such as these are protected not only against heavy-handed frontal attack, but also from being stifled by more subtle governmental interference." . . .

Once petitioners had filed an application in conformity with the requirements, the burden was upon the College administration to justify its decision of rejection. . . . It is to be remembered that the effect of the College's denial of recognition was a form of prior restraint, denying to petitioners' organization the range of associational activities described above. While a college has a legitimate interest in preventing disruption on the campus, which under circumstances requiring the safeguarding of that interest may justify such restraint, a "heavy burden" rests on the college to demonstrate the appropriateness of that action. . . .

But we are unable to conclude that no basis exists upon which nonrecognition might be appropriate. Indeed, based on a reasonable reading of the ambiguous facts of this case, there appears to be at least one potentially acceptable ground for a denial of recognition. Because of this ambiguous state of the record we conclude that the case should be remanded, and, in an effort to provide guidance to the lower courts upon reconsideration, it is appropriate to discuss the several bases of President James' decision. Four possible justifications for nonrecognition, all closely related, might be derived from the record and his statements. Three of those grounds are inadequate to substantiate his decision: a fourth, however, has merit.

From the outset the controversy in this case has centered in large measure around the relationship, if any, between petitioners' group and the National SDS. . . .

Although this precise issue has not come before the Court heretofore, the Court has consistently disapproved governmental action imposing criminal sanctions or denying rights and privileges solely because of a citizen's association with an unpopular organization. . . .

Students for a Democratic Society, as conceded by the College and the lower courts, is loosely organized, having various factions and promoting a number of diverse social and political views, only some of which call for unlawful action. Not only did petitioners proclaim their complete independence from this organization, but they also indicated that they shared only some of the beliefs its leaders have expressed. On this record it is clear that the relationship was not an adequate ground for the denial of recognition. . . .

The mere disagreement of the President with the group's philosophy affords no reason to deny its recognition. As repugnant as these views may have been, especially to one with President James' responsibility, the mere expression of them would not justify the denial of First Amendment rights. Whether petitioners did in fact advocate a philosophy of "destruction" thus becomes immaterial. The College, acting here as the instrumentality of the State, may not restrict speech or association simply because it finds the views expressed by any group to be abhorrent. . . .

President James . . . based rejection on a conclusion that this particular group would be a "disruptive influence at CCSC." . . .

If there were an evidential basis to support the conclusion that CCSC–SDS posed a substantial threat of mate-

rial disruption in violation of that command the President's decision should be affirmed.

The record, however, offers no substantial basis for
that conclusion. . . . There was no substantial evidence
that these particular individuals acting together would
constitute a disruptive force on campus. Therefore, insofar as nonrecognition flowed from such fears, it constituted little more than the sort of "undifferentiated fear
or apprehension of disturbance [which] is not enough to
overcome the right to freedom of expression." . . .

The College's Statement of Rights, Freedoms, and Responsibilities of Students contains . . . an explicit statement with respect to campus disruption. The regulation,
carefully differentiating between advocacy and action, is
a reasonable one, and petitioners have not questioned it
directly. Yet their statements raise considerable question
whether they intend to abide by the prohibitions contained therein. . . .

The critical line for First Amendment purposes must
be drawn between advocacy, which is entitled to full
protection, and action, which is not. Petitioners may, if
they so choose, preach the propriety of amending or even
doing away with any or all campus regulations. They
may not, however, undertake to flout these rules. . . .
Just as in the community at large, reasonable regulations
with respect to the time, the place, and the manner in
which student groups conduct their speech-related activities must be respected. A college administration may
impose a requirement, such as may have been imposed
in this case, that a group seeking official recognition affirm
in advance its willingness to adhere to reasonable campus
law. Such a requirement does not impose an impermissible condition on the students' associational rights. Their
freedom to speak out, to assemble, or to petition for

changes in school rules is in no sense infringed. It merely constitutes an agreement to conform with reasonable standards respecting conduct. This is a minimal requirement, in the interest of the entire academic community, of any group seeking the privilege of official recognition. . . .

Assuming the existence of a valid rule, however, we do conclude that the benefits of participation in the internal life of the college community may be denied to any group that reserves the right to violate any valid campus rules with which it disagrees.

We think the above discussion establishes the appropriate framework for consideration of petitioners' request for campus recognition. Because respondents failed to accord due recognition to First Amendment principles, the judgments below approving respondents' denial of recognition must be reversed. Since we cannot conclude from this record that petitioners were willing to abide by reasonable campus rules and regulations, we order the case remanded for reconsideration. . . .

MR. CHIEF JUSTICE BURGER, concurring.

I am in agreement with what is said in the Court's opinion and I join in it. I do so because I read the basis of the remand as recognizing that student organizations seeking the privilege of official campus recognition must be willing to abide by valid rules of the institution applicable to all such organizations. This is a reasonable condition insofar as it calls for the disavowal of resort to force, disruption and interference with the rights of others.

The District Judge was troubled by the lack of a comprehensive procedural scheme that would inform students of the steps to be taken to secure recognized standing, and by the lack of articulated criteria to be used in evaluating eligibility for recognition. It was for this reason, as I read the record, that he remanded the matter to the college for a factual inquiry and for a more orderly processing in a *de novo* hearing within the college administrative structure. It is within that structure and within the academic community that problems such as these should be resolved. The courts, state or federal, should be a last resort. Part of the educational experience of every college student should be an experience in responsible self-government and this must be a joint enterprise of students and faculty. . . .

MR. JUSTICE DOUGLAS, concurring.

The First Amendment does not authorize violence. But it does authorize advocacy, group activities, and espousal of change.

The present case is minuscule in the events of the 60's and 70's. But the fact that it has to come here for ultimate resolution indicates the sickness of our academic world, measured by First Amendment standards. Students as well as faculty are entitled to credentials in their search for truth. If we are to become an integrated, adult society, rather than a stubborn status quo opposed to change, students and faculties should have communal interests in which each age learns from the other. Without ferment of one kind or another, a college or university (like a federal agency or other human institution) becomes a useless appendage to a society which traditionally has reflected the spirit of rebellion. . . .

MR. JUSTICE REHNQUIST, concurring.

I find the implication clear from the Court's opinion that the constitutional limitations on the government's acting as administrator of a college differ from the limitations on the government's acting as sovereign to enforce its criminal laws. . . .

Prior cases dealing with First Amendment rights are not fungible goods, and I think the doctrine of these cases suggests two important distinctions. The government as employer or school administrator may impose upon employees and students reasonable regulations that would be impermissible if imposed by the government upon all citizens. And there can be a constitutional distinction between the infliction of criminal punishment, on the one hand, and the imposition of milder administrative or disciplinary sanctions, on the other, even though the same First Amendment interest is implicated by each.

Because some of the language used by the Court tends to obscure these distinctions, which I believe to be important, I concur only in the result.

26. Goss v. Lopez

419 U.S. 565 (1975)

An Ohio statute empowers the principal of a public school to suspend a pupil for misconduct for up to ten days, or to expel him. In either case, the principal must notify the student's parents within twenty-four hours and state the reasons for the action taken. One who has been expelled may appeal to the Board of Education, and after a hearing the Board may reinstate the pupil. There are no similar provisions for appeal in the case of suspensions. This case involved an action by nine high school students who had been suspended for up to ten days without a hearing. The suspensions were for disruptive or disobedient conduct which occurred during a period of widespread student unrest. The Court divided five to four in ruling that the lack of a hearing of some sort prior to suspension, or as soon thereafter as was practicable, denied these students due process of law.

Appeal from the United States District Court for the Southern District of Ohio.

MR. JUSTICE WHITE delivered the opinion of the Court.

At the outset, appellants contend that because there is no constitutional right to an education at public expense, the Due Process Clause does not protect against expulions from the public school system. This position misconceives the nature of the issue and is refuted by prior decisions. The Fourteenth Amendment forbids the State to deprive any person of life, liberty or property without due process of law. Protected interests in property are normally "not created by the Constitution. Rather, they are created and their dimensions are defined" by an independent source such as state statutes or rules entitling the citizen to certain benefits. . . .

Although Ohio may not be constitutionally obligated to establish and maintain a public school system, it has nevertheless done so and has required its children to attend. Those young people do not "shed their constitutional rights" at the schoolhouse door. . . . "The Fourteenth Amendment, as now applied to the States, protects the citizen against the State itself and all of its creatures. . . Boards of Education not excepted." . . . The authority possessed by the State to prescribe and enforce standards of conduct in its schools, although concededly very broad, must be exercised consistently with constitutional safeguards. Among other things, the State is constrained to recognize a student's legitimate entitlement to a public education as a property interest which is protected by the Due Process Clause and which may not be taken away for misconduct without adherence to the minimum procedures required by that clause.

The Due Process Clause also forbids arbitrary deprivations of liberty. "Where a person's good name, reputation, honor, or integrity is at stake because of what the government is doing to him," the minimal requirements of the Clause must be satisfied. . . . School authorities here suspended appellees from school for periods of up to 10 days based on charges of misconduct. If sustained and recorded, those charges could seriously damage the students' standing with their fellow pupils and their teachers as well as interfere with later opportunities for higher education and employment. It is apparent that the claimed right of the State to determine unilaterally and without process whether that misconduct has occurred immediately collides with the requirements of the Constitution.

Appellants proceed to argue that even if there is a right to a public education protected by the Due Process Clause generally, the clause comes into play only when the state subjects a student to a "severe detriment or grievous loss." The loss of 10 days, it is said, is neither severe nor grievous and the Due Process Clause is therefore of no relevance. Appellants' argument is again refuted by our prior decisions; for in determining "whether due process requirements apply in the first place, we must look not to the 'weight' but to the *nature* of the interest at stake." . . . A 10-day suspension from school is not *de minimis* in our view and may not be imposed in complete disregard of the Due Process Clause.

A short suspension is, of course, a far milder deprivation than expulsion. But, "education is perhaps the most important function of state and local governments," . . . and the total exclusion from the educational process for more than a trivial period, and certainly if the suspension is for 10 days, is a serious event in the life of the suspended child. Neither the property interest in educational benefits temporarily denied nor the liberty interest in reputation, which is also implicated, is so insubstantial that suspensions may constitutionally be imposed by any procedure the school chooses, no matter how arbitrary. . . .

At the very minimum, . . . students facing suspension and the consequent interference with a protected property interest must be given *some* kind of notice and afforded *some* kind of hearing. "Parties whose rights are to be affected are entitled to be heard; and in order that they may enjoy that right they must first be notified." . . .

It also appears from our cases that the timing and content of the notice and the nature of the hearing will depend on appropriate accommodation of the competing interests involved. . . . The student's interest is to avoid unfair or mistaken exclusion from the educational process, with all of its unfortunate consequences. The Due Process Clause will not shield him from suspensions properly imposed, but it disserves both his interest and the interest of the State if his suspension is in fact unwarranted. The concern would be mostly academic if the disciplinary process were a totally accurate, unerring process, never mistaken and never unfair. Unfortunately, that is not the case, and no one suggests that it is. Disciplinarians, although proceeding in utmost good faith, frequently act on the reports and advice of others; and the controlling facts and the nature of the conduct under challenge are often disputed. The risk of error is not at all trivial, and it should be guarded against if that may be done without prohibitive cost or interference with the educational process.

The difficulty is that our schools are vast and complex. Some modicum of discipline and order is essential if the educational function is to be performed. Events calling for discipline are frequent occurrences and sometimes require immediate, effective action. Suspension is considered not only to be a necessary tool to maintain order but a valuable educational device. The prospect of imposing elaborate hearing requirements in every suspension case is viewed with great concern, and many school authorities may well prefer the untrammeled power to act unilaterally, unhampered by rules about notice and hearing. But it would be a strange disciplinary system in an educational institution if no communication was sought by the disciplinarian with the student in an effort to inform him of his dereliction and to let him tell his side of the story in order to make sure that an injustice is not done. . . .

We do not believe that school authorities must be totally free from notice and hearing requirements if their schools are to operate with acceptable efficiency. Students facing temporary suspension have interests qualifying for protection of the Due Process Clause, and due process requires, in connection with a suspension of 10 days or less, that the student be given oral or written notice of the charges against him and, if he denies them, an explanation of the evidence the authorities have and an opportunity to present his side of the story. The Clause requires at least these rudimentary precautions against unfair or mistaken findings of misconduct and arbitrary exclusion from school.

There need be no delay between the time "notice" is given and the time of the hearing. In the great majority of cases the disciplinarian may informally discuss the alleged misconduct with the student minutes after it has occurred. We hold only that, in being given an opportunity to explain his version of the facts at this discussion, the student first be told what he is accused of doing and what the basis of the accusation is. . . . Since the hearing may occur almost immediately following the misconduct, it follows that as a general rule notice and hearing should precede removal of the student from school. We agree with the District Court, however, that there are recurring situations in which prior notice and hearing cannot be insisted upon. Students whose presence poses a continuing danger to persons or property or an ongoing threat of disrupting the academic process may be immediately removed from school. In such cases, the necessary notice and rudimentary hearing should follow as soon as practicable, as the District Court indicated.

In holding as we do, we do not believe that we have imposed procedures on school disciplinarians which are inappropriate in a classroom setting. Instead we have imposed requirements which are, if anything, less than a fair-minded school principal would impose upon himself in order to avoid unfair suspensions. . . .

We stop short of construing the Due Process Clause to require, countrywide, that hearings in connection with short suspensions must afford the student the opportunity to secure counsel, to confront and cross-examine witnesses supporting the charge or to call his own witnesses to verify his version of the incident. Brief disciplinary suspensions are almost countless. To impose in each such case even truncated trial-type procedures might well overwhelm administrative facilities in many places and, by diverting resources, cost more than it would save in educational effectiveness. Moreover, further formalizing the suspension process and escalating its formality and adversary nature may not only make it too costly as a regular disciplinary tool but also destroy its effectiveness as part of the teaching process.

On the other hand, requiring effective notice and informal hearing permitting the student to give his version of the events will provide a meaningful hedge against erroneous action. At least the disciplinarian will be alerted to the existence of disputes about facts and arguments about cause and effect. He may then determine himself to summon the accuser, permit cross-examination

and allow the student to present his own witnesses. In
more difficult cases, he may permit counsel. In any
event, his discretion will be more informed and we think
the risk of error substantially reduced.

Requiring that there be at least an informal give-and
take between student and disciplinarian, preferably prior
to the suspension, will add little to the factfinding func
tion where the disciplinarian has himself witnessed the
conduct forming the basis for the charge. But things
are not always as they seem to be, and the student will
at least have the opportunity to characterize his conduct
and put it in what he deems the proper context.

We should also make it clear that we have addressed
ourselves solely to the short suspension, not exceeding
10 days. Longer suspensions or expulsions for the re
mainder of the school term, or permanently, may require
more formal procedures. Nor do we put aside the possi
bility that in unusual situations, although involving only
a short suspension, something more than the rudimentary
procedures will be required. . . .

MR. JUSTICE POWELL, with whom CHIEF JUSTICE BURGER,
MR. JUSTICE BLACKMUN, and MR. JUSTICE REHNQUIST
join, dissenting.

The Court today invalidates an Ohio statute that per
mits student suspensions from school without a hearing
"for not more than ten days." The decision unnecessarily
opens avenues for judicial intervention in the operation
of our public schools that may affect adversely the quality
of education. The Court holds for the first time that the
federal courts, rather than educational officials and state
legislatures, have the authority to determine the rules
applicable to routine classroom discipline of children

d teenagers in the public schools. It justifies this un-
ecedented intrusion into the process of elementary and
condary education by identifying a new constitutional
ght: the right of a student not to be suspended for as
uch as a single day without notice and a due process
earing either before or promptly following the suspen-
on.

The Court's decision rests on the premise that, under
hio law, education is a property interest protected by
e Fourteenth Amendment's Due Process Clause and
erefore that any suspension requires notice and a hear-
g. In my view, a student's interest in education is not
fringed by a suspension within the limited period
escribed by Ohio law. Moreover, to the extent that
ere may be some arguable infringement, it is too specu-
tive, transitory and insubstantial to justify imposition
f a *constitutional* rule. . . .

State law . . . extends the right of free public school
ducation to Ohio students in accordance with the educa-
on laws of that State. The right or entitlement to edu-
ation so created is protected in a proper case by the Due
rocess Clause. . . . In my view, this is not such a
ase. . . .

The Ohio suspension statute allows no serious or sig-
ificant infringement of education. It authorizes only
maximum suspension of eight school days, less than
% of the normal 180-day school year. Absences of such
mited duration will rarely affect a pupil's opportunity
o learn or his scholastic performance. Indeed, the record
n this case reflects no educational injury to appellees.
ach completed the semester in which the suspension
ccurred and performed at least as well as he or she had
n previous years. Despite the Court's unsupported specu-
ation that a suspended student could be "seriously

damaged," . . . there is no factual showing of any su
damage to appellees. . . .

In prior decisions, this Court has explicitly recogniz
that school authorities must have broad discretiona
authority in the daily operation of public schools. Th
includes wide latitude with respect to maintaining d
cipline and good order. . . .

Moreover, the Court ignores the experience of ma
kind, as well as the long history of our law, recognizi
that there *are* differences which must be accommodat
in determining the rights and duties of children as co
pared with those of adults. Examples of this distincti
abound in our law: in contracts, in torts, in crimin
law and procedure, in criminal sanctions and rehabili
tion, and in the right to vote and to hold office. . . .

The State's interest, broadly put, is in the proper fur
tioning of its public school system for the benefit of
pupils and the public generally. Few rulings would i
terfere more extensively in the daily functioning
schools than subjecting routine discipline to the forma
ties and judicial oversight of due process. Suspensio
are one of the traditional means—ranging from keepir
a student after class to permanent expulsion—used
maintain discipline in the schools. It is common know
edge that maintaining order and reasonable decorum
school buildings and classrooms is a major education
problem, and one which has increased significantly i
magnitude in recent years. Often the teacher, in pr
tecting the rights of other children to an education (
not his or their safety), is compelled to rely on the pow
to suspend. . . .

The State's generalized interest in maintaining a
orderly school system is not incompatible with the ind
vidual interest of the student. Education in any mea

ngful sense includes the inculcation of an understanding
n each pupil of the necessity of rules and obedience
hereto. This understanding is no less important than
earning to read and write. One who does not compre-
end the meaning and necessity of discipline is handi-
apped not merely in his education but throughout his
ubsequent life. In an age when the home and church
lay a diminishing role in shaping the character and
alue judgments of the young, a heavier responsibility
alls upon the schools. When an immature student merits
ensure for his conduct, he is rendered a disservice if
ppropriate sanctions are not applied or if procedures
or their application are so formalized as to invite a
hallenge to the teacher's authority—an invitation which
ebellious or even merely spirited teenagers are likely to
iccept.

The lesson of discipline is not merely a matter of the
tudent's self-interest in the shaping of his own character
ind personality; it provides an early understanding of the
elevance to the social compact of respect for the rights
of others. The classroom is the laboratory in which this
esson of life is best learned. . . .

One of the more disturbing aspects of today's decision
s its indiscriminate reliance upon the judiciary, and the
idversary process, as the means of resolving many of the
nost routine problems arising in the classroom. In man-
lating due process procedures the Court misapprehends
the reality of the normal teacher–pupil relationship.
There is an ongoing relationship, one in which the
teacher must occupy many roles—educator, adviser,
friend and, at times, parent-substitute. It is rarely adversary in nature except with respect to the chronically
disruptive or insubordinate pupil whom the teacher must
be free to discipline without frustrating formalities. . . .

No one can foresee the ultimate frontiers of the ne "thicket" the Court now enters. Today's ruling appea to sweep within the protected interest in education multitude of discretionary decisions in the education process. Teachers and other school authorities are r quired to make many decisions that may have seriov consequences for the pupil. They must decide, fe example, how to grade the student's work, whether student passes or fails a course, whether he is to be promoted, whether he is required to take certain subject whether he may be excluded from interscholastic atl letics or other extracurricular activities, whether he ma be removed from one school and sent to another, wheth he may be bused long distances when available schoo are nearby, and whether he should be placed in a "ge eral," "vocational," or "college-preparatory" track.

In these and many similar situations claims of impai ment of one's educational entitlement identical in prir ciple to those before the Court today can be asserted wit equal or greater justification. Likewise, in many of thes situations, the pupil can advance the same types of specu lative and subjective injury given critical weight in thi case. . . .

If, as seems apparent, the Court will now require du process procedures whenever such routine school dec sions are challenged, the impact upon public educatio will be serious indeed. The discretion and judgment o federal courts across the land often will be substitute for that of the 50-state legislatures, the 14,000 schoo boards and the 2,000,000 teachers who heretofore hav been responsible for the administration of the America public school system. If the Court perceives a rationa and analytically sound distinction between the discre ionary decision by school authorities to suspend a pupil for a brief period, and the types of discretionary school decisions described above, it would be prudent to articulate it in today's opinion. Otherwise, the federal courts should prepare themselves for a vast new role in society. . . .

27. Wood v. Strickland

420 U.S. 308 (1975)

Two sixteen-year-old girls enrolled in the 10th grade of the high school at Mena, Arkansas, were expelled for a period of about three months on the grounds of their violation of a school regulation prohibiting the use or possession of intoxicating beverages at school activities. They brought a suit for damages against the members of the local school board, claiming that their federal constitutional rights to due process were infringed under color of state law, in that the board had acted without affording them a hearing. Suit was brought under 42 U.S.C. § 1983, which authorizes suits for damages or other relief in a federal court against "every person who, under color of any statute . . . of any State, . . . subjects any citizen of the United States or other person . . . to the deprivation of any rights, privileges or immunities secured by the Constitution and laws" of the federal government. The U.S. District Court in which the suit was filed gave a directed verdict for the defendants on the ground that the members of the school board were immune from damage suits of this sort in the absence of proof of malice or ill will. The court of appeals found on the facts that there had been a violation of the due process rights of the plaintiffs and remanded for a trial on the question of damages. On appeal, the Supreme Court Justices all agreed that the members of the school board had some immunity from lawsuits for damages

ought by expelled students, but they sharply disagreed,
e to four, as to how much immunity they had.

rtiorari to the United States Court of Appeals for the
Eighth Circuit.

R. JUSTICE WHITE delivered the opinion of the Court.

ommon-law tradition, recognized in our prior decisions,
id strong public-policy reasons also lead to a construc-
on of § 1983 extending a qualified good-faith immunity
school board members from liability for damages under
iat section. Although there have been differing em-
hases and formulations of the common-law immunity
public school officials in cases of student expulsion or
ispension, state courts have generally recognized that
ich officers should be protected from tort liability under
ate law for all good-faith, non-malicious action taken
fulfill their official duties.

As the facts of this case reveal, school board members
unction at different times in the nature of legislators
nd adjudicators in the school disciplinary process. Each
f these functions necessarily involves the exercise of
iscretion, the weighing of many factors, and the formu-
ition of long-term policy. "Like legislators and judges,
iese officers are entitled to rely on traditional sources
or the factual information on which they decide and
ct." . . . As with executive officers faced with instances
f civil disorder, school officials, confronted with student
ehavior causing or threatening disruption, also have an
obvious need for prompt action, and decisions must be
iade in reliance on factual information supplied by
thers."

Liability for damages for every action which is found

subsequently to have been violative of a student's cons
tutional rights and to have caused compensable inju
would unfairly impose upon the school decisionmak
the burden of mistakes made in good faith in the cour
of exercising his discretion within the scope of his offici
duties. School board members, among other duties, mu
judge whether there have been violations of school reg
lations and, if so, the appropriate sanctions for the viol
tions. Denying any measure of immunity in these ci
cumstances "would contribute not to principled an
fearless decision-making but to intimidation." . . . Th
imposition of monetary costs for mistakes which were no
unreasonable in the light of all the circumstances woul
undoubtedly deter even the most conscientious schoo
decisionmaker from exercising his judgment indepe
dently, forcefully, and in a manner best serving the long
term interest of the school and the students. The mos
capable candidates for school board positions might b
deterred from seeking office if heavy burdens upon thei
private resources from monetary liability were a likel
prospect during their tenure.

These considerations have undoubtedly played a prim
role in the development by state courts of a qualifie
immunity protecting school officials from liability fo
damages in lawsuits claiming improper suspensions o
expulsions. But at the same time, the judgment implici
in this common-law development is that absolute im
munity would not be justified since it would not suffi
ciently increase the ability of school officials to exercis
their discretion in a forthright manner to warrant the
absence of a remedy for students subjected to intentiona
or otherwise inexcusable deprivations. . . .

We think there must be a degree of immunity if the
work of the schools is to go forward; and, howeve
worded, the immunity must be such that public schoo

fficials understand that action taken in the good-faith
ılfillment of their responsibilities and within the bounds
f reason under all the circumstances will not be pun-
hed and that they need not exercise their discretion
ith undue timidity. . . .

The disagreement between the Court of Appeals and
he District Court over the immunity standard in this
ase has been put in terms of an "objective" versus a
subjective" test of good faith. As we see it, the appro-
riate standard necessarily contains elements of both.
The official must himself be acting sincerely and with a
elief that he is doing right, but an act violating a student's constitutional rights can be no more justified by
gnorance or disregard of settled, indisputable law on the
art of one entrusted with supervision of students' daily
ives than by the presence of actual malice. To be en-
itled to a special exemption from the categorical remedial language of § 1983 in a case in which his action
iolated a student's constitutional rights, a school board
member, who has voluntarily undertaken the task of
upervising the operation of the school and the activities
of the students, must be held to a standard of conduct
based not only on permissible intentions, but also on
knowledge of the basic, unquestioned constitutional
rights of his charges. Such a standard neither imposes
an unfair burden upon a person assuming a responsible
public office requiring a high degree of intelligence and
judgment for the proper fulfillment of its duties, nor an
unwarranted burden in light of the value which civil
rights have in our legal system. Any lesser standard
would deny much of the promise of § 1983. Therefore,
in the specific context of school discipline, we hold that
a school board member is not immune from liability for
damages under § 1983 if he knew or reasonably should
have known that the action he took within his sphere

of official responsibility would violate the constitution
rights of the student affected, or if he took the actic
with the malicious intention to cause a deprivation
constitutional rights or other injury to the student. Th
is not to say that school board members are "charge
with predicting the future course of constitutional law
. . . A compensatory award will be appropriate only
the school board member has acted with such an impe
missible motivation or with such disregard of the st
dent's clearly established constitutional rights that h
action cannot reasonably be characterized as being i
good faith. . . .

Given the fact that there *was* evidence supporting th
charge against respondents, the contrary judgment c
the Court of Appeals is improvident. It is not the role o
the federal courts to set aside decisions of school admin
istrators which the court may view as lacking a basis i
wisdom or compassion. Public high school students d
have substantive and procedural rights while at school
. . . But § 1983 does not extend the right to relitigate i
federal court evidentiary questions arising in school dis
ciplinary proceedings or the proper construction of schoo
regulations. The system of public education that ha
evolved in this Nation relies necessarily upon the discre
tion and judgment of school administrators and schoo
board members, and § 1983 was not intended to be a
vehicle for federal court correction of errors in the exer
cise of that discretion which do not rise to the level o
violations of specific constitutional guarantees. . . .

MR. JUSTICE POWELL, with whom CHIEF JUSTICE BURGER
MR. JUSTICE BLACKMUN, and MR. JUSTICE REHNQUIST
join, concurring in part and dissenting in part.

I join in Parts I, III, and IV of the Court's opinion, and
agree that the judgment of the Court of Appeals should

be vacated and the case remanded. I dissent from Part II which appears to impose a higher standard of care upon public school officials, sued under § 1983, than that heretofore required of any other official.

The holding of the Court on the immunity issue is set forth in the margin. It would impose personal liability on a school official who acted sincerely and in the utmost good faith, but who was found—after the fact—to have acted in "ignorance . . . of settled, indisputable law." . . . Or, as the Court also puts it, the school official must be held to a standard of conduct based not only on good faith "but also on knowledge of the basic, unquestioned constitutional rights of his charges." . . . Moreover, ignorance of the law is explicitly equated with "actual malice." . . . This harsh standard, requiring knowledge of what is characterized as "settled, indisputable law," leaves little substance to the doctrine of qualified immunity. The Court's decision appears to rest on an unwarranted assumption as to what lay school officials know or can know about the law and constitutional rights. These officials will now act at the peril of some judge or jury subsequently finding that a good-faith belief as to the applicable law was mistaken and hence actionable.

The Court states the standard of required knowledge in two cryptic phrases: "settled, indisputable law" and "unquestioned constitutional rights." Presumably these are intended to mean the same thing, although the meaning of neither phrase is likely to be self-evident to constitutional law scholars—much less the average school board member. One need only look to the decisions of this Court—to our reversals, our recognition of evolving concepts, and our five-to-four splits—to recognize the hazard of even informed prophecy as to what are "unquestioned constitutional rights." . . .

Less than a year ago, in *Scheuer* v. *Rhodes*, 416 U.S.

232 (1974), and in an opinion joined by all participating members of the Court, a considerably less demanding standard of liability was approved with respect to two of the highest officers of the State, the Governor and Adjutant General. In that case, the estates of students killed at Kent State University sued these officials under § 1983. After weighing the competing claims, the Court concluded:

These considerations suggest that in varying scope, a qualified immunity is available to officers of the executive branch of government, the variation being dependent upon the scope of discretion and responsibilities of the office and all the circumstances as they reasonably appeared at the time of the action on which liability is sought to be based. *It is the existence of reasonable grounds for the belief formed at the time and in light of all the circumstances, coupled with good-faith belief, that affords a basis for qualified immunity of executive officers for acts performed in the course of official conduct. . . .*

The italicized sentence from *Scheuer* states, as I view it, the correct standard for qualified immunity of a government official: whether in light of the discretion and responsibilities of his office, and under all of the circumstances as they appeared at the time, the officer acted reasonably and in good faith. This was the standard applied to the Governor of a State charged with maliciously calling out national guardsmen who killed and wounded Kent State students. Today's opinion offers no reason for imposing a more severe standard on school board members charged only with wrongfully expelling three teenage pupils.

There are some 20,000 school boards, each with five or more members, and thousands of school superintendents and school principals. Most of the school board members are popularly elected, drawn from the citizenry at large, nd possess no unique competency in divining the law. Few cities and counties provide any compensation for service on school boards, and often it is difficult to persuade qualified persons to assume the burdens of this important function in our society. Moreover, even if counsel's advice constitutes a defense, it may safely be assumed that few school boards and school officials have ready access to counsel or indeed have deemed it necessary to consult counsel on the countless decisions that necessarily must be made in the operation of our public schools.

In view of today's decision significantly enhancing the possibility of personal liability, one must wonder whether qualified persons will continue in the desired numbers to volunteer for service in public education.

Part V

THE FINANCING OF
PUBLIC SCHOOLS

28. San Antonio School District v. Rodriguez

411 U.S. 1 (1973)

All states but Hawaii support their public school systems through local property taxation. This produces substantial disparities among school districts in the revenue available per pupil. In Serrano v. Priest, 5 Cal. 3d 584, 96 Cal. Rptr. 601, 487 P. 2d 1241 (1971), the Supreme Court of California, currently one of the most innovative appellate courts in the country, ruled that a school financing system which invidiously discriminates among students on the basis of wealth violates the equal protection guaranty of the state constitution. The Court could find no compelling state interest to justify the relative handicaps endured by the poorer school districts. This decision created a great stir in the country, and soon thereafter a class action was brought in a federal district court by the parents of children attending elementary and secondary schools in San Antonio, in which the contention was pressed that the Texas school finance system, which is based largely on local property taxes, though supplemented by state grants which have an equalizing effect, violates the Equal Protection Clause of the Fourteenth Amendment. Among the seven school districts in the metropolitan San Antonio area, the average expenditure per pupil ranged from a low of $356 to a high of $594. The Supreme Court divided five to four in ruling that the Texas school finance system did not vio-

*late the federal Constitution. In doing so, it reversed
the decision of the district court.*

Appeal from the U.S. District Court for the Western
   District of Texas.

MR. JUSTICE POWELL delivered the opinion of the Court.

The wealth discrimination discovered by the District
Court in this case, and by several other courts that have
recently struck down school-financing laws in other States,
is quite unlike any of the forms of wealth discrimination
heretofore reviewed by this Court. Rather than focusing
on the unique features of the alleged discrimination, the
courts in these cases have virtually assumed their findings
of a suspect classification through a simplistic process of
analysis: since, under the traditional systems of financing
public schools, some poorer people receive less expensive
educations than other more affluent people, these systems
discriminate on the basis of wealth. This approach
largely ignores the hard threshold questions, including
whether it makes a difference for purposes of consideration under the Constitution that the class of disadvantaged "poor" cannot be identified or defined in customary equal protection terms, and whether the relative
—rather than absolute—nature of the asserted deprivation is of significant consequence. Before a State's laws
and the justifications for the classifications they create
are subjected to strict judicial scrutiny, we think these
threshold considerations must be analyzed more closely
than they were in the court below.

The case comes to us with no definitive description of
the classifying facts or delineation of the disfavored class.

Examination of the District Court's opinion and of appellees' complaint, briefs, and contentions at oral argument suggests, however, at least three ways in which the discrimination claimed here might be described. The Texas system of school financing might be regarded as discriminating (1) against "poor" persons whose incomes fall below some identifiable level of poverty or who might be characterized as functionally "indigent," or (2) against those who are relatively poorer than others, or (3) against all those who, irrespective of their personal incomes, happen to reside in relatively poorer school districts. Our task must be to ascertain whether, in fact, the Texas system has been shown to discriminate on any of these possible bases and, if so, whether the resulting classification may be regarded as suspect. . . .

First, in support of their charge that the system discriminates against the "poor," appellees have made no effort to demonstrate that it operates to the peculiar disadvantage of any class fairly definable as indigent, or as composed of persons whose incomes are beneath any designated poverty level. Indeed, there is reason to believe that the poorest families are not necessarily clustered in the poorest property districts. . . .

Second, neither appellees nor the District Court addressed the fact that . . . lack of personal resources has not occasioned an absolute deprivation of the desired benefit. The argument here is not that the children in districts having relatively low assessable property values are receiving no public education; rather, it is that they are receiving a poorer quality education than that available to children in districts having more assessable wealth. Apart from the unsettled and disputed question whether the quality of education may be determined by the amount of money expended for it, a sufficient answer to appellees' argument is that, at least where wealth is involved, the Equal Protection Clause does not require absolute equality or precisely equal advantages. Nor, indeed, in view of the infinite variables affecting the educational process, can any system assure equal quality of education except in the most relative sense. . . .

This brings us, then, to the third way in which the classification scheme might be defined—*district* wealth discrimination. Since the only correlation indicated by the evidence is between district property wealth and expenditures, it may be argued that discrimination might be found without regard to the individual income characteristics of district residents. Assuming a perfect correlation between district property wealth and expenditures from top to bottom, the disadvantaged class might be viewed as encompassing every child in every district except the district that has the most assessable wealth and spends the most on education. Alternatively, . . . the class might be defined more restrictively to include children in districts with assessable property which falls below the statewide average, or median, or below some other artificially defined level.

However described, it is clear that appellees' suit asks this Court to extend its most exacting scrutiny to review a system that allegedly discriminates against a large, diverse, and amorphous class, unified only by the common factor of residence in districts that happen to have less taxable wealth than other districts. The system of alleged discrimination and the class it defines have none of the traditional indicia of suspectness: the class is not saddled with such disabilities, or subjected to such a history of purposeful unequal treatment, or relegated to such a position of political powerlessness as to command extraordinary protection from the majoritarian political process.

We thus conclude that the Texas system does not operate to the peculiar disadvantage of any suspect class. . . .

It is not the province of this Court to create substantive constitutional rights in the name of guaranteeing equal protection of the laws. Thus, the key to discovering whether education is "fundamental" is not to be found in comparisons of the relative societal significance of education as opposed to subsistence or housing. Nor is it to be found by weighing whether education is as important as the right to travel. Rather, the answer lies in assessing whether there is a right to education explicitly or implicitly guaranteed by the Constitution. . . .

Education, of course, is not among the rights afforded explicit protection under our Federal Constitution. Nor do we find any basis for saying it is implicitly so protected. As we have said, the undisputed importance of education will not alone cause this Court to depart from the usual standard for reviewing a State's social and economic legislation. It is appellees' contention, however, that education is distinguishable from other services and benefits provided by the State because it bears a peculiarly close relationship to other rights and liberties accorded protection under the Constitution. Specifically, they insist that education is itself a fundamental personal right because it is essential to the effective exercise of First Amendment freedoms and to intelligent utilization of the right to vote. . . .

We need not dispute any of these propositions. The Court has long afforded zealous protection against unjustifiable governmental interference with the individual's rights to speak and to vote. Yet we have never presumed to possess either the ability or the authority to guarantee to the citizenry the most *effective* speech or the most *informed* electoral choice. That these may be

desirable goals of a system of freedom of expression and
of a representative form of government is not to be
doubted. These are indeed goals to be pursued by a
people whose thoughts and beliefs are freed from govern
mental interference. But they are not values to be im
plemented by judicial intrusion into otherwise legitimate
state activities.

Even if it were conceded that some identifiable quan
tum of education is a constitutionally protected pre
requisite to the meaningful exercise of either right, we
have no indication that the present levels of educational
expenditures in Texas provide an education that falls
short. Whatever merit appellees' argument might have
if a State's financing system occasioned an absolute denial
of educational opportunities to any of its children, that
argument provides no basis for finding an interference
with fundamental rights where only relative differences
in spending levels are involved and where—as is true in
the present case—no charge fairly could be made that the
system fails to provide each child with an opportunity to
acquire the basic minimal skills necessary for the enjoy
ment of the rights of speech and of full participation in
the political process.

Furthermore, the logical limitations on appellees'
nexus theory are difficult to perceive. How, for instance,
is education to be distinguished from the significant
personal interests in the basics of decent food and shelter?
Empirical examination might well buttress an assump
tion that the ill-fed, ill-clothed, and ill-housed are among
the most ineffective participants in the political process,
and that they derive the least enjoyment from the benefits
of the First Amendment. . . .

We need not rest our decision, however, solely on the
inappropriateness of the strict-scrutiny test. A century of

Supreme Court adjudication under the Equal Protection Clause affirmatively supports the application of the traditional standard of review, which requires only that the State's system be shown to bear some rational relationship to legitimate state purposes. This case represents far more than a challenge to the manner in which Texas provides for the education of its children. We have here nothing less than a direct attack on the way in which Texas has chosen to raise and disburse state and local tax revenues. We are asked to condemn the State's judgment in conferring on political subdivisions the power to tax local property to supply revenues for local interests. In so doing, appellees would have the Court intrude in an area in which it has traditionally deferred to state legislatures. This Court has often admonished against such interferences with the State's fiscal policies under the Equal Protection Clause. . . .

Thus, we stand on familiar ground when we continue to acknowledge that the Justices of this Court lack both the expertise and the familiarity with local problems so necessary to the making of wise decisions with respect to the raising and disposition of public revenues. Yet, we are urged to direct the States either to alter drastically the present system or to throw out the property tax altogether in favor of some other form of taxation. No scheme of taxation, whether the tax is imposed on property, income, or purchases of goods and services, has yet been devised which is free of all discriminatory impact. In such a complex arena in which no perfect alternatives exist, the Court does well not to impose too rigorous a standard of scrutiny lest all local fiscal schemes become subjects of criticism under the Equal Protection Clause.

In addition to matters of fiscal policy, this case also involves the most persistent and difficult questions of educational policy, another area in which this Court's lack of specialized knowledge and experience counsels against premature interference with the informed judgments made at the state and local levels. Education, perhaps even more than welfare assistance, presents a myriad of "intractable economic, social, and even philosophical problems." . . . The very complexity of the problems of financing and managing a statewide public school system suggests that "there will be more than one constitutionally permissible method of solving them," and that, within the limits of rationality, "the legislature's efforts to tackle the problems" should be entitled to respect. . . .

It must be remembered, also, that every claim arising under the Equal Protection Clause has implications for the relationship between national and state power under our federal system. Questions of federalism are always inherent in the process of determining whether a State's laws are to be accorded the traditional presumption of constitutionality, or are to be subjected instead to rigorous judicial scrutiny. While "[t]he maintenance of the principles of federalism is a foremost consideration in interpreting any of the pertinent constitutional provisions under which this Court examines state action," it would be difficult to imagine a case having a greater potential impact on our federal system than the one now before us, in which we are urged to abrogate systems of financing public education presently in existence in virtually every State.

The foregoing considerations buttress our conclusion that Texas' system of public school finance is an inappropriate candidate for strict judicial scrutiny. These same considerations are relevant to the determination whether that system, with its conceded imperfections, nevertheless bears some rational relationship to a legitimate state purpose. . . .

In an era that has witnessed a consistent trend toward centralization of the functions of government, local sharing of responsibility for public education has survived. . . .

The persistence of attachment to government at the lowest level where education is concerned reflects the depth of commitment of its supporters. In part, local control means . . . the freedom to devote more money to the education of one's children. Equally important, however, is the opportunity it offers for participation in the decisionmaking process that determines how those local tax dollars will be spent. Each locality is free to tailor local programs to local needs. Pluralism also affords some opportunity for experimentation, innovation, and a healthy competition for educational excellence. An analogy to the Nation–State relationship in our federal system seems uniquely appropriate. . . . No area of social concern stands to profit more from a multiplicity of viewpoints and from a diversity of approaches than does public education. . . .

The people of Texas may be justified in believing that other systems of school financing, which place more of the financial responsibility in the hands of the State, will result in a comparable lessening of desired local autonomy. That is, they may believe that along with increased control of the purse strings at the state level will go increased control over local policies. . . .

Any scheme of local taxation—indeed the very existence of identifiable local government units—requires the establishment of jurisdictional boundaries that are inevitably arbitrary. It is equally inevitable that some localities are going to be blessed with more taxable assets than others. Nor is local wealth a static quantity. Changes in the level of taxable wealth within any district may result from any number of events, some of which local residents can and do influence. For instance, commercial and industrial enterprises may be encouraged to locate within a district by various actions—public and private.

Moreover, if local taxation for local expenditures were an unconstitutional method of providing for education then it might be an equally impermissible means of providing other necessary services customarily financed largely from local property taxes, including local police and fire protection, public health and hospitals, and public utility facilities of various kinds. We perceive no justification for such a severe denigration of local property taxation and control as would follow from appellees' contentions. It has simply never been within the constitutional prerogative of this Court to nullify statewide measures for financing public services merely because the burdens or benefits thereof fall unevenly depending upon the relative wealth of the political subdivisions in which citizens live.

In sum, to the extent that the Texas system of school financing results in unequal expenditures between children who happen to reside in different districts, we cannot say that such disparities are the product of a system that is so irrational as to be invidiously discriminatory. . . . The Texas plan is not the result of hurried, ill-conceived legislation. It certainly is not the product of purposeful discrimination against any group or class. On the contrary, it is rooted in decades of experience in Texas and elsewhere, and in major part is the product of responsible studies by qualified people. In giving substance to the presumption of validity to which the

Texas system is entitled, . . . it is important to remember that at every stage of its development it has constituted a "rough accommodation" of interests in an effort to arrive at practical and workable solutions. . . . One also must remember that the system here challenged is not peculiar to Texas or to any other State. In its essential characteristics, the Texas plan for financing public education reflects what many educators for a half century have thought was an enlightened approach to a problem for which there is no perfect solution. We are unwilling to assume for ourselves a level of wisdom superior to that of legislators, scholars, and educational authorities in 50 States, especially where the alternatives proposed are only recently conceived and nowhere yet tested. The constitutional standard under the Equal Protection Clause is whether the challenged state action rationally furthers a legitimate state purpose or interest. . . . We hold that the Texas plan abundantly satisfies this standard. . . .

The consideration and initiation of fundamental reforms with respect to state taxation and education are matters reserved for the legislative processes of the various States, and we do no violence to the values of federalism and separation of powers by staying our hand. We hardly need add that this Court's action today is not to be viewed as placing its judicial imprimatur on the status quo. The need is apparent for reform in tax systems which may well have relied too long and too heavily on the local property tax. And certainly innovative thinking as to public education, its methods, and its funding is necessary to assure both a higher level of quality and greater uniformity of opportunity. These matters merit the continued attention of the scholars who already have contributed much by their challenges. But the ultimate solutions must come from the lawmakers and from the democratic pressures of those who elect them. . . .

MR. JUSTICE STEWART, concurring.

The method of financing public schools in Texas, as in almost every other State, has resulted in a system of public education that can fairly be described as chaotic and unjust. It does not follow, however, and I cannot find, that this system violates the Constitution of the United States. I join the opinion and judgment of the Court because I am convinced that any other course would mark an extraordinary departure from principled adjudication under the Equal Protection Clause of the Fourteenth Amendment. . . .

MR. JUSTICE BRENNAN, dissenting.

Although I agree with my Brother WHITE that the Texas statutory scheme is devoid of any rational basis, and for that reason is violative of the Equal Protection Clause, I also record my disagreement with the Court's rather distressing assertion that a right may be deemed "fundamental" for the purposes of equal protection analysis only if it is "explicitly or implicitly guaranteed by the Constitution." . . .

MR. JUSTICE WHITE, with whom MR. JUSTICE DOUGLAS and MR. JUSTICE BRENNAN join, dissenting.

The Equal Protection Clause permits discrimination between classes but requires that the classification bear some rational relationship to a permissible object sought to be attained by the statute. It is not enough that the Texas system before us seeks to achieve the valid, rational purpose of maximizing local initiative; the means chosen by the State must also be rationally related to the end sought to be achieved. . . .

Requiring the State to establish only that unequal treatment is in furtherance of a permissible goal, without also requiring the State to show that the means chosen to effectuate that goal are rationally related to its achievement, makes equal protection analysis no more than an empty gesture. . . .

Mr. Justice Marshall, with whom Mr. Justice Douglas concurs, dissenting.

The Court today decides, in effect, that a State may constitutionally vary the quality of education which it offers its children in accordance with the amount of taxable wealth located in the school districts within which they reside. The majority's decision represents an abrupt departure from the mainstream of recent state and federal court decisions concerning the unconstitutionality of state educational financing schemes dependent upon taxable local wealth. More unfortunately, though, the majority's holding can only be seen as a retreat from our historic commitment to equality of educational opportunity and as unsupportable acquiescence in a system which deprives children in their earliest years of the chance to reach their full potential as citizens. The Court does this despite the absence of any substantial justification for a scheme which arbitrarily channels educational resources in accordance with the fortuity of the amount of taxable wealth within each district.

In my judgment, the right of every American to an equal start in life, so far as the provision of a state service as important as education is concerned, is far too vital to permit state discrimination on grounds as tenuous as those presented by this record. Nor can I accept the notion that it is sufficient to remit these appellees to the vagaries of the political process which, contrary to the majority's suggestion, has proved singularly unsuited to the task of providing a remedy for this discrimination. I, for one, am unsatisfied with the hope of an ultimate "political" solution sometime in the indefinite future while, in the meantime, countless children unjustifiably receive inferior educations that "may affect their hearts and minds in a way unlikely ever to be undone." . .

In my view, then, it is inequality—not some notion of gross inadequacy—of educational opportunity that raises a question of denial of equal protection of the laws. I find any other approach to the issue unintelligible and without directing principle. Here appellees have made a substantial showing of wide variations in educational funding and the resulting educational opportunity afforded to the school children of Texas. This discrimination is, in large measure, attributable to significant disparities in the taxable wealth of local Texas school districts. This is a sufficient showing to raise a substantial question of discriminatory state action in violation of the Equal Protection Clause. . . .

The fundamental importance of education is amply indicated by the prior decisions of this Court, by the unique status accorded public education by our society, and by the close relationship between education and some of our most basic constitutional values.

The special concern of this Court with the educational process of our country is a matter of common knowledge. . . .

Education directly affects the ability of a child to exercise his First Amendment interests, both as a source and as a receiver of information and ideas, whatever interests he may pursue in life. . . .

Of particular importance is the relationship between education and the political process. "Americans regard the public schools as a most vital civic institution for the preservation of a democratic system of government." . . .

On this record, it is apparent that the State's purported concern with local control is offered primarily as an excuse rather than as a justification for interdistrict inequality. . . .

In conclusion, it is essential to recognize that an end to the wide variations in taxable district property wealth inherent in the Texas financing scheme would entail none of the untoward consequences suggested by the Court or by the appellants.

First, affirmance of the District Court's decisions would hardly sound the death knell for local control of education. It would mean neither centralized decisionmaking nor federal court intervention in the operation of public schools. Clearly, this suit has nothing to do with local decisionmaking with respect to educational policy or even educational spending. It involves only a narrow aspect of local control—namely, local control over the raising of educational funds. In fact, in striking down interdistrict disparities in taxable local wealth, the District Court took the course which is most likely to make true local control over educational decisionmaking a reality for *all* Texas school districts.

Nor does the District Court's decision even necessarily eliminate local control of educational funding. The District Court struck down nothing more than the continued interdistrict wealth discrimination inherent in the present property tax. Both centralized and decentralized plans for educational funding not involving such inter-district discrimination have been put forward. The choice among these or other alternatives would remain with the State, not with the federal courts. . . .

The Court seeks solace for its action today in the possibility of legislative reform. The Court's suggestions of legislative redress and experimentation will doubtless be of great comfort to the school children of Texas' disadvantaged districts, but considering the vested interests of wealthy school districts in the preservation of the status quo, they are worth little more. The possibility of legislative action is, in all events, no answer to this Court's duty under the Constitution to eliminate unjustified state discrimination. In this case we have been presented with an instance of such discrimination, in a particularly invidious form, against an individual interest of large constitutional and practical importance. To support the demonstrated discrimination in the provision of educational opportunity the State has offered a justification which, on analysis, takes on at best an ephemeral character. Thus, I believe that the wide disparities in taxable district property wealth inherent in the local property tax element of the Texas financing scheme render that scheme violative of the Equal Protection Clause.

APPENDIXES

Meek v. Pittenger

421 U.S. 349 (1975)

*n this case, the constitutionality, under the Establish-
ment of Religion Clause of the First Amendment, of
several Pennsylvania statutes was challenged by several
residents and organizations in the state. These statutes
authorized the public school authorities (1) to lend textbooks and instructional material and equipment (e.g.,
maps, charts, films, laboratory equipment) and (2) to
supply professional staff and supportive materials for
such auxiliary services as remedial instruction, counseling, testing, hearing, and speech services to nonpublic
schools, including primarily parochial schools. The Supreme Court, dividing six to three, upheld the textbook
loan provisions on the basis of* Board of Education v.
Allen, *392 U.S. 236 (1968). The other statutory provisions were held to be unconstitutional, also by a six-to-
three vote. Since portions of the* Allen *opinion are re-
printed elsewhere in this book, the selection in the opin-
on of the Court dealing with the textbook issue has been
omitted.*

MR. JUSTICE STEWART delivered the opinion of the Court.

n judging the constitutionality of the various forms of
assistance authorized, . . . the District Court applied the

three-part test that has been clearly stated, if not easil
applied, by this Court in recent Establishment Claus
cases. . . . First, the statute must have a secular legisla
tive purpose. . . . Second, it must have a "primar
effect" that neither advances nor inhibits religion. . .
Third, the statute and its administration must avoi
excessive government entanglement with religion. . . .

These tests constitute a convenient, accurate distilla
tion of this Court's efforts over the past decades to evalu
ate a wide range of governmental action challenged a
violative of the constitutional prohibition against law
"respecting an establishment of religion," and thus pro
vide the proper framework of analysis for the issues pre
sented in the case before us. It is well to emphasize
however, that the tests must not be viewed as setting th
precise limits to the necessary constitutional inquiry, bu
serve only as guidelines with which to identify instance
in which the objectives of the Establishment Clause hav
been impaired. . . .

Although textbooks are lent only to students, Act 19
authorizes the loan of instructional material and equip
ment directly to qualifying nonpublic elementary an
secondary schools in the Commonwealth. . . .

We agree with the appellants that the direct loan o
instructional material and equipment has the unconstitu
tional primary effect of advancing religion because of th
predominantly religious character of the schools benefi
ing from the Act. . . .

It is, of course, true that as part of general legislatio
made available to all students, a State may includ
church-related schools in programs providing bus trans
portation, school lunches, and public health facilities—
secular and nonideological services unrelated to the pri
mary, religious-oriented educational function of the sec

:arian school. The indirect and incidental benefits to church-related schools from those programs do not offend the constitutional prohibition against establishment of religion. . . . But the massive aid provided the church-related nonpublic schools of Pennsylvania by Act 195 is neither indirect nor incidental.

For the 1972–1973 school year the Commonwealth authorized just under $12 million of direct aid to the predominantly church-related nonpublic schools of Pennsylvania through the loan of instructional material and equipment pursuant to Act 195. To be sure, the material and equipment that are the subjects of the loan—maps, charts, and laboratory equipment, for example—are "self-polic[ing], in that starting as secular, nonideological and neutral, they will not change in use." . . . But faced with the substantial amounts of direct support authorized by Act 195, it would simply ignore reality to attempt to separate secular educational functions from the predominantly religious role performed by many of Pennsylvania's church-related elementary and secondary schools and to then characterize Act 195 as channeling aid to the secular without providing direct aid to the sectarian. Even though earmarked for secular purposes, "when it flows to an institution in which religion is so pervasive that a substantial portion of its functions are subsumed in the religious mission," state aid has the impermissible primary effect of advancing religion. . . .

The church-related elementary and secondary schools that are the primary beneficiaries of Act 195's instructional material and equipment loans typify such religion-pervasive institutions. The very purpose of many of those schools is to provide an integrated secular and religious education, the teaching process is, to a large extent, devoted to the inculcation of religious values and belief. . . . Substantial aid to the educational function of such schools, accordingly, necessarily results in aid to the sectarian school enterprise as a whole. . . . For this reason, Act 195's direct aid to Pennsylvania's predominantly church-related, nonpublic elementary and secondary schools, even though ostensibly limited to wholly neutral, secular instructional material and equipment, inescapably results in the direct and substantial advancement of religious activity, . . . and thus constitutes an impermissible establishment of religion. . . .

Unlike Act 195, which provides only for the loan of teaching material and equipment, Act 194 authorizes the Secretary of Education, through the intermediate units, to supply professional staff, as well as supportive materials, equipment, and personnel, to the nonpublic schools of the Commonwealth. The "auxiliary services" authorized by Act 194—remedial and accelerated instruction, guidance counseling and testing, speech and hearing services—are provided directly to nonpublic schoolchildren with the appropriate special need. But the services are provided only on the nonpublic school premises, and only when "requested by nonpublic school representatives." . . .

We need not decide whether substantial state expenditures to enrich the curricula of church-related elementary and secondary schools, like the expenditures of state funds to support the basic educational program of those schools, necessarily results in the direct and substantial advancement of religious activity. For decisions of this Court make clear that the District Court erred in relying entirely on the good faith and professionalism of the secular teachers and counselors functioning in church-related schools to ensure that a strictly nonideological posture is maintained. . . .

The prophylactic contacts required to ensure that teachers play a strictly nonideological role . . . necessarily give rise to a constitutionally intolerable degree of entanglement between church and state. . . .

Whether the subject is "remedial reading," "advanced reading," or simply "reading," a teacher remains a teacher, and the danger that religious doctrine will become intertwined with secular instruction persists. The likelihood of inadvertent fostering of religion may be less in a remedial arithmetic class than in a medieval history seminar, but a diminished probability of impermissible conduct is not sufficient: "The State must be certain, given the Religion Clauses, that subsidized teachers do not inculcate religion." . . . And a state-subsidized guidance counselor is surely as likely as a state-subsidized chemistry teacher to fail on occasion to separate religious instruction and the advancement of religious beliefs from his secular educational responsibilities.

The fact that the teachers and counselors providing auxiliary services are employees of the public intermediate unit, rather than of the church-related schools in which they work, does not substantially eliminate the need for continuing surveillance. To be sure, auxiliary services personnel, because not employed by the nonpublic schools, are not directly subject to the discipline of a religious authority. . . . But they are performing important educational services in schools in which education is an integral part of the dominant sectarian mission and in which an atmosphere dedicated to the advancement of religious belief is constantly maintained. . . . The potential for impermissible fostering of religion under these circumstances, although somewhat reduced, is nonetheless present. To be certain that auxiliary teachers remain religiously neutral, as the Constitution demands, the State would have to impose limitations on the activities of auxiliary personnel and then engage in some form of continuing surveillance to ensure that those restrictions were being followed. . . .

In addition, Act 194 . . . creates a serious potential for divisive conflict over the issue of aid to religion—"entanglement in the broader sense of continuing political strife." . . . The recurrent nature of the appropriation process guarantees annual reconsideration of Act 194 and the prospect of repeated confrontation between proponents and opponents of the auxiliary services program. The Act thus provides successive opportunities for political fragmentation and division along religious lines, one of the principal evils against which the Establishment Clause was intended to protect. . . . This potential for political entanglement, together with the administrative entanglement which would be necessary to ensure that auxiliary services personnel remain strictly neutral and nonideological when functioning in church-related schools, compels the conclusion that Act 194 violates the constitutional prohibition against laws "respecting an establishment of religion." . . .

MR. JUSTICE BRENNAN, with whom MR. JUSTICE DOUGLAS and MR. JUSTICE MARSHALL join, dissenting in part.

A three factor test by which to determine the compatibility with the Establishment Clause of state subsidies of sectarian educational institutions has evolved over 50 years of this Court's stewardship in the field. The law in question must, first, reflect a clearly secular legislative purpose, second, have a primary effect that neither advances nor inhibits religion, and, third, avoid excessive government entanglement with religion. But four years ago, the Court, albeit without express recognition of the fact, added a significant fourth factor to the test: "A broader basis of entanglement of yet a different character is presented by the divisive political potential of these state programs." . . .

The Court, in considering the constitutionality of Act 195 says not a single word about the political divisiveness factor in Part III of the opinion upholding the textbook loan program created by that Act, and makes only a passing footnote reference to the factor, without evaluation of its bearing on the result. . . .

The Court notes that the total 1972–1973 appropriation under Act 195 was $16,660,000, of which $4,670,000 was appropriated to finance the textbook program. . . . The Court obviously must attach determinative weight to the factor as respects both the textbook loan and instructional materials and equipment loan provisions, since both are inextricably intertwined in Act 195. For in light of the massive appropriations involved, the Court would be hard put to explain how the factor weighs determinatively against the validity of the instructional materials loan provisions, and not also against the validity of the textbook loan provisions. The Court therefore would extricate itself from the horns of the dilemma by simply ignoring the factor in the weighing process. . . .

First, it is pure fantasy to treat the textbook program as a loan to students. It is true that, like the New York statute in *Allen,* Act 195 in terms talks of loans by the State of acceptable secular textbooks directly to students attending nonpublic schools. But even the Court acknowledges that "the administrative practice is to have student requests for the books filed initially with the nonpublic school and to have the school authorities prepare collective summaries of these requests which they forward to the appropriate public officials. . . ." Further, "the nonpublic schools are permitted to store on their premises the textbooks being lent to students." . . . Even if these practices were also followed under the New York statute, the regulations implementing Act 195 make clear, as the record in *Allen* did not, that the nonpublic school in Pennsylvania is something more than a conduit between the State and pupil. The Commonwealth has promulgated "Guidelines for the Administration of Acts 194 and 195" to implement the statutes. These regulations, unlike those upheld in *Allen,* constitute a much more intrusive and detailed involvement of the State and its processes into the administration of nonpublic schools. The whole business is handled by the schools and public authorities and neither parents nor students have a say. The guidelines make crystal clear that the nonpublic school, not its pupils, is the motivating force behind the textbook loan, and that virtually the entire loan transaction is to be, and is in fact, conducted between officials of the nonpublic school, on the one hand, and officers of the state, on the other. . . .

Clearly, in the context of application of the factor of political divisiveness, it is wholly irrelevant whether the loan is to the children or to the school. A divisive political potential exists because aid programs, like Act 195, are dependent on continuing annual appropriations, and Act 195's textbook loan program, even if we accepted it as a form of loans to students, involves increasingly massive sums now approaching $5,000,000 annually. It would blind reality to treat massive aid to nonpublic schools, under the guise of loans to the students, as not creating "a serious potential for divisive conflict over the issue of aid to religion." . . .

MR. CHIEF JUSTICE BURGER, concurring in part and dissenting in part.

There is absolutely no support in this record or, for that matter, in ordinary human experience to support the concern some see with respect to the "dangers" lurking in extending common, nonsectarian tools of the education process—especially remedial tools—to students in private schools. . . . Indeed, I see at least as much potential for divisive political debate in opposition to the crabbed attitude the Court shows in this case. . . .

To hold, as the Court now does, that the Constitution permits the States to give special assistance to some of its children whose handicaps prevent their deriving the benefit normally anticipated from the education required to become a productive member of society and, at the same time, to deny those benefits to other children *only because* they attend a Lutheran, Catholic or other church-sponsored school does not simply tilt the Constitution against religion; it literally turns the Religion Clause on its head. . . .

The melancholy consequence of what the Court does today is to force the parent to choose between the "free exercise" of a religious belief by opting for a sectarian education for his child or to forego the opportunity for his child to learn to cope with—or overcome—serious congenital learning handicaps, through remedial assistance financed by his taxes. Affluent parents, by employing private teaching specialists, will be able to cope with this denial of equal protection, which is, for me, a gross violation of Fourteenth Amendment rights, but all others will be forced to make a choice between their judgment as to their children's spiritual needs and their temporal need for special remedial learning assistance. One can only hope that, at some future date, the Court will come to a more enlightened and tolerant view of the First Amendment's guarantee of free exercise of religion, thus eliminating the denial of equal protection to children in church-sponsored schools, and take a more realistic view that carefully limited aid to children is not a step toward establishing a state religion—at least while this Court sits. . . .

MR. JUSTICE REHNQUIST, with whom MR. JUSTICE WHITE joins, concurring in part and dissenting in part.

The failure of the majority to justify the differing approaches to textbooks and instructional materials and equipment . . . is symptomatic of its failure even to attempt to distinguish the Pennsylvania textbook loan program, which it upholds, from the Pennsylvania instructional materials and equipment loan program, which it finds unconstitutional. . . .

I am disturbed as much by the overtones of the Court's opinion as by its actual holding. The Court apparently believes that the Establishment Clause of the First Amendment not only mandates religious neutrality on the part of government but also requires that this Court go further and throw its weight on the side of those who believe that our society as a whole should be a purely secular one. Nothing in the First Amendment or in the cases interpreting it requires such an extreme approach to this difficult question, and "[a]ny interpretation of [the Establishment Clause] and constitutional values it serves must also take account of the free exercise clause and the values it serves." . . .

Milliken v. Bradley
418 U.S. 717 (1974)

That the road to racial desegregation of the public schools is a rocky one is reflected in this five-to-four decision of the Supreme Court. After the U.S. District Court concluded that the Board of Education of the City of Detroit had engaged in de jure segregation in the city school district, it ordered the submission of desegregation plans not only for the city but also for the three-county metropolitan area, even though there was no claim that the suburban school districts had committed any constitutional violations. The district court, following a hearing in which the suburban school districts participated only on the issue of the form of the desegregation plan, ordered an interdistrict metropolitan desegregation plan. The plan would involve a great deal of busing among the city and fifty-three suburban school districts. The court of appeals affirmed on the theory that the City of Detroit did in fact engage in de jure racial segregation and that a metropolitan remedy was appropriate since the state had the authority to control all local school districts. A bare majority of the Supreme Court reversed.

Certiorari to the United States Court of Appeals for the Sixth Circuit.

MR. CHIEF JUSTICE BURGER delivered the opinion of the Court.

We granted certiorari in these consolidated cases to determine whether a federal court may impose a multi-district, areawide remedy to a single district *de jure* segregation problem absent any finding that the other included school districts have failed to operate unitary school systems within their districts, absent any claim or finding that the boundary lines of any affected school district were established with the purpose of fostering racial segregation in public schools, absent any finding that the included districts committed acts which effected segregation within the other districts, and absent a meaningful opportunity for the included neighboring school districts to present evidence or be heard on the propriety of a multidistrict remedy or on the question of constitutional violations by those neighboring districts. . . .

Viewing the record as a whole, it seems clear that the District Court and the Court of Appeals shifted the primary focus from a Detroit remedy to the metropolitan area only because of their conclusion that total desegregation of Detroit would not produce the racial balance which they perceived as desirable. Both courts proceeded on an assumption that the Detroit schools could not be truly desegregated—in their view of what constituted desegregation—unless the racial composition of the student body of each school substantially reflected the racial composition of the population of the metropolitan area as a whole. The metropolitan area was then defined as Detroit plus 53 of the outlying school districts. . . .

Here the District Court's approach to what constituted "actual desegregation" raises the fundamental question . . . as to the circumstances in which a federal court may order desegregation relief that embraces more than a single school district. The court's analytical starting point was its conclusion that school district lines are no more than arbitrary lines on a map drawn "for political convenience." Boundary lines may be bridged where there has been a constitutional violation calling for interdistrict relief, but the notion that school district lines may be casually ignored or treated as a mere administrative convenience is contrary to the history of public education in our country. No single tradition in public education is more deeply rooted than local control over the operation of schools; local autonomy has long been thought essential both to the maintenance of community concern and support for public schools and to quality of the educational process. . . .

The Michigan educational structure involved in this case, in common with most States, provides for a large measure of local control and a review of the scope and character of these local powers indicates the extent to which the interdistrict remedy approved by the two courts could disrupt and alter the structure of public education in Michigan. The metropolitan remedy would require, in effect, consolidation of 54 independent school districts historically administered as separate units into a vast new super school district. . . . Entirely apart from the logistical and other serious problems attending large-scale transportation of students, the consolidation would give rise to an array of other problems in financing and operating this new school system. Some of the more obvious questions would be: What would be the status and authority of the present popularly elected school boards? Would the children of Detroit be within the jurisdiction and operating control of a school board elected by the parents and residents of other districts? What board or boards would levy taxes for school operations in these 54 districts constituting the consolidated metropolitan area? What provisions could be made for assuring substantial equality in tax levies among the 54 districts, if this were deemed requisite? What provisions would be made for financing? Would the validity of long-term bonds be jeopardized unless approved by all of the component districts as well as the State? What body would determine that portion of the curricula now left to the discretion of local school boards? Who would establish attendance zones, purchase school equipment, locate and construct new schools, and indeed attend to all the myriad day-to-day decisions that are necessary to school operations affecting potentially more than three-quarters of a million pupils? . . .

It may be suggested that all of these vital operational problems are yet to be resolved by the District Court, and that this is the purpose of the Court of Appeals' proposed remand. But it is obvious from the scope of the interdistrict remedy itself that absent a complete restructuring of the laws of Michigan relating to school districts the District Court will become first, a *de facto* "legislative authority" to resolve these complex questions, and then the "school superintendent" for the entire area. This is a task which few, if any, judges are qualified to perform and one which would deprive the people of control of schools through their elected representatives.

Of course, no state law is above the Constitution. School district lines and the present laws with respect to local control, are not sacrosanct and if they conflict with the Fourteenth Amendment federal courts have a duty to prescribe appropriate remedies. . . . But our prior holdings have been confined to violations and remedies within a single school district. We therefore turn to address, for the first time, the validity of a remedy mandating cross-district or interdistrict consolidation to remedy a condition of segregation found to exist in only one district.

The controlling principle consistently expounded in our holdings is that the scope of the remedy is determined

by the nature and extent of the constitutional violation.
. . . Before the boundaries of separate and autonomous
school districts may be set aside by consolidating the separate units for remedial purposes or by imposing a cross-
district remedy, it must first be shown that there has
been a constitutional violation within one district that
produces a significant segregative effect in another district. Specifically, it must be shown that racially discriminatory acts of the state or local school districts, or
of a single school district have been a substantial cause
of interdistrict segregation. Thus an interdistrict remedy
might be in order where the racially discriminatory acts
of one or more school districts caused racial segregation
in an adjacent district, or where district lines have been
deliberately drawn on the basis of race. In such circumstances an interdistrict remedy would be appropriate to
eliminate the interdistrict segregation directly caused by
the constitutional violation. Conversely, without an interdistrict violation and interdistrict effect, there is no
constitutional wrong calling for an interdistrict remedy.

The record before us, voluminous as it is, contains
evidence of *de jure* segregated conditions only in the Detroit schools; indeed, that was the theory on which the
litigation was initially based and on which the District
Court took evidence. . . . With no showing of significant
violation by the 53 outlying school districts and no evidence of any interdistrict violation or effect, the court
went beyond the original theory of the case as framed
by the pleadings and mandated a metropolitan area
remedy. To approve the remedy ordered by the court
would impose on the outlying districts, not shown to
have committed any constitutional violation, a wholly
impermissible remedy based on a standard not hinted at
in *Brown* I and II or any holding of this Court. . . .

Disparate treatment of white and Negro students occurred within the Detroit school system, and not elsewhere, and on this record the remedy must be limited to that system. . . .

MR. JUSTICE STEWART, concurring.

In this case the Court of Appeals approved the concept of a remedial decree that would go beyond the boundaries of the district where the constitutional violation was found, and include schools and schoolchildren in many other school districts that have presumptively been administered in complete accord with the Constitution.

The opinion of the Court convincingly demonstrates . . . that traditions of local control of schools, together with the difficulty of a judicially supervised restructuring of local administration of schools, render improper and inequitable such an interdistrict response to a constitutional violation found to have occurred only within a single school district.

This is not to say, however, that an interdistrict remedy of the sort approved by the Court of Appeals would not be proper, or even necessary, in other factual situations. Were it to be shown, for example, that state officials had contributed to the separation of the races by drawing or redrawing school district lines, . . . by transfer of school units between districts, . . . or by purposeful, racially discriminatory use of state housing or zoning laws, then a decree calling for transfer of pupils across district lines or for restructuring of district lines might well be appropriate. . . .

MR. JUSTICE DOUGLAS, dissenting.

No new principles of law are presented here. Metropolitan treatment of metropolitan problems is commonplace.

If this were a sewage problem or a water problem, or an energy problem, there can be no doubt that Michigan would stay well within federal constitutional bounds if it sought a metropolitan remedy. . . . Here the Michigan educational system is unitary, maintained and supported by the legislature and under the general supervision of the State Board of Education. The State controls the boundaries of school districts. The State supervises school site selection. The construction is done through municipal bonds approved by several state agencies. Education in Michigan is a state project with very little completely local control, except that the schools are financed locally, not on a statewide basis. Indeed the proposal to put school funding in Michigan on a statewide basis was defeated at the polls in November 1972. Yet the school districts by state law are agencies of the State. State action is indeed challenged as violating the Equal Protection Clause. Whatever the reach of that claim may be, it certainly is aimed at discrimination based on race.

Therefore as the Court of Appeals held there can be no doubt that as a matter of Michigan law the State itself has the final say as to where and how school district lines should be drawn. . . .

MR. JUSTICE WHITE, with whom MR. JUSTICE DOUGLAS, MR. JUSTICE BRENNAN, and MR. JUSTICE MARSHALL, join, dissenting.

Regretfully, and for several reasons, I can join neither the Court's judgment nor its opinion. The core of my disagreement is that deliberate acts of segregation and their consequences will go unremedied, not because a remedy would be infeasible or unreasonable in terms of the usual criteria governing school desegregation cases, but because an effective remedy would cause what the Court considers to be undue administrative inconvenience to the State. The result is that the State of Michigan, the entity at which the Fourteenth Amendment is directed, has successfully insulated itself from its duty to provide effective desegregation remedies by vesting sufficient power over its public schools in its local school districts. If this is the case in Michigan, it will be the case in most States. . . .

This Court now reverses the Court of Appeals. It does not question the District Court's findings that *any* feasible Detroit-only plan would leave many schools 75 to 90 percent black and that the district would become progressively more black as whites left the city. Neither does the Court suggest that including the suburbs in a desegregation plan would be impractical or infeasible because of educational considerations, because of the number of children requiring transportation, or because of the length of their rides. Indeed, the Court leaves unchallenged the District Court's conclusion that a plan including the suburbs would be physically easier and more practical and feasible than a Detroit-only plan. Whereas the most promising Detroit-only plan, for example, would have entailed the purchase of 900 buses, the metropolitan plan would involve the acquisition of no more than 350 new vehicles.

Despite the fact that a metropolitan remedy, if the findings of the District Court accepted by the Court of Appeals are to be credited, would more effectively desegregate the Detroit schools, would prevent resegregation, and would be easier and more feasible from many standpoints, the Court fashions out of whole cloth an arbitrary rule that remedies for constitutional violations occurring in a single Michigan school district must stop at the school district line. Apparently, no matter how much less burdensome or more effective and efficient in many respects, such as transportation, the metropolitan plan might be, the school district line may not be crossed. Otherwise, it seems, there would be too much disruption of the Michigan scheme for managing its educational system, too much confusion, and too much administrative burden.

The District Court, on the scene and familiar with local conditions, had a wholly different view. The Court of Appeals also addressed itself at length to matters of local law and to the problems that interdistrict remedies might present to the State of Michigan. . . .

I am surprised that the Court, sitting at this distance from the State of Michigan, claims better insight than the Court of Appeals and the District Court as to whether an interdistrict remedy for equal protection violations practiced by the State of Michigan would involve undue difficulties for the State in the management of its public schools. . . .

I am even more mystified as to how the Court can ignore the legal reality that the constitutional violations, even if occurring locally, were committed by governmental entities for which the State is responsible and that it is the State that must respond to the command of the Fourteenth Amendment. . . .

Nor does the Court's conclusion follow from the talismanic invocation of the desirability of local control over education. Local autonomy over school affairs, in the sense of the community's participation in the decisions affecting the education of its children, is, of course, an important interest. But presently constituted school district lines do not delimit fixed and unchangeable areas of a local educational community. If restructuring is required to meet constitutional requirements, local authority may simply be redefined in terms of whatever configuration is adopted, with the parents of the children attending schools in the newly demarcated district or attendance zone continuing their participation in the policy management of the schools with which they are concerned most directly. The majority's suggestion that judges should not attempt to grapple with the administrative problems attendant on a reorganization of school attendance patterns is wholly without foundation. . . .

Mr. Justice Marshall, with whom Mr. Justice Douglas, Mr. Justice Brennan, and Mr. Justice White join, dissenting:

After 20 years of small, often difficult steps toward that great end, the Court today takes a giant step backwards. Notwithstanding a record showing widespread and pervasive racial segregation in the educational system provided by the State of Michigan for children in Detroit, this Court holds that the District Court was powerless to require the State to remedy its constitutional violation in any meaningful fashion. Ironically purporting to base its result on the principle that the scope of the remedy in a desegregation case should be determined by the nature and the extent of the constitutional violation, the Court's answer is to provide no remedy at all for the violation proved in this case, thereby guaranteeing that Negro children in Detroit will receive the same separate and inherently unequal education in the future as they have been unconstitutionally afforded in the past.

I cannot subscribe to this emasculation of our constitutional guarantee of equal protection of the laws and must respectfully dissent. Our precedents, in my view, firmly establish that where, as here, state-imposed segregation has been demonstrated, it becomes the duty of the State to eliminate root and branch all vestiges of racial discrimination and to achieve the greatest possible degree of actual desegregation. I agree with both the District Court and the Court of Appeals that, under the facts of this case, this duty cannot be fulfilled unless the State of Michigan involves outlying metropolitan area school districts in its desegregation remedy. Furthermore, I perceive no basis either in law or in the practicalities of the situation justifying the State's interposition of school district boundaries as absolute barriers to the implementation of an effective desegregation remedy. Under established and frequently used Michigan procedures, school district lines are both flexible and permeable for a wide variety of purposes, and there is no reason why they must now stand in the way of meaningful desegregation relief.

The rights at issue in the case are too fundamental to be abridged on grounds as superficial as those relied on by the majority today. We deal here with the right of all of our children, whatever their race, to an equal start in life and to an equal opportunity to reach their full potential as citizens. Those children who have been denied that right in the past deserve better than to see fences thrown up to deny them that right in the future. Our Nation, I fear, will be ill served by the Court's refusal to remedy separate and unequal education, for unless our children begin to learn together, there is little hope that our people will ever learn to live together. . . .

Since the Court chooses, however, to speculate on the feasibility of a metropolitan plan, I feel constrained to comment on the problem areas it has targeted. To begin with, the majority's questions concerning the practicality of consolidation of school districts need not give us pause. The State clearly has the power, under existing law, to effect a consolidation if it is ultimately determined that this offers the best prospect for a workable and stable desegregation plan. . . . And given the 1,000 or so consolidations of school districts which have taken place in the past, it is hard to believe that the State has not already devised means of solving most, if not all, of the practical problems which the Court suggests consolidation would entail.

Furthermore, the majority ignores long-established Michigan procedures under which school districts may enter into contractual agreements to educate their pupils in other districts using state or local funds to finance nonresident education. Such agreements could form an easily administrable framework for interdistrict relief short of outright consolidation of the school districts. The District Court found that interdistrict procedures like these were frequently used to provide special educational services for handicapped children, and extensive statutory provision is also made for their use in vocational education. Surely if school districts are willing to engage in interdistrict programs to help those unfortunate children crippled by physical or mental handicaps, school districts can be required to participate in an interdistrict program to help those children in the city of Detroit whose educations and very futures have been crippled by purposeful state segregation. . . .

Desegregation is not and was never expected to be an easy task. Racial attitudes ingrained in our Nation's childhood and adolescence are not quickly thrown aside in its middle years. But just as the inconvenience of some cannot be allowed to stand in the way of the rights of others, so public opposition, no matter how strident, cannot be permitted to divert this Court from the enforcement of the constitutional principles at issue in this case. Today's holding, I fear, is more a reflection of a perceived public mood that we have gone far enough in enforcing the Constitution's guarantee of equal justice than it is the product of neutral principles of law. In the short run, it may seem to be the easier course to allow our great metropolitan areas to be divided up each into two cities—one white, the other black—but it is a course, I predict, our people will ultimately regret. I dissent.

DAVID FELLMAN, Vilas Professor of Political Science at the University of Wisconsin, was born in Omaha, Nebraska, in 1907. He received his B.A. and M.A. from the University of Nebraska, and his Ph.D. from Yale University. Professor Fellman taught political science at the University of Nebraska from 1934 until 1947, when he joined the faculty of the University of Wisconsin. He has also held several positions in the Wisconsin state government and has served as Chairman of the Committee on Academic Freedom and Tenure of the American Association of University Professors, and also as President of the Association. Professor Fellman has written numerous articles for scholarly journals in law and political science, and was the first editor of the *Midwest Journal of Political Science.* His books include *The Defendant's Rights* (1958), *The Limits of Freedom* (1959), *The Constitutional Right of Association* (1963), *Religion in American Public Law* (1965), *The Defendant's Rights under English Law* (1966), and *The Defendant's Rights Today* (1976).